ROYAL HISTORICAL SOCIETY
STUDIES IN HISTORY
SERIES
No. 24

THE POLITICAL CAREER OF
SIR ROBERT NAUNTON 1589-1635

Recent volumes published in this series include

For a complete list of the series please see pp. 191-2

THE POLITICAL CAREER OF SIR ROBERT NAUNTON 1589-1635

Roy E. Schreiber

LONDON
ROYAL HISTORICAL SOCIETY
1981

© Roy E. Schreiber 1981

ISBN 0 901050 79 2

The Society records its gratitude to the following, whose generosity made possible the initiation of this series: The British Academy; The Pilgrim Trust; The Twenty-Seven Foundation; The United States Embassy bicentennial funds; The Wolfson Trust; several private donors.

Printed in England
by Swift Printers (Sales) Ltd
London E.C.1.

To the S.K.G.S. Foundation
and the London firm that
provided its funds

ACKNOWLEDGEMENTS

Any attempt to acknowledge the help of those who aided me with the preparations for this book must begin with my friends at London University. At the head of the list goes Professor Joel Hurstfield, who originally suggested that I investigate Naunton's life. Professor J.E. Neale and the other members of the Tudor seminar at the Institute of Historical Research put their knowledge at my disposal, as did those in the Stuart seminar then under the direction of Robert Latham, Ian Roy and Henry Rosevere. Among the many people who passed through these seminars I would especially like to single out Terry Hartley, Robert Zaller, Robert Bonner, Alan McGowan, Birget Jenson and A.J. Loomie. All of them brought numerous sources to my attention, and spent many hours listening to my pet theories. A word of thanks must also go to Professors S.T. Bindoff and G.E. Aylmer who gave me some excellent advice on how to improve my work.

A variety of people were kind enough to let me see their private collections. They included the Duke of Rutland, the Duke of Buccleuch, the Marquis of Downshire and Baron Sackville. In every instance I was extended unfailing courtesy and consideration by the staffs of these peers.

Finally I would like to thank those friends and colleagues who helped me to prepare this book. Louis Knafla, Paul Scherer, Leo Solt, Felicity Nussbaum, Paul Parrish, John Lewis and John Penikis all read semi-finished portions of the work and gave me useful criticisms. The last person in this category is Margaret Wiltrout, who braved the perils of both seventeenth-century spelling and my now somewhat unusual ideas on this subject, to proof read and edit this work.

Roy E. Schreiber
Indiana University at South Bend

CONTENTS

ABBREVIATIONS

APC	*Acts of the Privy Council*
Add.	Additional Manuscript
Bodley	Bodleian Library, Oxford
BL	British Library, London
	Calendars of State Papers:
CSPD	*Domestic*
CSP, Irish	*Ireland*
CSP, Ven.	*Venetian*
DNB	*Dictionary of National Biography*
Eg.	Egerton Manuscripts
Harl.	Harleian Manuscripts
HMC	Historical Manuscripts Commission
Lans.	Lansdowne Manuscripts
PRO	Public Record Office
SP	State Papers

Note

Unless otherwise indicated, the dates used in this book are the old style pre-Gregorian form. New Year's day is, however, reckoned as 1 January. With the exception of modernizing the use of the letters u and i, the spellings within the quotations have been left in their contemporary form.

INTRODUCTION

When Benjamin Disraeli, upon becoming prime minister, said, 'I have climbed to the top of a long, greasy pole,' he spoke not only for himself, but for the thousands of politicians before and since who have tried to make their mark in governmental affairs. Even for those who achieved something less than Disraeli, the ability to maintain any place at all was often accomplishment enough. It was the more so for those who did not seek a place for its own sake, but who sought it in order to forward a programme in which they believed.

The political climate of early seventeenth-century England produced both kinds of men and many grades in between. It was, however, the changing nature of the Stuart monarchy that determined the framework in which these men would operate. Putting the emphasis on change is important, for there has been a tendency among historians to view James I and Charles I as essentially one person with two names and by this process to make the Civil Wars inevitable from the moment of Elizabeth's death. Yet whatever the differences between the last Tudor and the first Stuart, equally profound divergences existed between James and his son. The subtle flexibility of James I contrasts profoundly with the alternating tenacious certainty and weak unpredictability of Charles I. Attempting to cope with such a situation while maintaining both place and integrity is the focus of this study of Sir Robert Naunton.

Naunton is little known today, but his relative anonymity provides him with virtues for the historian. He represents the mainstream of Stuart government; he was neither eminent enough to attract an undue number of enemies, nor inconsequential enough to be out of the main thrust of important business. In James I's reign Sir Robert, as Secretary of State, played a major role in the foreign policy decisions that dominated the last years of the reign. Under Charles I, as Master of the Court of Wards, Naunton was in charge of one of the nation's major revenue-producing institutions and was thus a mainstay of the king's personal government.

Despite these shifts of office, Sir Robert was not a mindless automaton reprogrammed at his master's convenience to carry out any governmental function. He had quite decided opinions on the issues of his day, and a major reason for his seeking office was to help institute his viewpoint as governmental policy. Naunton was adamantly against toleration for English Roman Catholics and he wished to see the major Romanist countries in Europe, especially those controlled by the Habsburgs, either severely limited in their influence, or, if possible, destroyed altogether. By the standards of our time, Naunton's goals strike a somewhat sour note, but it is not our age that is important here; it is his. Once again he proves a model for the other governmental officials of his era. The concept of a multi-religioned state seemed so subversive to an ordered society as they knew it, that they rejected the possibility. They had been raised with the doctrine that there was only one truth, and for them, this truth was Protestantism as the English practised it. Naunton shared all these beliefs, but they did not spring into his head; they were developed through many years and numerous experiences with the political life of his day.

It would be satisfying if this process could be traced through Sir Robert and his family on a day by day basis from their first entry into England, but they only emerge from obscurity for very brief periods before the Jacobean era. The Naunton family was based in Suffolk and had members among the knightly ranks as far back as the fourteenth century.[1] It was not, however, until the sixteenth century that any member of the family achieved anything that remotely resembled political prominence. The individual involved was Sir Robert's grandfather, William. After attending Gray's Inn in 1525, he became associated with Henry VIII's favourite, the duke of Suffolk, becoming treasurer of his household. By 1550 William was a marshal of the King's Bench. Three years earlier the widow of the duke of Suffolk, Catherine, Baroness Willoughby had used her influence to help elect him MP for Boston, Lincolnshire in Edward VI's first parliament. William's marriage to one of Sir Anthony Wingfield's daughters was also a major accomplishment. Wingfield was a Knight of the Garter, a chief servant of Henry VIII and the head of Suffolk's most prestigious knightly house.[2]

William's eldest surviving son, Henry, fell into the more traditional Naunton obscurity. All that is known of Henry is that he continued the family's association with the Baroness Willoughby by serving as her master of horse, and that in 1562 he married Elizabeth Asheby of Hornsby, Leicestershire. A year later the subject of this study, Robert, was born.

Robert's first half century, though it has a few prominent landmarks, remains largely merged with the rest of the landscape. In his early days he was attracted to the academic life, and periodically, over a twenty-five year time span, he would return to Cambridge University

[1]BL. Add. 17098.

[2]Information obtained from the manuscript biography of William Naunton (History of Parliament Trust), edited by S.T. Bindoff.

where he received his BA in 1582 and his MA in 1586.[3] Naunton was first associated with Trinity College but later transferred his fellowship to Trinity Hall and rose to the post of Public Orator of Cambridge.[4] What kept drawing him away from scholarly pursuits was the lure of political life. The lure must have been a very strong one because all his early endeavours in this direction were failures.

Naunton began his political pursuits by joining his uncle, Sir William Asheby, the English ambassador in Scotland. Ironically, his first mission shortly after arriving, in 1589, was to arrange for Asheby's retirement.[5] The scholar waited six years at his university before he found another political opportunity. The next venture was for Elizabeth I's favourite, the earl of Essex. Under the guise of acting as tutor to a young member of the earl's connection named Robert Vernon, Naunton was sent to France in February 1596 to make contact with a renegade secretary of Philip II named Antonio Perez.[6] For nearly two years Naunton attempted to pump useful information out of this cagey old Spanish rogue in an effort to prove to Essex that he was more than a scholar. The result was a near nervous breakdown,[7] and no political appointment. All Naunton had to show for his time was a heartfelt loathing for the French, who had given him rough passage on numerous occasions,[8] a profound fear of the Spanish, who seemed capable of keeping Europe in continual chaos,[9] and a lawsuit. Naunton had proved a poor judge of character when he entrusted the £1,065 in cash that he had thus far acquired to three men who tried to cheat him out of it. It took him three years and the intervention of Sir Robert Cecil to get his money back.[10]

Naunton's contact with Cecil provided him with yet another opportunity to advance his political career. The man who had been the chief beneficiary of the Essex débâcle, who held the important posts

---

[3]J. and J.A. Venn, *Alumni Cantabrigienses* (Cambridge, 1924), III, 232.

[4]*Ibid.*

[5]Naunton to Asheby, 13 July 1589, BL Eg. 2598, fo. 12.

[6]T. Birch, *Memoirs of the Reign of Queen Elizabeth* (London, 1756), 1, 368, citing Bacon Papers, VIII, fol. 63.

[7]Naunton to Essex, Rouen 29 November 1596, *ibid.*, II, 213, citing Bacon Papers, XIV, fol. 62.

[8]Naunton to Essex, Rouen 10 January 1597, Lambeth Palace Bacon Papers, MS. 654, fo. 203; 17 January 1597, *ibid.*, fo. 191, and Paris 14 March 1597, Birch, *Memoirs,* II, 300, citing Bacon Papers, XV, fol. 54.

[9]Naunton to Coke, Paris 9 November [1597], HMC, *Cowper,* I, 25.

[10]Huntington Library, MS. EL 6055; J. Duport to R. Cecil, 25 April 1602, HMC, *Salisbury,* XII, 124 and PRO SP/12/284, no. 74. It is unfortunate that the records do not indicate more about where Naunton got this money. His father was alive when the trust was established so it was not the family estate but rather his own personal funds.

of Secretary of State and Master of the Court of Wards and who was chiefly responsible for James I's peaceful accession to the English throne, was a patron worth having. On the other side, Cecil was never averse to using talent whenever he found it. Thus when James entered England for the first time, it is not entirely surprising to find Naunton there to greet him as the royal party came south to Hinchinbrook. He was acting in his capacity as University Orator, but it could not have hurt to have Cecil whispering in the king's ear as he performed.[11]

Here was the first of several attempts by the earl of Salisbury (as Cecil shortly became) to help his new protégé, but for various reasons Naunton was never able to make the best of the aid given. Undoubtedly through Salisbury's efforts, in the sumer of 1604 Robert was appointed orator of the earl of Rutland's extraordinary embassy to King Christian IV of Denmark. Unfortunately on his first audience he only managed to come out with a few words before he became utterly panic-stricken and had to beat a hasty retreat.[12] A year later Salisbury found Naunton a seat in the House of Commons for the Cornish borough of Helston.[13] If the secretary had hoped to start a great parliamentary career by his action, he was disappointed. Although Naunton did gradually receive important committee assignments including the committees on grievances and the Great Contract,[14] he did not become one of the great orators of the Commons. In fact no speech given by him was noted by his contemporaries. Nonetheless, Salisbury still kept his faith in the Cambridge Orator for in February 1612 Naunton became one of the earl's personal assistants for the Secretary of State's office.[15] As luck would have it, in less than six months, Salisbury was dead and Cambridge once more seemed to beckon. Yet Naunton had by now become too much involved in the political world to go back. Despite his impressive list of failures, he felt he had a start, and he did not intend to give up his position, such as it was, on the greasy pole.

Others had the same idea. Salisbury's body had scarcely been laid to rest before the scramble for his offices began. The problem for those interested in improving themselves was to find the means of convincing James that their improvement was to his benefit as well. Several were available. Besides the Scottish favourites brought to England, there

[11]*DNB. sub* Naunton, Sir Robert citing *Sydney Papers,* II, 325.

[12]J. Howell, *Epistolae Ho-elianae, The Familiar Letters,* ed. J. Jacobs (London, 1890), p. 294.

[13]*Official Return - Members of Parliament,* 1213-1702 (1878), I, 442; J.E. Neale, *The Elizabethan House of Commons* (London, 1949), pp. 242-3.

[14]*Commons Journal,* I, 393, 404 & 445.

[15]Salisbury to the king, Whitehall, 9 February 1612, CSPD., *1611-18,* p. 119.

were two rather amorphous groups at court that hoped for royal favour. The first centred around the Howard family and was led by the Lord Privy Seal, the earl of Northampton. The members of this group were often crypto-Catholics or favourable to friendly ties with Spain. The second faction was led by men such as Lord Ellesmere (the Lord Chancellor), George Abbot (archbishop of Canterbury) and the earl of Pembroke. Before the death of Prince Henry, James's eldest son, in 1612 this group had looked to him as their inspiration, if not their leader. Henry had been a militant Protestant who favoured releasing Sir Walter Raleigh from the Tower, presumably in preparation for an attack on Spanish America. Even without the prince's flamboyant personality, the group maintained its anti-Spanish and anti-Roman Catholic focus.

The pivot between these two groups was James's young Scottish favourite, Robert Carr, Viscount Rochester, and Sir Thomas Overbury, Carr's friend and adviser. Their attitudes were not a cut and dried matter. Carr was deeply involved with Frances Howard; once she divorced her husband, the earl of Essex (the son of Elizabeth's beheaded favourite), he hoped to marry her, thus bringing him into the Howard faction. On the other hand, Overbury tended to have ideas about the balancing of Protestant and Roman Catholic Europe which more closely resembled the attitude of the anti-Spanish group. Just how much actual influence these two young men had with the king either jointly or individually is open to question, but their contemporaries thought they had a good deal when it came to the selection of officials and so besieged them with requests.

As Naunton prepared to take part in the race for office and preferment, he had to choose the best point of entry. Philosophically the anti-Spanish group was to his liking, and he made his first efforts in their direction. The contact he chose was a distant relative, Sir Ralph Winwood, English ambassador at The Hague.[16] Winwood was an ardent Protestant with decided puritan leanings who had his eye on the post of Secretary of State. Sir Ralph's enforced absence from the court made it necessary for him to act through intermediaries, and there was nothing more natural than the use of his 'cousin', Naunton, as one of his agents. From Naunton's point of view, acting for Winwood was an excellent opportunity to make himself better known to those who counted: 'When you write to my Lord of Rochester or to Sir Thomas Overbury, if it please you to use me for delivery of your letter, it may happily occasion me some further overture.'[17] There was

[16]*The Letters of John Chamberlain,* ed., N. E. McClure (Philadelphia, 1939), I, 365-6.

[17]Naunton to Winwood, Holebourne, 15-25 September [1612], HMC., *Buccleuch,* I, 114.

more than a little self-interest involved in Naunton's work for Winwood, for he was after his cousin's job at The Hague. Here Naunton proved his own worst enemy, for he made a devious yet ineffectual attempt to mask his plans from Sir Ralph.

In September 1612, probably as part of this effort, Naunton related the story of his first meeting with the Scot James, Lord Hay, one of the king's early favourites. After explaining how the baron had offered to act as his patron, Naunton added that he considered himself a man 'who, as much drowned as he hath been and sunk in the eye of the world, yet would not catch at every bough to clamber up by'.[18] Winwood was too experienced a courtier to be fooled by his cousin's oblique pledge to stick with him no matter who offered to help. Naunton further tried to distract Sir Ralph's attention in November by informing him that he hoped Sir Thomas Lake would give up his post of Latin Secretary and move on to become the other Secretary of State besides Winwood.[19] Though this statement by Naunton was probably not a complete fabrication, it certainly was not the whole truth.

All of the connivance was a mistake. By February 1613, if not sooner, Winwood discovered what his cousin was trying to do and resented it.[20] A month later Naunton was so confident of replacing Sir Ralph that he applied for a licence to travel abroad for four years.[21] Under the circumstances, his action was an affront to Winwood and was duly reported to him.[22] Had Naunton been open about his intentions, he could probably have obtained the ambassador's cooperation. After all, if the man became secretary and was helped by Naunton, he had nothing to lose by such a gesture. But the conspiratorial atmosphere of the court and perhaps Naunton's fears that he was not Sir Ralph's first choice as a successor got the better of him. He decided to use the less forthright route and paid the price. By May 1614, Naunton had become so desperate according to John Chamberlain, the famous Jacobean letter writer and friend of Winwood's,[23] that he was using 'a contrarie course, and such as I thought the other wold have taken but that there hath ben a bracke of late among them.'[24] This contrary course can only have been the earl of Somerset (as Rochester had become) and the Howard faction.

[18]*Ibid.*, 113.

[19]17 November [1612], *ibid.*, 119.

[20]2 July 1612, *Chamberlain Letters*, I, 365-6, and Wake to Carleton, London, 10 February 1613 (new style) PRO SP/99/12, fo. 63.

[21]HMC. *Buccleuch*, I, 129.

[22]*Ibid.*

[23]12 May 1614, *Chamberlain Letters*, I, 529.

[24]*Ibid.*, Sir Dudley Digges is the 'other' referred to by Chamberlain.

Following Naunton's convoluted path towards that ever elusive office does little to raise one's opinion of his character or his methods. He did not treat with his friends honestly, and he evidently betrayed his principles by using the Howards. Yet something should be pointed out in mitigation. In 1613 Naunton was fifty years old, the beginning of old age for a Jacobean gentleman. This factor was especially important since he was on barely the first rung of the ladder to preferment. Time could run out at any minute; he was becoming desperate that he should not be passed by.

The irony is that it was all for nothing. Though Winwood was appointed Secretary of State in March 1614, James did not appoint his replacement at The Hague until two years later when Sir Dudley Carleton, formerly ambassador to Venice, assumed the post. Carleton was in turn replaced at Venice by Naunton's friend, Sir Henry Wotton. Even the prospects for Latin Secretary proved illusionary when Sir Thomas Lake was made the second Secretary of State in 1616, but retained the Latin secretaryship as well. The only sops to Naunton's ego were that in March 1614 he received an appointment to the commission that recommended approval of Alderman Cockayne's disastrous scheme for the exporting of dyed and dressed cloth,[25] and on 7 September 1615, a knighthood was bestowed upon him at Windsor.[26] For what it was worth, the Royal managers of such matters found him a seat in the Addled Parliament of 1614 for Camelford, a Cornish borough.[27]

Though Naunton did not think so at the time, the disappointments he suffered during these years ultimately worked to his advantage. Had he succeeded in obtaining the ambassadorial post at The Hague, he would have removed himself from the centre of power. This action would have meant an end to his advancement. Winwood, who was far wealthier and more influential than Naunton, was forced to return from The Hague to obtain the secretaryship, and even then it took him two years. Sir Dudley Carleton, whose political connections were quite extensive, was never able to use intermediaries effectively to advance his cause for higher office. His attempts to leave his post for the purpose were frowned upon by James. What is more, as will be discussed in detail in a later chapter, the pay for the ambassadors was either in arrears or totally absent during this period. For all these reasons, for a man of Naunton's relatively modest means, an

[25]T. Albery to W. Trumbull, 15 March 1614, HMC., *Downshire-Trumbull,* IV, 338.

[26]J. Nichols, *The Progressess, etc. of James the First* (London, 1828), III, 99.

[27]*Commons Journal,* I, 465, 487, 492; T. Moir, *The Addled Parliament of 1614* (Oxford, 1958), p. 48. I am grateful to Vivienne Hodges for information on Duchy of Cornwall patronage.

ambassadorship could have proved a serious blow and effectively thwarted any further hopes for preferment. Thus one is forced to the conclusion that failure in this case was Naunton's best friend.

But the failure was at an end. In June 1616 he was made a Master of Requests. The post had opened up when Sir John Dacombe became Chancellor of the Duchy of Lancaster and vacated his former position.[28] Dacombe had been active in the successful campaign to bring down the earl of Somerset for the murder of his former friend, Overbury. Sir John had played a relatively small part in the business, but he still received his reward.[29]

Why and how Naunton moved up to this post is not entirely clear. There is no record that he played any part, even a small one, in Somerset's disgrace. Given his apparent use of the former favourite and the Howard faction, it is difficult even to gauge his reaction to the affair. The only clue that exists as to Sir Robert's sudden success is a brief mention in July 1616, by John Chamberlain that the new Master of Requests acted as one of the godparents for John Packer's daughter.[30] Acting as a godfather is certainly as much an indication of political favour as of a close personal relationship, and Packer was a man who knew all about political favour. He must have been one of the more adept politicians of his day, for, after serving as Somerset's secretary, he managed to abandon his declining master and take up the same post with the new favourite, George Villiers. Just when and for how long Naunton and Packer knew each other it is difficult to say. There was a John Packer in the Essex faction who was in France at the same time as Sir Robert;[31] they could well have met then.

Whatever the circumstances, it would be surprising if Packer had not had something to do with Naunton's appointment. He was, of course, in no position to directly arrange to grant anyone a post, but his new master, the rising star of the Jacobean scene, was. Villiers was initially sponsored at court by the anti-Spanish group, but his rise was so meteoric that, in the wake of Somerset's disgrace, he rapidly outgrew their sponsorship. Naunton was quick to travel this path to influence. Sir Robert discovered that his mother was actually Villiers's cousin (they both came from Leicestershire), and this connection enabled him to ingratiate himself. If one of the stories that made the rounds at this time is accurate, it was principally through

[28] 24 June 1616, APC, *1615-16*, p. 630.

[29] D. Nicholas, *Mr Secretary Nicholas (1593-1669): His Life and Letters* (London, 1955), p. 18.

[30] *Chamberlain Letters*, II, 16.

[31] J. Packer to E. Reynolds, Orleans 3 September 1598, HMC., *Salisbury*, VIII, 329.

Lady Compton, the favourite's mother, that Sir Robert had his links with the family.[32]

The result of this favourable reception from the new powers of the court was yet another office. On 4 November 1616, Naunton replaced Sir Sydney Montagu as Surveyor of the Court of Wards.[33] The appointment was not popular. A variety of people, several of whom had considered themselves Naunton's friends, were not at all pleased. James Whitelock, the parliamentarian and common lawyer, had been quite thankful for Sir Robert's assistance with the dean and canons of Canterbury.[34] Nonetheless he bristled noticeably when Naunton, a scholar and 'meer stranger to the law,' took over a post that had previously been held by noted lawyers.[35] John Chamberlain had more personal objections; he marvelled that 'in his declining age, when neither his eyes nor his eares *satis officium suum faciunt,* he shold be so ambitious to come upon the stage and shew his defects.'[36]

Perhaps it was the resentment of others in and around the court, or perhaps it was that the surveyorship had not been officially confirmed,[37] but whatever the reason, in late October 1616, Naunton was very cautious of an assignment that came his way. The task stemmed from James's anger at a book called *Corna Regia*: it had been written by a resident of the Spanish Netherlands and was anything but favourable to the English monarch. The king therefore decided to send a special agent abroad to discover the author and see to his punishment. It was probably Naunton's enemies who put his name forward as the agent, but the new surveyor knew his way around the court well enough to see the pitfalls of the mission; he side-stepped the job.[38] The assignment ultimately fell to Sir John Bennet who discovered that it was no easy task. Four years later the author was still at large.[39]

Once all these alarms and difficulties were surmounted, Sir Robert settled down into his new posts; however, precisely what he did in them is something of a question. As one of the four Masters of Request in Ordinary, he was supposed to work under the supervision

[32]*Chamberlain Letters,* II. 30.

[33]PRO. Wards 9/535. p. 543.

[34]J. Whitlock. *Liber Famelicus,* ed. J. Bruce (Camden Society: Westminster, 1858), p. 29.

[35]*Ibid.,* p. 54.

[36]26 October 1616. *Chamberlain Letters,* II, 30.

[37]HMC. *Buccleuch,* I, 250.

[38]9 November 1616. *Chamberlain Letters,* II, 33.

[39]W. Trumbull to Naunton. 30 June 1620, PRO SP/77/14, fol. 148.

of the Lord Privy Seal, the earl of Worcester.[40] It is the matter of work that
is at issue. Although there are various letters written by Sir Robert
as he went about his tasks,[41] there is no evidence in the official records
of the Court of Requests that he was particularly conscientious in his
duties. Most of the cases were heard by Sir Christopher Parkins (or
Perkins), who was usually assisted by Sir Sydney Montague, another
master. Naunton was hardly ever there.[42] The impression that Sir
Robert was not particularly active as a Master of Requests is
confirmed by the statements of contemporaries. In one instance a
gentleman was trying to obtain a 'diet' (meals) at court. He had used
Naunton in his effort only to find that the master had not done
anything about the matter for two months and was returning his
gratuity because of the lack of progress.[43]

There is, of course, the possibility that Sir Robert's work as
surveyor occupied so much of his time that he never really had a
chance to become involved in the Court of Requests. That does not
seem to have been the case. The role of surveyor had become an
anachronism. In the early sixteenth century the surveyor had been in
charge of his own court; he handled cases involving suits for livery.
That meant that when a person came of age, a suit was filed with the
Court of Liveries to take possession of the lands in question (or more
properly to hold them from the king) in the plaintiff's own right. By the
mid-sixteenth century the Court of Liveries had been merged with the
Court of Wards, and the surveyor placed in a position subordinate to
the Master of the Wards.[44] Only the legal talents of the earlier
surveyors had made their post important, and, as Whitelock had
properly pointed out, it was precisely legal training that Naunton
lacked. He was qualified in neither common nor civil law.

The records of the Court of Wards show practically no evidence of
Sir Robert's participation, even in livery cases. In June 1617 there
was a complicated case and in it the Attorney of the Court, Sir James

[40]Although Worcester was a Roman Catholic, Sir Robert seems to have respected
him and said some kind things about his life.Earl of Monmouth, *Memoirs of
Robert Cary* and Sir Robert Naunton, *Fragmenta Regalia* (Edinburgh, 1808), *sub* earl
of Worcester.

[41]BL. Add. 38170, fol. 288 and *Egerton Papers,* ed. J.P. Collier (Camden Society:
Westminster, 1840), p. 491.

[42]PRO, Req. 1/28 lists the cases for this period. The clerk or registrar, Hugh Alington,
put the initials of the masters who heard each case along side the record of the decisions.

[43]Reynolds to F. Mills, 1 January 1617, PRO SP/17/90, no. 2.

[44]J. Hurstfield, *The Queen's Wards* (Cambridge, 1958), pp. 211, 213.

Ley, not Naunton went over the documents with the local official.[45] The pattern repeated itself in October when once again Ley rather than Naunton consulted with the chief judges of England and communicated their decision to the Court of Wards.[46] In short, whatever function the surveyor once had, was in large measure assumed by the attorney.

It was, perhaps, because Naunton was not especially active in his offices that he engaged in other affairs that seemed to have little relationship to his posts. In September 1616, he received a letter from Sir Henry Wotton, the English ambassador to Venice, concerning the election of cardinals in the Roman Catholic Church. The nature of the letter is such that it appears to be an official dispatch intended for the king's service. What is more, this comunication was evidently not some whim of Wotton's; Sir Robert had written requesting the information.[47] One can only conclude that in Naunton's spare time he reverted to his old post of assistant to the Secretary of State.

Given Sir Robert's failure to perform the tasks of his offices and his dabbling in other areas, what was the good of him holding office? From the crown's point of view he was not much more useful now than as a jobless courtier. In so far as one can detect that he did anything of value for his royal master, it was mainly acting as a messenger or mediator.[48] What his post gave him was a little extra prestige, a little extra security, and a very respectable income. Sir Robert had achieved about as much as many courtiers ever aspired to; he was often near the king, had ready access to most of the other people who counted, and had a chance to turn a nice profit. The fact that he used his posts as sinecures was not particularly upsetting either to the functioning of the royal government or, apparently, to him.

Whether Naunton assumed that he had reached his ultimate in the royal service or whether these preferments and the favour of the Villiers family simply sharpened his appetite for more is unknown. He must have felt that his position as a royal servant was now relatively secure because he finally resigned his fellowship at Trinity Hall in 1616.[49] As circumstance developed, cutting his links with Cambridge was not a move that he had cause to regret. At age fifty-four his political career had only begun.

[45] 15 James, Trinity, 26 June 1617, PRO Wards 9/93, fol. 125.

[46] Michelmas, 24 October 1617, *ibid.*, fol. 149.

[47] Wotton to Naunton, 20/30 September 1616, Bodley Tanner 74, fol. 81.

[48] For an example see *Egerton Papers,* p. 491.

[49] *Warren's Book,* ed. A. Dale (Cambridge, 1911), p. 193.

1

SECRETARY OF STATE: SETTLING IN

Appointment as Secretary

Sir Robert Naupton was a fortunate man. He might have spent the rest of his life as Master of Requests and Surveyor of the Wards, a largely unnoticed member of the ranks of middle level bureaucracy. But fortune touched him when Sir Ralph Winwood died on 27 October 1617 creating a vacancy in the office of Secretary of State.

Winwood had been a forceful, competent secretary, and there was need for more like him. Vagueness and drift characterized the times and no one was completely satisfied. The parliamentary interests worried because the king would not call a parliament, while courtiers such as the Howards were concerned that he might. The pro-Spanish faction feared the results of Raleigh's voyage, whereas the anti-Spanish faction feared the influence of the Spanish ambassador, Gondomar, even more.

Winwood's death, in the midst of all this uncertainty, did more than create a blank spot in the central administration: it meant the loss of an ardent spokesman for the anti-Spanish party. A dedicated, not to say militant, Protestant, Winwood had not hesitated to pursue his ideological goals while in office. Among other accomplishments, he had brought about Prince Henry's dream, the release of Sir Walter Raleigh to search for a lost gold mine in Spanish controlled South America.[1] It is much to the secretary's credit that he made progress while the Howards were still powerful at court.

Members of the anti-Spanish group obviously wanted someone with Winwood's politics to fill his now vacant position. Their hopes did not, however, centre on one individual. Several candidates began manoeuvres in an effort to secure the post. The chief of these was Sir Dudley Carleton, who was still ambassador to the Dutch Republic. Like the late secretary, Carleton had extensive diplomatic experience, several well-placed friends at court and a hunger for higher office. As a long time associate of Winwood's and a man of more than a little diplomatic skill, Sir Dudley considered himself the logical successor to his late friend.

Another candidate was Sir Thomas Edmonds, the Treasurer of the Household and a former ambassador to France. His diplomatic qualifications were at least as good as Carleton's, but he was operating under a serious drawback. Buckingham differed with

[1] F.M.G. Evans, *The Principal Secretary*, p. 71.

Edmonds over a successor to the latter's old ambassadorial post in France. The favourite wanted William Beecher, but Edmonds did not care for the man.[2] The conflict put Sir Thomas at a major disadvantage vis-á-vis Carleton, but it did not discourage him from making the effort.

Other names were mentioned as well. Sir John Bennet, the civil lawyer, lately turned diplomatic envoy, and Sir Fulk Greville, the Chancellor of the Exchequer, were among the better known.[3] Neither of these was a serious contender despite their prominence. Bennet was working under the handicap of having failed in his diplomatic mission.[4] As for Greville, if Naunton's own evaluation of his personality is correct,[5] he probably did not try very hard for the post.

In the end, whatever plans ambitious men had, the choice of secretary was in the king's hands. Whether or not he would choose an anti-Spaniard for the post depended as much on the political complexion of the time as on the men available. The *leit motiv* of the latter half of James's reign, the magnet that constantly pulled at his mind, was a Spanish marriage for the Prince of Wales and peace and friendship with Spain. Ever since the appearance of the Condé Gondomar, the Spanish ambassador to England, the prospects for this policy had been very good.[6] With this view in mind, James might want to choose a secretary who would not interfere with these plans.

On the other side, in the last months of 1617 Raleigh was still on his final voyage in search of South American gold. Given a successful outcome of the venture, James most likely planned to use the gold mines as a bargaining-counter in the Spanish marriage negotiations.[7] He would only part with the mines to secure favourable conditions for the match, and to increase the value of the Infanta's dowry. Spanish unhappiness at such a turn of events was a foregone conclusion, and thus a Secretary of State who would not be averse to helping strike a hard bargain with King Philip would also be useful.

What this situation called for was a neutral, a man who had no strong opinions either way. The problem was, when it came to foreign policy, most of those with real competence had strong opinions. The

[2]3 November 1617, PRO SP/105/95.

[3]Sir Edward Cecil to Carleton, London, 31 October 1617, PRO SP/84/79, fo. 247 & 3 November 1617, SP/105/95.

[4]*Chamberlain Letters,* II, 109-110, and PRO, SP/84/79, fo. 247.

[5]*Fragmenta Regalia,* Greville.

[6]G. Mattingly, *Renaissance Diplomacy,* (London, 1955), p. 245.

[7]See V.T. Harlow, *Raleigh's Last Voyage,* (London, 1932), introduction.

Lord Keeper, Francis Bacon, was perhaps an exception, but he was not about to abandon the Great Seal for the signet, and James was not about to create a first minister as powerful as the late Lord Salisbury by giving him both.

Another alternative was open. In 1612, the last time the king had been faced with the problem of finding a Secretary of State, he had avoided the issue. He did the work and used the earl of Somerset as a combination confidant and scribe. Somerset's weaknesses as a man of business precluded the success of the scheme. Now, however, with Buckingham on the scene, there were those who thought that the old 'temporary' arrangements would be restored,[8] perhaps on a more permanent basis.

There was one last possibility. When Sir Thomas Lake was appointed secretary two years after Winwood, James kept Spanish business in the new appointee's hands, as he was most sympathetic to it. Anti-Spanish business, such as the persecution of Roman Catholics and diplomacy with Protestant Germany, was given to the senior secretary.[9] As for the large area of neutral business that was neither pro nor anti-Spanish, it could be divided up as the king decided or as custom or circumstances dictated.

In the end, it was the final alternative that appealed most to James. Yet there was some tinkering with the system or rather its personnel. The king wanted someone who would follow his lead better than Winwood had, regardless of any anti-Spanish bias, and this consideration made him look away from forceful men such as Carleton and Edmonds and towards Sir Robert Naunton.

Buckingham's growing influence was another factor in Naunton's favour. Any Secretary of State would have to deal with the favourite quite frequently, for he often acted as the king's agent. Thus it made good sense to avoid any built-in conflict between the two. With Buckingham acting as Naunton's patron and with the favourite's strong sense of family loyalty, James had every reason to expect that there would be little friction between them.

Such considerations do not mean that the favourite, rather than the king, was the final judge of royal appointees. Buckingham no doubt had his opinions on who belonged where, and he was by and large successful in looking out for members of his family such as Naunton. Given the nature of his relationship with the king, such an arrangement is not surprising. Yet in 1617 Buckingham had no monopoly on

[8] 3 November 1617, PRO SP/105/95.
[9] Evans, *The Principal Secretary,* pp. 71-2.

patronage. The Howards, despite Somerset's disgrace, were far from powerless in this area. The Lord Chamberlain, the earl of Pembroke, was also a factor. He helped place Sir Benjamin Rudyerd in Naunton's old office of Surveyor of the Wards after assisting the previous surveyor, Sir Humphrey May, to the post of Chancellor of the Duchy of Lancaster.[10] The favourite's supposed monopoly on patronage was not yet even a political rallying point.

Even without considering the patronage involved, Naunton had some very practical qualifications. He had a long career in both foreign and domestic affairs (though one hesitates to use the adjective 'distinguished' that is so frequently inserted into such a description). Nonetheless, from age twenty-five to thirty-five he had been involved with foreign affairs quite extensively. His work for Salisbury as an assistant to the Secretary of State had renewed this contact, and even as Master of Requests, diplomatic correspondence passed through his hands.[11]

On the domestic side, Naunton had been a courtier, MP, Master of Requests and Surveyor of the Wards. Except for the first-named occupation, he had served in none of these capacities for very long nor with any great show of brilliance. Yet, if none of these posts gave Naunton the highly intensive experience that Carleton and Edmonds had, nor did they give him the pretensions to power and superior knowledge that might have caused clashes with the king. Naunton's experience was a sufficient base upon which to build; an instant source of wisdom and power it was not.

As far as Sir Robert's politics or ideology went, James must have known about his connection with both Essex and Cecil and also of his flirtation with the Howard group. Thus, besides having the blessings of Buckingham, Naunton's appointment might be acceptable to the still-powerful Howards. This situation in turn gave hope that Sir Robert would not be as narrowly anti-Spanish as his predecessor and might support a Spanish marriage if the wind was blowing that way. To James, Naunton must have seemed the near-perfect compromise candidate: a man with anti-Spanish and anti-Catholic leanings who had shown a certain flexibility when the need arose. As a result, on 8 January 1618, to Dudley Carleton's and doubtless to several others' chagrin, Sir Robert Naunton was sworn in as Secretary of State.

If the king had ideas about what to expect of Naunton as secretary, it is not entirely surprising that the new appointee should have his own

[10]See *DNB, sub* May, Sir Humphrey and Rudyerd, Sir Benjamin.

[11]See for example Wotton to Naunton, Venice, 20/30 September 1616, Bodley Tanner. 74, fo. 81.

16

expectations about his post. Three days after he took office, he unburdened himself of these feelings to his good friend and future Secretary of State, John Coke:

> It hath pleased God to incline the King's Majesty to call their unworthy servant to the place of one of his Secretaries. The first advertisement hereof that my own pen hath given is this to yourself (whose fear of God and love of his dear Church and of our dear country my soul hath so long embraced). The choice of the two places I held had they been in my disposal should have been your own before any man's living; but I hear they are both forestalled. You may give me leave out of my true love to invite you a little nearer the sun, specially being endowed as you are with such powers as will abide the sun and the light so well, and are indeed peculiarly complexionated and interested to inhabit and improve themselves therein, as in their proper tabernacle.[12]

Besides Naunton's concern for church and state, it is also interesting that he believed he would be in a position to help Coke (and by implication other friends) to obtain posts of honour and profit. Although the tone is restrained, one gets the impression that Naunton felt he would now be able to do a good deal along this line. He was not entirely mistaken.

One further point arises in the letter that deserves some consideration: what did Sir Robert do to get his office, or, to put it more bluntly, what was the cash price? Naunton makes a reference to having to give up his offices without the right of naming a successor, but there was other talk of a more direct kind of payment. The rumour was that Christopher 'Kit' Villiers, Buckingham's younger brother, would receive £500 a year in land from Naunton in the form of a bequest in the latter's will.[13] The truth of this charge must remain an open question because the evidence has not survived. In Naunton's official will there is no record of such a bequest,[14] but this fact does not conclusively disprove the rumour. Both Buckingham and his brother died before Naunton which may have cancelled the obligation. Furthermore, when Sir Robert gave up his office as secretary after serving only three active years, all previous arrangements may have ended, or there may have been a cash settlement for which no record exists. One sidelight does emerge on the question of a cash payment. When Naunton left the secretariat, Buckingham proposed setting his

[12]HMC, *Cowper*, I, 95-6.

[13]S. R. Gardiner, *History of England. . .* (London, 1901), III, 101, citing Chamberlain to Carleton, 8 November 1617 and Salvetti's *News-Letter*, 14/24 January 1618.

[14]See appendix D.

pension at the very interesting figure of £500 a year in land.[15] Until some further proof is unearthed, the Scottish verdict of 'not proven' seems the most appropriate.

The First Year: the Howards, Raleigh and the New Arrangements

If anyone was pleased with the new secretary's first months, it must have been James rather than Naunton (or Lake for that matter). What the king had done was to take a potential power centre, the secretaryship, and weaken it through division. Lake was in charge of the major section of the business, especially the supervision of the Privy Council. The nature of the work meant that he had to remain at Whitehall or at least not much further afield than Greenwich. He was thus separated from the king whose constant progresses from hunting lodge to hunting lodge seldom put him in the London area. As a result, Lake could bring little direct influence to bear on the king and had to deal with him by means of an intermediary or by correspondence.

Naunton was Lake's alter-ego, staying with the court and king as they left their trail of disembowelled stags throughout the English countryside. The new secretary presented James with letters and dispatches that Lake had sent and saw to it that, as often as circumstances permitted, important business was dispatched promptly.[16] Naunton was thus getting most of his information second-hand by means of Lake, which meant that the travelling secretary had the king's ear, but lacked first-hand knowledge. This system had the virtue of working both ways, for the king might instruct Naunton to carry out various pieces of business that Lake would only learn of secondhand. It was like a card game in which James was the dealer who knew all the cards and thus kept the other players from getting a really good hand.

Whatever the advantages of the system from the point of view of royal control, it did have definite weaknesses. It was certainly inefficient with respect to time, and it was vulnerable to further difficulties if the two secretaries did not work well as a team. In fact, despite their diverse viewpoints, Naunton and Lake cooperated. Either James was fortunate, or, in this case, he was a good judge of men.

With regard to Naunton personally, there is no doubt that initially

[15]Discussed below pp. 92-3.

[16]When Naunton had the post of principal secretary he was at least once quite upset with Calvert, the junior secretary, for not pressing the king to dispatch important matters. Naunton to W. Trumbull, Whitehall, 6 May 1619, Berkshire Record Office, Trumbull MS. 33, no. 13.

the king's expectations of him were fully realized. He was the 'second' secretary just as James had promised Gondomar he would be.[17] A few days after Naunton took office, he wrote to Sir Lionel Cranfield about a picture the king wanted copied from the Barber-Surgeons' Hall in London,[18] a piece of business more fit for a scribe than for a Secretary of State. Sir Robert's duties were so light that he found time to look after his friends and relations. Not long after his adventures as an art dealer, he recommended a relative to Sir Dudley Carleton for service with one of the English regiments to the Dutch Republic.[19] As late as 5 May 1618 Chamberlain wrote to Carleton: 'I heare no newes nor speach of Secretarie Nanton, no more in a manner then yf there were no such man in *rerum natura,* which is a straunge kind of obscuritie for a man of his place to lie so close and hidden that he shold scant be seen or heard of at home.'[20] The only thing that can be said in mitigation of Chamberlain's observation is that by March 1618 Naunton began to attend the Privy Council meetings on a fairly regular basis.[21] But with the summer progresses about to lead the court away from Whitehall, how long this attendance would have lasted under ordinary circumstances is a matter for question.

More rapidly than anyone could have predicted the circumstances ceased being ordinary. By April 1618 Sir Thomas Lake was about to have his political career ended. A family dispute between his daughter and son-in-law, Lady and Lord Roos, took on political implications. Then there were charges that Lake made unethical use of his position as secretary to advance his family's financial position. The matter took some time to develop, but for a good six months Sir Thomas was held in a state of suspended animation and was secretary in name only.

In May 1618, as Lake became conscious of the net tightening about him, he appealed to Naunton: 'I had hoped that I should from your honor had some comfort by meanes of my Lady Margerie [Lake's wife] wherein I pray you persist. No man knoweth my case more then you, and I hope that myne own assertions shalbe of as much creditt as theirs, who in bringing me to this question have broken the

[17]Gondomar to Philip III, 12 January 1618 (new style), *Documentos Ineditos para la Historia de Espana* (Madrid, 1936), I, 211.

[18]Naunton to Cranfield, Newmarket, 17 January 1618, Kent Record Office, Sackville MS. M1007, fo. 46.

[19]Naunton to Carleton, Whitehall, 10 March 1618, PRO SP/84/83, fo. 33.

[20]*Chamberlain Letters,* II, 161.

[21]*APC., 1618-1619,* pp. 57 ff.

fayth and honour they gave me.'[22] Lake's plea was no more effective than the rest he must have made to people a good deal more influential than his fellow secretary. Within a week of the appeal to Naunton, Sir Thomas stopped attending Privy Council meetings, and with one or two exceptions his signature disappeared from council documents.[23]

No direct evidence exists about Naunton's attitude towards his fellow secretary's decline. The nature of the letter written in May, especially the remark, 'no man knoweth my case more than you', leads one to suspect that Sir Robert's connection with the Howards may not have ended with Somerset's disgrace. Yet how much truth lies in a desperate man's cry for help?

As far as the members of the court were concerned, Naunton's behaviour towards Lake was all that could be expected. On 1 July 1618, Thomas, Viscount Fenton wrote to his friend, the earl of Mar, 'Secreterrye Nenton is a verrye honnest man and hes bein a good frind to his fellow'.[24] In later years Sir Robert prided himself on his loyalty,[25] and perhaps his support of Sir Thomas was part of the reason for his attitude. He may also have realized that the bell could toll for him one day, as it had for his fellow secretary. Nonetheless one can only wonder just how sorry a militant Protestant like Naunton was to see a crypto-Romanist and pro-Spaniard such as Lake fade from the scene.

Whatever Naunton's personal involvement may have been, there is no doubt that Sir Thomas's gradual eclipse had a marked effect on the newer man's role as Secretary of State. The first and most obvious effect was on Naunton's dealings with the Privy Council. In the summer of 1618 when James went on progress, the council followed him. Though it was not uncommon for various councillors to join the king for his summer hunting, it was not standard procedure for the Privy Council as a body to do so; the summer of 1618 was the only time during Naunton's tenure as secretary that it happened. Evidently James did not want Lake supervising the council at a time when he was under suspicion, and the result was that Naunton took over the responsibility for organizing the council's business. He retained this role as Privy Council co-ordinator for nearly three years until his own disgrace brought it and many other things to an end.

The other effect Lake's disappearance had on Naunton's role as

[22]Lake to Naunton, received 25 May [1618], PRO SP/78/68, fo. 61.

[23] *APC, 1618-1619*, pp. 148 & 155.

[24]HMC, *Mar Supplement*, p. 85.

[25]*Fragmenta Regalia*, conclusion.

secretary was to substantially increase the diplomatic correspondence he handled.[26] Although Sir Thomas continued to receive dispatches almost until the time of his Star Chamber trial, after the sumer of 1618 the major part of the diplomatic work passed through Naunton's hands.

This development was not entirely due to a decision made by James. The ambassadors may have been stationed all over Europe, but they made every attempt to keep in close touch with events at court. The Chamberlain-Carleton letters are good evidence of ambassadorial interest in domestic happenings. There were definite advantages to corresponding with a Secretary of State who was in the king's good graces. Thus it is not entirely surprising that the ambassadors seized whatever opportunity they could to write to Naunton once it was clear that Lake was in disgrace. Sir Thomas was anything but pleased about his loss of popularity, and at one point complained to Buckingham that Carleton was not writing to him. Carleton heard of the complaint and blandly replied that the king had instructed him to direct his dispatches to Naunton the last time he was in England (the summer of 1618), and he was only following orders.[27] In the case of William Trumbull at Brussels, Lake's protests had more effect. As late as 21 December 1618, Naunton wrote him that he should direct his dispatches to Sir Thomas unless he received the king's or Sir Thomas's permission to do otherwise.[28]

During the period of transition there were items of business that fell to Sir Robert only because of the nebulous state of affairs. One of these was Raleigh's execution.

By all the standards thus far set, Raleigh's trial and execution should not have been a matter for Naunton. Sir Walter's last voyage, whatever else it was calculated to do, was not the sort of venture that would endear him to the Spanish. Given the role one would expect Naunton to play as secretary — that of the anti-Spaniard — sympathy for Sir Walter and his project would be the most predictable attitude for him to take. Yet it was Sir Robert who was charged with overseeing Raleigh's destruction. There are several possible reasons for this unexpected role. First and foremost was Lake's position at the time of Sir Walter's return. Although the disgraced secretary was not yet dismissed from his post, when Raleigh landed in the summer of

[26]See appendix A.
[27]Carleton to Buckingham, The Hague, 29 October 1618, PRO SP/84/86, fo. 230.
[28]Berkshire Record Office, Trumbull MS. 33, no. 26.

1618, James had no inclination to put the suspect Lake in charge. The matter of Sir Walter's examination and arraignment was politically too sensitive. Therefore Naunton had to take the responsibility. Another factor was Raleigh's own actions. He came ashore at Plymouth and tried to reach the king who was then at Salisbury. If he had landed at one of the ports near London, it would have made all the difference. Since Naunton was accompanying James when Sir Walter turned up in the West Country, it made sense to let the secretary in residence deal with him. Had Raleigh arrived in London, Lake could have interposed himself, or he might even have been ordered to handle matters simply because there was no one else around.

Raleigh's last months have been related many times;[29] the focus here, however, is on Naunton's role. Basically his duties consisted of supervising Sir Thomas Wilson's interrogation of Raleigh and of keeping an eye on any foreign power (especially France) which might interfere in the proceedings. There was special concern with someone attempting to spirit the fugitive out of England. Of necessity Naunton was also a member of the Privy Council committee assigned to examine Raleigh on his actions during his last voyage.[30]

Sir Robert's supervision of the interrogation placed him in a position he would fill with increasing frequency, that of intermediary between the king and some other party. In practice he not only passed on information, but also acted as a filter for the complaints and problems that arose. When Wilson was upset because the Lieutenant of the Tower, Sir Allen Apsley, was not cooperating with him[31] it was Naunton who procured the necessary warrant from the king to overcome the difficulty.[32] Likewise, when James thought Wilson had promised Raleigh too much, it was Naunton who questioned Wilson, and later reassured the king.[33] The initiative for these duties came from parties other than Sir Robert, and his role was to carry them out with a minimum of friction.

[29]Harlow, *Raleigh's Last Voyage* is probably the best account, while W. E. Wallace gives a fairly objective view of Raleigh's life as a whole in *Sir Walter Raleigh* (Princeton, 1959).

[30]The other members of the committee were Archbishop Abbot, Francis Bacon (Lord Chancellor), the earl of Worcester (Lord Privy Seal), Sir Julius Caesar (Master of the Rolls) and Sir Edward Coke. J. Spedding, *The Letters and the Life of Francis Bacon* (London, 1872), VI, 356.

[31]Harlow, *Raleigh's Last Voyage,* p. 262, citing SP/14/99, no. 9.

[32]Harlow, *Raleigh's Last Voyage,* p. 266, citing SP/14/99. no. 11.

[33]SP/14/99, no. 292.

22

When it came to the direction of the counter-espionage, Naunton had more latitude for independent action. He ordered all ports closed to outgoing transport,[34] a move which sealed off any possible escape and denied foreign agents easy access to their superiors abroad. He also formulated an elaborate plan based on the liberal use of wine for relieving some French agents of their dispatches.[35]

Sir Robert's actions alone give no clue to his attitude towards Raleigh. Contemporaries, however, formed a rather definite opinion on where Naunton stood. A wealthy goldsmith named Edward Wymark, a 'Paul's walker' and a friend of John Chamberlain,[36] said publicly after Raleigh's execution that Sir Walter's head should be on Naunton's shoulders. This rather rash statement was reported to the Privy Council, and Wymark found himself rapidly brought before that board to explain himself.[37] It is not inconceivable that his loose tongue could have cost him a few weeks in the Fleet or a large fine. With such a prospect in mind, and hoping that Naunton had a sense of humour, Wymark made light of the whole affair and claimed that all he meant was that two heads were better than one. The councillors must have laughed, for Wymark was let off.[38]

Contemporary opinion about Naunton's attitude is largely confirmed by a statement he made to Wilson: 'I hope you will evry day get grownd of that hypocrite that is so desirous to dye, mortified man that he is.'[39] Though it is possible that Naunton's comment was made for the record and does not reflect his true opinion, it has the ring of truth about it. Whatever else Naunton was, he was not overtly hypocritical. He could have remained silent (he did so on other occasions when he objected to royal policy), and it would have cost him nothing. His speaking out must mean that he did not like Raleigh.

The dislike of Sir Walter in all likelihood did not have political motivation. Raleigh was not especially popular until after his death,

[34]Lord Zouch [Lord Warden of the Cinque Ports] to the mayor of Dover, 12 October 1618, *CSPD, 1611-1618*, p. 584.

[35]Naunton to Buckingham, Whitehall, 11 December 1618, *Fortescue Papers*, ed. S.R. Gardiner (Camden Society: Westminster, 1871), pp. 71-3.

[36]W. Notestein, *Four Worthies* (London, 1956), p. 41.

[37]Sir Thomas Wynn to Carleton, 9 December 1618, *CSPD, 1611-1618*, p. 601.

[38]The story does not end here. Some years later the goldsmith was appointed to the commission for the repair of St Paul's Cathedral. In order to show his good will, Wymark offered to donate £100 of his own money, whereat Naunton, who was also on the commission, changed the donation to £200. The goldsmith protested, but Naunton silenced him with the remark: 'Surely you remember that two is better than one'. T. Fuller, *Worthies*, III, 175.

[39]Harlow, *Raleigh's Last Voyage*, p. 266, citing SP/14/99, no. 11.

and this lack of popularity was not necessarily because his politics were suspect. Sir Dudley Carleton, whose Protestant and anti-Spanish sympathies were well known, wrote to John Chamberlain that the best thing that could be said about Raleigh's life was that he died well.[40]

With respect to Sir Robert, as a member of both the Essex and Cecil factions in his earlier days, he may well have absorbed some of their dislike of the man. In addition, during Elizabeth's reign Raleigh was thrown into the Marshalsea for duelling with a man named Wingfield.[41] Since the Wingfields were closely related to the Nauntons, there may have been a long-time family feud involved in Naunton's attitude.

Whatever motivated Naunton's feelings towards Raleigh, it must have been a relief to him when the furore over the execution died down, and he could return to the more routine aspects of being a Secretary of State. What Sir Robert found, however, was that the routine had rather radically altered. Sir Thomas Lake was dismissed from office by February 1619, and the temporary duties of managing the Privy Council and handling the diplomatic correspondence became permanent tasks for Naunton. He was now the senior Secretary of State, and just to complete the picture, Sir George Calvert, another former secretary to the earl of Salisbury and a man sympathetic to the Roman Catholics, was appointed junior secretary within a few weeks of Lake's dismissal. As had been the case with Naunton, as junior secretary, Calvert stayed with the king as much as possible while the senior secretary was pretty much tied to Whitehall.

The turnover of personnel in the secretariat was a reflection of a much broader change that was occurring within the English government. The Howard faction was being driven from its offices and was no longer a major political influence at the national level. Not only Lake but Suffolk, the Lord Treasurer, Wallingford, the Master of the Court of Wards, and finally Yelverton, the Attorney General, were all forced from their posts. Even the old earl of Nottingham, the Lord Admiral, turned his office over to the man who was the ultimate beneficiary of the Howards' decline, Buckingham. Until his death in 1628, this favourite of two kings controlled the most effective patronage machine at court.

Such a shift in power at court was bound to have an effect on Naunton beyond his elevation to the post of senior secretary. He had

[40]Carleton to Chamberlain, The Hague, 15 November 1618, PRO SP/84/87, fo. 36.

[41]Wallace, *Sir Walter Raleigh*, pp. 14-5.

24

been an adherent of Buckingham's since the young man's first success at court. Naunton's dependence bound him to a cautious policy wherever his patron's basic interests were involved. Having no power base of his own, if he offended Buckingham, all further hope of promotions, or perhaps even of retention, were in jeopardy.

Equally important, Naunton had seen Somerset's decline and fall and had seen its effects on those such as Sir Robert Cotton who were dependent on him. He had also seen what had just happened to the Howard faction and its adherents. The message was clear; no faction or favourite could last forever. When these large oaks fell in the forest, many smaller trees were damaged beyond all hope of recovery.

These considerations meant that Sir Robert would be well advised to find a person or group that he could rely upon in case the need arose. The person would have to be well-established in the court and in the King's affections. Presumably he also would have to be someone whose religious and political views roughly coincided with Naunton's. Sir Robert reached back nearly a decade into his past and chose James, Lord Hay (now Viscount Doncaster) to fill the role.

Naunton and Doncaster

Even from a non-political point of view, Naunton's efforts to improve his relationship with Doncaster are quite understandable. The man was one of the few important court figures of his day who was well liked by nearly everyone. He must have been a person of genuine charm, for he overcame the large initial disadvantage of being a Scot seeking favour in England, and became a universal favourite with the court. He even managed to gain the respect of his father-in-law, the 'Wizard' earl of Northumberland, whose family, the Percys, had virtually built its reputation by defending the northern borders against the Scots.[42] There is thus every reason to believe Naunton when he wrote Doncaster that he missed their walks in Whitehall gardens.[43]

Charm, of course, has its political uses, and early in 1619 James decided to utilize Doncaster's by appointing him ambassador extraordinary to mediate the dispute between Ferdinand, king of Bohemia, and his rebel subjects. The mission was the English king's first of many attempts to prevent the outbreak of the Thirty Years War. It was also Naunton's first important project as senior secretary; what is more, it provided Sir Robert with an opportunity to prove his usefulness to Doncaster.

[42] See *DNB sub* Percy, Henry, 9th earl of Northumberland.
[43] Naunton to Doncaster, Whitehall, 10 June 1619, BL Eg. 2592, fo. 133.

It is not entirely surprising to find that Naunton played the role of intermediary for the embassy: he passed James's instructions to Doncaster and the latter's reports back to his master. It was a frustrating job. Naunton had strong views on war and peace with the Habsburgs, which had to remain unadvocated for the sake of the mission. In addition dealing with the idiosyncrasies and troubles of both the king and his ambassador became the secretary's most unwilling province.

Right from the start, Doncaster was nervous about the prospect of an extended separation from James and the court. He no sooner left his first stop, Brussels, than he asked Sir Robert to check on rumours that there was dissatisfaction with his performance. The secretary probably would have been more than delighted to carry out his request, but he ran into the problem of James's style of doing business:

> To the first I must aunswer breifly thus, that I never heard of any the least mislike in his Majestie for your Lordships stay in Bruxells; who if he mislike any thing in your Lordship I see I am not likely to heare it from him. If I had, your Lordship should not have beene unacquainted with it. I am tied here to the counsell boord and committees that have the government of all [t]his state at home, so as I can not attend his Majesty personally, but when I am sent for; and am faine to send him away your Lordships lettres post, being so much longed for before they arrive. And when I am sent for to receive directions how to aunswer your Lordship and others, I finde his Majesty so full of distractions with the multiplicities of buisinesses which he alwayes directs by deluges, as I am faine to spend all my soule in attention to carry away what he directs, and have no freedome to offer any thing to his consideracion as from my selfe, may not scarcely so much as to conceive any doubt of mistaking what he speaketh so much as may give him occasion to repeate any one word of his torrents of instructions, which ar delivered with such sodaines as a man may safelier adventure to mistake then question or interrupt the swiftness and course of his discourses.[44]

Within Naunton's cry of frustration are the factors that dominated his life as senior Secretary of State. He was separated from the king, and he had the responsibility for running the Privy Council and its committees. The rest of the commentary about his position must not be taken too seriously. Naunton was quite capable of presenting his point of view to James when the circumstances were somewhat less chaotic than he described.

[44]Naunton to Doncaster, Whitehall, 20 July 1619, Eg. 2592 fo. 231.

Nonetheless, it must have been something of a blow when Sir Robert discovered that the office of Secretary of State was not in and of itself a powerful office. Its previous occupants in James's reign, Salisbury and, to a lesser extent, Winwood, had been influential men and had, by their presence in the post raised its prestige. Even leaving aside personal capabilities, Naunton lacked his predecessors' wealth and their supporting factions. He always had to deal with the king and Buckingham from a very much subordinate position. His only tools for gaining his ends were patience and persuasion. It is no wonder that he sometimes struck out at people in frustration.[45]

Under these circumstances whatever success Naunton achieved must have been of particular satisfaction to him. One such success occurred during Doncaster's mission and involved the ambassador and another special object of Naunton's devotion, Elizabeth, Princess Palatine, James's daughter.[46] Given the princess's charm and her staunch Protestantism, it is hard to imagine Naunton not falling under her spell. The high regard with which Doncaster held her could not have hurt either. By helping Elizabeth, he also helped himself with Doncaster, and in the Elphinstone affair she needed help. Elphinstone was part of that impecunious troop of Scots which had attached itself to the Stuarts in England. He himself had gone to Germany with the Princess Elizabeth and had subsequently fallen into some disfavour with her. His solution to this problem was to extricate himself with the help of a little forgery.

The post of secretary to Elizabeth was open, and she had made it a practice to let her father choose the man who took the job. Since the individual often acted as a go-between for both father and daughter, James had the intelligence to try to pick someone who met with his daughter's approval. What Elphinstone did was convince another Scot, Francis Galbraith, to write a letter recommending the said Elphinstone and sign Elizabeth's name to the letter. Since Galbraith had been trained by the princess to imitate her handwriting in order to save her the trouble of personally answering all her mail this note must have been quite convincing.[47]

Though no one ever said so in so many words, James apparently had no great love for Elphinstone and was upset that his daughter appeared taken with the man. He also had more than a slight suspicion

[45] In one instance Naunton let go a blast at a messenger who was too slow in returning to Doncaster. *Ibid.*, fo. 232.

[46] Naunton once commented: 'I have made a religion of it to serve hir Highness towards his Maiestie for the eradicating of that scruple which I ioy much to see it done.' BL, Naunton to Doncaster, Whitehall, 20 August 1619, BL Eg. 2592, fo. 259.

[47] Naunton to Doncaster, Whitehall, 25 August 1619, BL Eg. 2593, fo. 8.

that, even if the letter was forged, Elizabeth was more closely connected with its writing than she let on, and with obvious distress the king told Naunton as much:

> Two thinges ther ar in this [Elphinstone's] account which resolve one of the truthe of it because they agree so punctually with his Majesties own secreet and confident relacion which in the bitternesse of his sowle he intimated to my self; which were that the lettre was of hir Highness own hand writing or exceeding dexterously counterfeitted. . . .[48]

Naunton was plainly upset by the rift between his master and his master's daughter, and he did his best to resolve the king's fears:

> I feare his Majesty would not well allow my selfe to prye thus searchingly into this buisinesse further then himself was pleased of himself to admitt and let me into it, but I know it knowingly that it will joye his sowle to see that noble lady cleered and righted, and therefore I am resolved to make it my owne way with him when I shall have the first leave and happinesse to attend him, to move him to make this whole discoverie his own worke &c. . . [Marginal note] as a tricke intended to have bene put as well upon himselfe as upon that deare daughter of his &c.[49]

In and of itself, the Elphinstone affair is of little importance: the man was not given the post, James more or less forgave Elizabeth, and Sir Francis Nethersole, Doncaster's secretary, eventually became Elizabeth's. Yet Naunton's handling of the matter does reveal some interesting features about his attitude towards his duties as Secretary of State. It is clear that Naunton was reluctant to jump too rapidly to Elizabeth's defence because of the king's feelings. A line existed, and he felt he must not step over it, despite his enthusiasm for the princess. Still, Sir Robert was also not easily discouraged from his goal. When his first effort seemingly failed, he merely changed tack and suggested that James make the discoveries on his own, presumably with Naunton laying out the trail for him. The secretary's actions show a certain awareness about the king's nature. Though the awareness was by no means complete, in the coming conflicts it would prove sufficient.

Beyond Naunton's attitude towards his job, the Elphinstone affair demonstrates the king's attitude towards his secretary. In a fit of exasperation Sir Robert had complained that James never told him anything.[50] Yet the king was willing to bare his soul to his secretary on

[48] *Ibid.*
[49] *Ibid.* fos. 8-9.
[50] BL, Eg. 2592, fo. 231.

what was, after all, a rather personal matter. James must have liked and trusted Sir Robert to do what he did. What is more, the king proved perfectly willing to hear the man out, the earlier fears notwithstanding. Nonetheless, James felt under no obligation either to inform Naunton of every aspect of royal affairs or to ask for or take his advice on all matters. Sir Robert was aware of this ambiguity in his master's attitude, but never detected the motivation for it. It did not occur to Naunton that James could not, if he expected to stay master in his own house for very long, put all his trust and confidence in one minister or one party.

It was in the aftermath of Doncaster's mission that Naunton's confusion about the king comes out most clearly. In September 1619 Frederick, Elizabeth's husband, was on the verge of agreeing to the displacement of Ferdinand (now the Holy Roman Emperor) and accepting the Bohemian throne for himself; war among the German states was a real possibility. The prince's plans were hailed by many influential English ministers. Naunton, Doncaster and Archbishop Abbot, to name only a few, had reached the conclusion that it was necessary for the militant, united Protestant Church to triumph over the forces of Roman Catholicism (particularly over its Spanish-Habsburg-Jesuit contingents). That the English should be in the forefront of this movement was to them a foregone conclusion.

Their blend of religion and nationalism ran directly counter to James's orientation towards peace and maintenance of the *status quo*. The tragedy for Naunton and other Englishmen like him was that they never accepted the idea that their king was governed by motives different from their own. For them maintaining the *status quo* was permitting Satan to live on earth unmolested,[51] and, as they saw it, James would never accept such a situation.

When Frederick was elected king of Bohemia, he requested James's advice before he took the proffered crown. The enemies of Satan thought their moment had come and were certain of the English king's enthusiastic approval. Naunton for one showed just how much he had misjudged James, for in a letter written to Doncaster late in August 1619, he wrote: 'Now of my selfe I must in the freedome which I owe your Lordship say this, that for those reportes of the Transilvanian in Hungarie,[52] or of the new election in Bohemia I finde his

---

[51]For a full discussion of this question see Elmar Weiss, *Die Unterstützung Friedrichs V. von de Pfalz durch Jacob I und Karl I von England in Dreissigjährigen Krieg* (Stuttgart, 1966), pp. 12-17.

[52]Bethlen Gabor, Prince of Transylvania.

Majestie is slowe of beleefe as if he tasted them to be too good to be true . . .'.[53] One can only marvel at Sir Robert's isolation from the king's true line of thought. Here was James filled with apprehension and dismay at what his son-in-law was contemplating, and there was Naunton writing to his friend that their master thought it was all too good to be true. Once Sir Robert realized that the king would not leap at the chance to weaken Romanist power, he tried to mobilize his allies to increase the pressure for support of Frederick's venture. Among other actions, the secretary called on Doncaster to come home as quickly as possible.[54] Debates were going on in the Privy Council over the question of what Frederick should do and Naunton wanted his friend's support.[55]

From the political point of view, Sir Robert's efforts were a failure. Doncaster did not come home immediately, and James did not come out in support of Frederick's venture. The cause was too dangerous. The displacement of one king by the will of the people was contrary to everything James believed in; he would not even give covert support. Yet James was too clever a politician to cut off all hope from the ultra-Protestant faction. What he did was put the burden of proof on them. He asked them to show him that the displacement of Ferdinand by Frederick was compatible with the law of monarchies. This device delayed matters and permitted James time to reorganize his peace efforts. Like his secretary, James was not easily deterred from his goals.

Naunton's efforts to gain Doncaster as a friend and potential patron were not nearly so disappointing as their joint efforts to influence the king. There can be little doubt that it was their unity on the subject of Frederick that played the decisive part in joining Naunton and the viscount in an alliance of friendship and inclination. Sir Robert's recent marriage to Doncaster's widowed sister-in-law, Penelope Perrot Lower, could only have strengthened this bond.[56] Sir Robert was still Buckingham's man, but as later events were to demonstrate, Doncaster was a useful ally at times when many other people had deserted him.

---

[53]Naunton to Doncaster, Whitehall, BL Eg. 2593, fo. 8.

[54]BL, Eg. 2593, fo. 13.

[55]Naunton to Doncaster, Whitehall, 3 September 1619, BL Eg. 2593 fo. 15.

[56]Naunton married Penelope Perrot Lower, the half-sister of Lucy Percy. Their mother was Dorothy Devereux, the sister of the 2nd earl of Essex, who first married Sir Thomas Perrot and then the 9th earl of Northumberland.

2

SECRETARY OF STATE: DUTIES

Domestic affairs

Naunton's role in domestic affairs while he was Secretary of State was, if nothing else, an extremely varied one. It ranged as far afield as being a member of the committee that decided whether or not Christopher Villiers could have a monopoly for engrossing wills,[1] to writing to Lord Clifford for a report on the middle marches.[2] Broadly speaking, however, Sir Robert's domestic interests and duties largely concerned the Privy Council, the Treasury Commission, and the distribution of patronage and the use of influence.

The first of these, the Privy Council, was the most important, consuming vast amounts of Naunton's time. The nature of the councillors increased his difficulties. They were a diverse lot composed of nobles and gentlemen, bureaucrats and ecclesiastics, Puritans and Roman Catholics. It was Naunton's task to co-ordinate their duties and, when necessary, prod them to action.

Procedurally, Sir Robert was in charge of calling council meetings.[3] He also had a certain amount of responsibility for setting the agenda.[4] These tasks made him the *de facto,* if not the *de jure,* chairman of the council, for there was no Lord President of the Privy Council while he was active as secretary. As for Calvert, it is not inconceivable that, when he could get away from the court, he also brought orders from the king to call meetings, but there is no way of knowing if he acted as chairman for the meetings he called.

Despite his role as organizer, or possibly because of it, Naunton was not exempt from the committees set up by the council to deal with specific problems. In fact he was on many of them ranging from permanent ones such as the committee on the wool trade[5] to *ad hoc* ones such as the committee on the dispute over the lead trade between the merchants of Hull and the Merchant Adventurers of London.[6]

---

[1] Bacon, Naunton and Sir H. Montagu to James, 15 November 1620, Lambeth Palace, MS 936, fo. 134b.

[2] *HMC, 3rd Report,* p. 39.

[3] Rules to be observed in the Councills and Committees made 20 February 1627. BL Add. 38861, fo. 3.

[4] *Ibid.,* fo. 5.

[5] *APC, 1619-21,* pp. 197-8.

[6] *Ibid.,* 90.

Whether it was the nature of these duties or their sheer volume, Naunton found them wearisome and restraining. In the summer of 1619 he often complained to Doncaster about how burdensome the council and its committees were,[7] and at one point described himself as 'being tyed here like Epimetheus to the Caucasus of Whitehall'.[8] As a result, whenever the opportunity arose, Naunton avoided these committees.[9] From his point of view, these opportunities did not arise nearly often enough.

On the surface at least, the role of co-ordinator of the Privy Council seems like an influential one, but in practice it was much less so. Naunton was principally an intermediary between the king and council, and the greater percentage of his work was simply conveying information from one to the other. It was not uncommon for Sir Robert's letters to the court to consist almost entirely of Privy Council business.[10]

The role of man-in-the-middle was not an easy one. Naunton's status as a bureaucrat rather than a factional leader meant that he had to tread lightly with all concerned. What is more, wherever there was a dispute or misunderstanding between the crown and the Privy Council, Sir Robert was in the unenviable position of having to face both sides with information they did not want to hear.

Despite such a severe handicap, occasionally Naunton did manage to persuade either the king or the council to change its mind. In one instance, Sir Robert reminded the council of the king's pleasure: 'This inclosed peticion of the Earl of Ormond's was almost given way unto. But I remembered their Lordships that he stood out prisoner in contempt against his Majesties decree made by his own royal person, and moved that his Majestie might be acquainted herewith and declare his pleasur before they gave any order herein.'[11] No one likes to be reminded what his duty is, and the magnates of the Privy Council responded accordingly, for about a week later Naunton wrote:

'let me know his Majesties pleasure touching the Earl of Ormond's peticion, which I sent inclosed in that dispatch, for which I

[7]BL, Eg. 2592, fo. 231.

[8]*Ibid.*

[9]Naunton to Carleton, Whitehall, 3 January 1619, PRO SP/84/88, fo. 7a.

[10]*Fortescue Papers,* 129-32.

[11]*Ibid.,* 115.

suffer envie, having turned the resolucion of the table by putting them and myselfe in minde of our dueties and respects to his Majestie. . .'.[12]

Because of his inherently weak position, it is unlikely that Naunton interposed himself any more than was absolutely necessary. When he did so, he draped himself heavily with the king's authority. If James had chosen Sir Robert with the idea that he would not have to worry about a masterful man like Salisbury or Winwood who might oppose his will, he had indeed chosen well.

Nonetheless, Naunton's greatest success came when he acted as the council's voice to the king, for it was in this capacity that he was able to help bring about the 1621 Parliament.[13] As anyone who had ever dealt with James must have known, he did not find the holding of parliaments a pleasant experience. But once the council had decided that a parliament was desirable, it was only natural that the councillors should encourage Naunton to continue his role as intermediary, if only to shield themselves from the king's wrath. Under other circumstances Naunton might have found such a task distasteful. In this case, however, he had very much wanted the council to give him just such a commission.[14]

Naunton may have used his role on the Treasury Commission to pursue personal goals as well, but much less is known about his work here than that with the Privy Council. The Treasury was put in commission in 1618 when Suffolk, the Lord Treasurer, was disgraced. The commission lasted until Sir Henry Montagu's appointment as treasurer in December 1620. Archbishop Abbot acted as chairman of the commission. In so far as anything can be said about Naunton's role on this board, the nature of the work was similar in many respects to that of the Privy Council. Once again he was responsible for calling the meetings and for informing the king and commissioners of the other's respective wishes. The first of these duties was not always an easy assignment, and it would appear that Naunton was not the only English royal servant who was averse to avoiding his more burdensome duties:

> There could be no proceeding in the Threasury this afternoone because Mr. Chauncellor who onely is of the Quorum was absent, my Lord of Canterbury stayed at home by the gout, my

---

[12]*Ibid.*, 116.

[13]Although James was no doubt putting on something of an act to upset the Habsburgs who distrusted the English parliament, he is reported as saying, 'I may well thank Naunton as were it not for him, I should not have summoned parliament.' Lando to the Doge and Senate, 11 June 1621, (new style), *CSP, Ven, 1621-23.* p. 64.

[14]See below, p. 75.

> Lord Chancellor sat not in the afternoone but went from the Starr
> Chamber home to dinner my Lord of Winchester was gone
> before all the rest of the concell rise and the master of the Rolls
> and Sir Edward Coke and I being left alone were under the
> number limited in the commission.[15]

Quite clearly, the reluctant were leading the unwilling, and it is not
inconceivable that Naunton had more difficulty trying to keep the
Treasury Commission functioning than he did the Privy Council.

Because of the lack of documentation concerning the role played
by each of the treasury commissioners, one gets only an impressionistic
picture of Naunton's part. So far as anyone can tell, he knew little
about financial affairs, and, except in the way of most gentlemen of the
period, he had little experience with them.[16] These facts, such as they
are, lead one to conclude that Sir Robert functioned mainly as an
over-qualified messenger rather than an influential member of the
commission. This impression is at least in part confirmed by his
cautious behaviour when trying to obtain a more efficient system of
payment for English diplomats, a matter upon which he had quite
strong feelings.[17] When the commission was dissolved in December
1620, and the duties turned over to the new Lord Treasurer, Sir
Henry Montagu (who was created Viscount Mandeville, for the
occasion), Naunton must have felt relieved that there was one less
matter for him to look after, rather than hurt that he had lost some of
his power or prestige.

Though the Privy Council and the Treasury Commission were
sides of Naunton's domestic duties as Secretary of State that he
performed without relish, there were other aspects of the office that
he viewed with much greater favour, namely the distribution of
patronage and the use of his influence.[18] In fact, Sir Robert had very
little of the former to distribute. Strictly speaking there was no post
within the government that was in the gift of the Secretary of State by
virtue of his office alone. However, just as Salisbury had done,

[15] Naunton to Buckingham, Whitehall, 23 April 1619, BL Harl. 1581, fo. 105.

[16] Naunton was quite reluctant to risk money on the more speculative opportunities
provided by the joint stock companies that were springing up in the early part of the
seventeenth century. T. Rabb, *Enterprise and Empire* (Cambridge, Mass., 1967), p.
347.

[17] See below, pp. 41-44.

[18] Although patronage and influence are often used interchangeably, it is best to
differentiate between them here. Patronage will be defined as the ability, by virtue of
one's office and/or political prestige, to place others in governmental posts or to obtain
concessions such as money, privileges or honours. Influence will be defined as the
ability to convince people who have patronage to use it on someone's behalf.

Naunton employed assistants at his own expense.[19] He used two men, George Verney and Thomas Lord, who remained with him until his death in 1635. The former was probably a member of the Verney family, with whom Naunton had had dealings while at Cambridge, and thus was related to John Coke.[20] The latter had connections in Kent, but just how he came to Naunton's attention is unknown.

Even though the patronage side was rather bleak, when it came to influence, the story appears quite different. It is fair to say that as long as Sir Robert did not try to aim too high for major offices such as Secretary of State,[21] he was a reasonably influential man.

Following what had become the accepted pattern of the time, Naunton occasionally helped obtain posts for men he claimed he had never met but who presumably came well recommended from some source. In one case the individual involved was Sir Adam Loftus, a man who subsequently developed a rather dubious reputation in the post for which Sir Robert recommended him.[22] Nonetheless, Naunton devoted a considerable proportion of one of his letters to Buckingham explaining why Loftus was the best man to fill the vacant chancellorship of Ireland.[23] About a month after Naunton's intercession, Sir Adam was made Lord Chancellor of Ireland.[24]

Fortunately for Naunton's reputation, Loftus represents something of an exception. Sir Robert usually had direct knowledge of the abilities of the people he recommended. John Coke is a good example. As already mentioned, almost from the moment Naunton became Secretary of State, he wanted to do something for Coke.[25] Sir Robert may have helped his friend obtain a post on the temporary naval commission set up in the summer of 1618. He definitely interceded with Buckingham on Coke's behalf to hear naval business in October of that year.[26] At about this same time, Naunton arranged for his friend to have his first audience with the king.[27]

[19]Whether Naunton paid these men a salary or whether they relied on tips from those who wanted access to their master is unknown. In all likelihood, they received both with the bulk of their income coming from the latter source.

[20]HMC, *Cowper,* I, 47.

[21]Logan Pearsall Smith, *The Life and Letters of Sir Henry Wotton* (Oxford, 1907), II, 166.

[22]C.V. Wedgwood, *Thomas Wentworth, First Earl of Strafford, 1593-1641*: A *Revaluation* (London, 1961), p. 133.

[23]Naunton to Buckingham, Whitehall, 2 April 1619, BL Harl. 1581, fo. 103.

[24]J. Haydn, *The Book of Dignities,* ed. H. Ockerby, (London, 1894), 3rd edition, p. 576.

[25]HMC, *Cowper,* I, 95.

[26]*Ibid.,* 98.

[27]*Ibid.,* 104.

Naunton was putting Coke in a position where he could make the most of his opportunities, and he did so. When the permanent navy commission was formed in 1619, Coke was on it. Perhaps it should also be added that John Coke was one of the principal driving forces in making the commission a success and restoring the navy to a state of efficiency that at least resembled the days of the Armada.[28]

It was not only in secular affairs that Naunton used his influence. From the time he was a young man, he had had a fair amount of success in placing friends at Canterbury. In 1594 he placed Martin Fotherby, a future bishop of Salisbury, in a prebend there.[29] As Secretary of State Naunton helped Sir Henry Wotton's chaplain, Isaac Bargrave, on the road to another prebend and an eventual deanery at the same see.[30] Yet even in this area, he had his limitations. When Sir Robert recommended Dr Field to Buckingham, or rather reminded him of his own previous recommendation, his efforts proved useless, and the deanery in question went to one John Boys instead. Evidently, the combination of the Boys family's local influence in Canterbury and Archbishop Abbot's own preference was too much for Naunton.[31]

Influence, of course, is a nebulous quality. So many factors are involved. John Coke is a good example once again. He was related to Sir Fulk Greville, the Chancellor of the Exchequer, and used Greville's influence as much as Naunton's.[32] In addition, Coke had previous experience with naval administration and was thus one of the best qualified men available for a place on the naval commission. How much all these factors individually or collectively influenced the king it would be impossible to know. About all one can say is that, judging by the existing evidence, Naunton was either a fairly good judge of whom the king would pick for various posts, or he was reasonably successful at convincing Buckingham and the king to appoint the men he sponsored. Whatever the case, he had a political talent that cannot be dismissed lightly.[33]

[28] See A.P. McGowan, 'The Royal Navy under the First Duke of Buckingham, Lord High Admiral 1618-1628', Univ. of London, unpublished doctoral thesis, 1967.

[29] CSPD, 1591-94, p. 569.

[30] J. Le Neve, Fasti Ecclesiae Anglicaniae, ed. T.D. Hardy (Oxford, 1854), 1, 52 and Smith, Wotton, II, 462.

[31] Le Neve, Fasti, I, 33; Naunton to Buckingham, Whitehall, 31 January 1620. BL Harl. 1581, fo. 109 & P. Clark, English Provincial Society from the Reformation to the Revolution (Hassocks, Sussex, 1977), pp. 289, 322.

[32] HMC, Cowper, I, 110.

[33] The matter of what Naunton received for recommending these various individuals is, of course, pertinent here. To save duplication, however, it is discussed below pp. 90-2 along with the matter of his earnings as Secretary of State.

Yet when Sir Robert's part in the domestic side of government is considered, it does not present a particularly inspiring picture. He found the work tedious and only did what he absolutely had to do. There is never any hint that he was anxious to experiment with improving the efficiency of the operations under his control or that he even had any thought-out policy on domestic matters. In the one area in which he showed some genuine interest, the use of influence, the burden of his other work and his long separation from the king kept his participation down to a minimum. Naunton lamented his limitations,[34] but there was little he could do about them.

Nonetheless, on the purely administrative level, the indications are that Naunton did a capable job, especially with respect to the Privy Council. Though he may have disliked the work, he did it competently. His occasional ability to influence both the king and the council indicates that his skill and judgement were not entirely discounted by his contemporaries. When it came to international affairs, especially those relating to the English ambassadors and agents abroad, Naunton was able to put these abilities to a more congenial use.

English ambassadors and agents

Jacobean diplomats were as close as any group in England to being full-time professionals. With the exception of Sir Walter Aston in Spain, the other diplomats were either well schooled in their craft or intimately knew the country to which they were assigned. In the case of men such as Sir Henry Wotton and Sir Dudley Carleton their experience was well over a decade in duration by the time Naunton became secretary.

As Secretary of State, Sir Robert dealt with almost all of these men at one time or another, but for a variety of reasons he tended to deal with some much more frequently than others. After Calvert's appointment in 1619, Carleton (Dutch Republic), Wotton (Venice), Sir Isaac Wake (Savoy), Sir William Trumbull (Spanish Netherlands), Sir Edward Herbert (France) and Sir Francis Nethersole (Princes of the Germanic Union) corresponded almost entirely with Naunton.[35] These men had one thing in common; their assignments were unfavourable to the interests of Spain. They were either assigned to posts where the courts were antagonistic to the Spanish interest, such as Wotton in Venice and Carleton in the Dutch Republic, or else they

[34] BL, Eg. 2592, fo. 231.
[35] See appendix A.

were working against Spanish plans in the countries to which they were assigned, such as Trumbull in the Spanish Netherlands. He was attempting to recover a large debt due to James and to spy on the Irish, Scottish and English Roman Catholics in his area. The archduke's troop movements also interested him.[36]

As might be expected, those ambassadors with whom Naunton did not correspond regularly represented the other point of view. Cottington and Aston were both on missions friendly to Spain, including the Spanish marriage negotiations. What is significant here is that during the whole course of Sir Robert's term as secretary no information on James's secret affairs with Spain was sent through him nor did he receive any. There was not, however, a total lack of communication. When Phillip III first showed an interest in James acting as mediator in Bohemian affairs, Cottington transmitted the information to Naunton.[37] It is interesting that this event occurred while Lake was out of favour. What is more, it was a matter about which the anti-Spanish party would have to be informed. Nonetheless, if there had been a pro-Spanish secretary functioning normally, it is doubtful whether Sir Robert would have received the initial correspondence. As to whether Naunton ever saw Spanish secrets, there is no certain way to tell. Yet since he would only show anti-Spanish confidential information to the king, it is not beyond the realm of possibility that the pro-Spanish ministers acted in a similar manner. Certainly none of the surviving dispatches written by Naunton contain anything that might be called a secret Spanish matter.[38]

James's policy of divided government has been criticized,[39] but there is much to recommend it. For a king such as James, who formed alliances with both the Protestant princes of the Union and the Roman Catholic king of Spain, it was necessary to keep open all possible channels of information. If all the nations with whom England was friendly were to be kept happy, it was necessary to have others in the

[36]PRO, SP/77/13, fos. 59, 396 and 410.

[37]Cottington to Naunton, Madrid, 3/13 December 1618, *Letters and Documents Illustrating Relations between England and Germany,* ed. S.R. Gardiner (Camden Society: Westminster, 1865), I, 25-6.

[38]PRO, SP/75/5, fos. 188-9, 203 and 207. These documents Illustrate the only exception to the pro- and anti-Spanish division, Sir Rober Anstruther in Denmark. During the three years that Naunton was active as secretary, Anstruther did not correspond with him. On the other hand, he did not write to Calvert either. For some reason (and the survival of documents could be that reason), the extant letters on Danish affairs in this period are exchanged by James and Christian.

[39]D.H. Willson, *Privy Councillors,* p. 22 citing Gardiner, III, 72-83.

38

English government besides the king with whom they could communicate. It is true that this system often gave the appearance of stimulating the English ministers involved to corruption, particularly because they frequently accepted money from the nations with which they dealt. It is, however, important to remember that these countries needed some assurance that the people in England with whom they had regular contact would be sympathetic to their cause. If it made the Spanish (and presumably the Dutch, French, and Venetians as well) more content to put some of the people who favoured them on their pensions lists, James was the last one to object. It saved him the expense of raising their salaries and gave these countries confidence in their English associates.[40]

As was the case of so much else that went on in Jacobean government, the system also had the advantage of keeping the king in full control. He was the only one with all the information about foreign policy. Each of the two factions with whom he worked and their various sub-divisions corresponded with their own people on secret matters and passed the information on to James. He could dispose of it as he saw fit without reference to anyone else.

There is no doubt that this delicately balanced system could have backfired badly if the two factions became so antagonistic that they were constantly at sword's point and refused to co-operate in any way with one another. The same would have been true if they had become too friendly and had begun putting all the pieces together. But for whatever reasons, be they James's skill as a politician or just good luck, such a situation did not occur while Sir Robert was Secretary.

It would, however, be a mistake to regard these factions as closely knit, unified, or even vigorously led bodies. As the competition for Winwood's place demonstrated, there was little, if any, real cohesion in the anti-Spanish faction, and the relations among its members were often strained. It is very much to Sir Robert's credit that, while he was secretary, he did a great deal to minimize these differences and even to co-ordinate their anti-Spanish activities. He accomplished his ends by using two of his greatest assets: his desire to please and his cautious, steady approach to solving problems.

Naunton's relations with Sir Dudley Carleton are especially illustrative of just how much the secretary did achieve. In the beginning their relationship was poor. At an earlier time, Carleton had

[40] See *Documentos Ineditos*, II, 183-9 and G. Mattingly, *Renaissance Diplomacy*, pp. 246-9.

known Sir Robert and indeed considered him a friend.[41] Yet the friendship was somewhat unequal, for both Sir Dudley and his letter-writing associate, John Chamberlain, felt Naunton to be a cut below the really first-rate people in government.[42] Carleton thus had a double burden to bear: dealing with a man he considered second class, and dealing with a man who had taken 'his' post.[43] Nonetheless, once it was generally known that Naunton was the new secretary, Carleton was intelligent enough to know that it would not pay to antagonize him. Before official confirmation came, the ambassador wrote to Sir Robert to congratulate him on his new post. Despite the fact that the note was a kind of form letter that Sir Dudley sent to all successful candidates who might do him some good, a certain amount of pique shows through:

> Rather then be waunting in a necessary duty I lay hold of the comon report of your being preferred to a place neere his Majesty to which we forregyne ministers have our reference and salute the same with all due affection presenting unto your honor the best of my poor abilytyes both for the publique and your private servyce, which you may please to embrace with a favorable regard of the present condition of my imployment which affordes as smale contentment here as meanes to valew my selfe at home.[44]

Having got these remarks off his chest, Carleton then proceeded to a long discourse about Arminianism and its evils, tacitly implying that Naunton had never heard of it before.[45]

While Lake was still in favour, Carleton's and Naunton's relationship at least had no chance to grow worse; the bulk of Carleton's routine dispatches continued to go to the senior secretary. Once Sir Robert had established himself in his new office, this system probably would have changed. In any case Sir Thomas's rapidly deteriorating position threw Naunton and the ambassador into closer contact.

Carleton returned to England in the summer of 1618 hoping to administer the *coupe de grace* to Lake and have the last laugh on Sir Robert after all. Not only did he fail in his efforts, but he was also told

---

[41] Carleton to Chamberlain, Spa, 23 July 1616, PRO, SP/84/73, fo. 109.

[42] Chamberlain, *Letters*, I, 365-6.

[43] For his efforts to obtain the post see PRO, 3 November 1617, 20 November 1617 and 28 December 1617, SP/105/95.

[44] Carleton to Naunton, The Hague, 4 February 1618, PRO, SP/84/82, fo. 138.

[45] *Ibid.*, fos. 138-9.

to return to The Hague and to direct his correspondence to Naunton.[46] Whatever the secretary's personal feelings about Sir Dudley's attempt to condescend to him, he chose publicly to keep their relationship cordial. When Carleton first delayed his return to The Hague, Sir Robert gently prodded him to be on his way before he angered James:

> I will this evening prepare another lettre to the States of Zeland and offer it to be signed to morrow morning. I forbare to tell him [the king] of your attending him to morrow at Wimbeldon which he wold have taken for an expresse contradiction of the haste with which he expects you shold dispatche away his lettres and your owne to wayte on them.[47]

Attempting to hurry Carleton along and keeping him away from the king may not have been entirely altruistic; no doubt Naunton knew of his desire to take Lake's post. Nonetheless, the remarks were still polite, even after two months, when once again Sir Dudley was encouraged to return to The Hague:

> His Majestie asked me this morning when you went. I tould him I knew not. Why is he not gone then? I sayd I made accompt you were, for you had received both his Majesty's lettres and your mony and had gotten a vessel for your transportacion from my Lord Admiral and taken your leave of me as upon Thursday last . . . This I thought fitt to advertise you with all the speed I could that you might not be found in England, nor I refuted, that to shunne his misconceipt of you, take upon me to thinke confidently you were gone and so indeed I do, howsoever, I use *abundantia cautelae* in this my thus writing to you.[48]

Carleton could not have been pleased by Sir Robert's efforts to get him out of England, and doing it for the ambassador's 'own good', must have made a wound already raw smart slightly more.

A quiet battle was going on to see who would be master and who servant. In the long run the big battalions were all on the secretary's side, for if he had the ability to shield the ambassadors from the king's wrath, he could also let it come through at its full intensity. In December 1618 Naunton proved his point.

For many years James had been trying to negotiate his differences with the Dutch Republic but was habitually stalled when ambassadors

[46]Carleton to Buckingham, The Hague, 29 October 1618, PRO, SP/84/86, fo. 230.

[47]Naunton to Carleton, Greenwich, 10 June 1618, PRO, SP/84/84, fo. 94.

[48]Naunton to Carleton, Salisbury, 2 August 1618, PRO, SP/84/85, fo. 135.

were sent to him without full authority to reach a settlement. In 1618 the Dutch were due to send another group of ambassadors over, and the king had taken special pains to warn the States through Carleton that this time he expected men empowered to make decisions.[49] To his chagrin James discovered that this set of negotiators had no more authority than the last. The anger he felt over this state of affairs was, to some extent, directed at his ambassador in The Hague. It was Naunton's task to let him know his master's feelings:

> And for your selfe his Majesty bad me tell you that he must either thinke you an idle ambassador or els litle respected and ill used by them that being a councellor of that State[50] you shold not have more particular accompt and knowledge given you of their doings and theyr so slight and impertinent proceedings . . . .[51]

Carleton, of course, protested the unfairness of what was said,[52] but the message of what Naunton could do was too plain to miss. Just so there was no mistake, Sir Robert attempted to place Sir Dudley's arch-rival, Sir Henry Wotton, in Lake's vacant post.[53]

Though the situation between the secretary and the ambassador was more akin to intermittent sniping than open warfare, a victory was achieved nonetheless. In early 1619 Carleton acknowledged his defeat and threw himself on the mercy of the victor:

> I wish Sir George Calvert all happines in his preferment and your honour all contentment in his assistance, and with all I besiech your Honour (though this expectacion fayles me) to procure me some honest condition of his Majesty to which I may retire my self which want of health, decay of my poore estate and over-long absence from my native soile (not any ambition I will assure your Honour) makes me thirst after . . .[54]

Naunton had that quality that he so much admired in others, magnanimity,[55] and responded with good grace to Sir Dudley's submission. He promised to seek a peerage for the ambassador,[56] an especially generous gesture since it would place Carleton above Sir

[49]Naunton to Carleton, Windsor, 8 September 1618, PRO, SP/84/86, fo. 28 and Carleton to Naunton, The Hague, 28 September 1618, *Ibid.*, fo. 114.

[50]Carleton was a member of the Council of State of the Dutch Republic.

[51]Naunton to Carleton, Whitehall, 21 December 1618, PRO, SP/84/87, fo. 172.

[52]Carleton to Naunton, The Hague, 30 December 1618, PRO, *ibid.*, fo. 200.

[53]Smith, *Wotton*, II, 166.

[54]Carleton to Naunton, The Hague, 9 March 1619, PRO, SP/84/89, fo. 12.

[55]Sir Robert Naunton, *Fragmenta Regalia, sub* Willoughby and Perrot.

[56]T. Locke to Carleton, 5 June 1619, PRO, SP/13/109, no. 77.

Robert on the social hierarchy. Of more general importance, he made a genuine effort to see that not only Carleton but all the other ambassadors had their salaries paid regularly from specific funds in the Exchequer set aside for that purpose.[57] Naunton was not a wily man, but he was sharp enough to discern that the regular payment of the diplomatic corps would assure him of its members' loyalty. There were many good causes to which this loyalty could be put.

However, wishing for money from the Jacobean government was not a notably lucrative pursuit. What is more, the situation with the diplomats was complex. Their rates of pay were not uniform and depended upon whether the individuals were ambassadors or agents, and upon the countries to which they were assigned. At the bottom of the scale were the agents who received £1 day for diet and no regular allowance for secret service expenses.[58] At the other end was the ambassador to Spain who received £6 per day for diet and £500 per year for secret service.[59]

During the earl of Salisbury's time, the standard procedure was to pay the diets in the middle of the quarter in which it was due. The secret service funds were kept in arrears and were paid at the end of each quarter for the preceding one. With Salisbury's death regularity ceased. Salaries began to run in arrears and systematic payment for all but a few ambassadors fell by the wayside.[60] James made some attempt to set matters right by borrowing from the financier and merchant, Philip Burlamachi,[61] but the loans had little overall effect. When Naunton took over as Secretary of State, though some effort had been made to pay the long-standing arrears,[62] the decay of the previous half decade was still very much in evidence.

Naunton's efforts to find money should have been aided by his place on the Treasury Commission.[63] Unfortunately neither assertiveness nor finance were Sir Robert's strong points. After his initial promise to Carleton, he bided his time, watching for an opportunity to raise the matter.

[57]Wotton to Carleton, London, 16 November 1619, PRO, SP/14/111, no. 26.

[58]By Naunton's time this system had changed somewhat, and they received secret service money when they needed it. For a while these funds became a regular part of their pay, but by Charles's reign the procedure was discontinued. Naunton to Trumbull, Whitehall, 27 November 1619, Berkshire Record Office, Trumbull MS. 33, no. 24 and Isaac Wake, 6 July 1618, PRO, E/403/1724.

[59]18 July 1611, PRO, E/403/1711.

[60]See appendix B.

[61]12 January 1614, PRO, E/403/1716.

[62]See appendix B.

[63]Naunton to Carleton, 20 November 1619, PRO, SP/84/93, fo. 90.

Some of the ambassadors did not make Naunton's task an easy one. Sir Edward Herbert and Sir Walter Aston (significantly enough, the least experienced of the diplomatic corps) were quite adept at causing problems. Herbert took it into his head to be the extraordinary ambassador as well as the resident in France for a ceremonial treaty renewal.[64] His demand for extra money, when it was nearly impossible to find the funds for regular salaries, must have embarrassed Naunton, who passed the matter on to Buckingham.[65]

Aston's demands were even more phenomenal. He called upon both Naunton and the favourite for £7,000 for his first year's expenses and transportation to Madrid.[66] Either the outrageousness of the demand or the lack of a suitable advocate at court (Aston was, after all, one of the pro-Spanish ambassadors with whom Naunton had little to do) prevented Aston from getting the bulk of his money until the summer of 1621. It may be significant that Naunton was no longer active as secretary when the payment was made.[67]

Despite these awkward moments and set-backs, Sir Robert did succeed in improving the regularity of pay for the diplomatic corps. He did not, however, succeed in fully regularizing the situation, though in Carleton's case, he came close.[68] What he did do was keep a steady flow of money going out to almost all the ambassadors and agents, even though it was not in the amounts he desired.

Sir Robert remained dissatisfied with even this marked improvement and tried in his steady, quiet way to restore the situation to where it had been in Salisbury's day. By December 1620 or January 1621 Naunton apparently achieved his aim. Sir Lionel Cranfield, the Master of the Wards and the moving force behind much of the financial reform in the latter half of James's reign, and the new Lord Treasurer, Viscount Mandeville, both agreed in principle that £10,000 or £12,000 per year should be set aside from the Exchequer for the salaries and allowances of the resident ambassadors and agents. They also agreed to take the matter up with the king and obtain his formal approval.[69] The exact details, regrettably, must not have been worked out. Before they could be, Sir Robert was under house arrest and his

[64]Herbert to Naunton, Paris, 8 January 1620, BL Add. 7082, fo. 92.

[65]*Fortescue Papers,* p. 111.

[66]Aston to Buckingham, Madrid, 7 May 1620, BL Harl. 1580, fo. 1.

[67]See appendix B and 20 July 1621, PRO, E/403/1728.

[68]See appendix B.

[69]Naunton to Carleton, Whitehall, 2 January 1621, PRO, SP/84/99, fo. 4.

place suspended. The result of the abrupt end to Naunton's effective career as Secretary of State was that the ambassadors' and agents' pay continued along in a sporadic and wholly disorganized manner, with money spewing forth from the Exchequer in fits and starts.[70] Six months more might well have permitted Sir Robert to achieve his ends.

In some ways, it is surprising that Naunton was forced to take any special action for the diplomats. James was, after all, a king who took pride in his peacemaking and diplomatic skill. In the actual course of events he relied very slightly on personal negotiations and depended on the talents of his men on the spot. Much in the same way a king with military aspirations set the strategy but left the tactics to his generals. To follow the analogy, just as it was incumbent on the soldier-king to adequately arm his forces, so it was equally as incumbent upon James to see to it that his diplomats were properly supplied with their chief weapon, money. That the king was largely indifferent to their situation must have affected his efficiency in the diplomatic sphere.

Since James did not care, why did his Secretary of State? Political power played a part. Obtaining regular pay for these men would increase Naunton's own authority and make them subservient to him. Yet there was more to it than that; Sir Robert was especially concerned with the uses that a well paid, highly efficient diplomatic corps could serve in the Protestant cause. Naunton wanted nothing more than to build up England's position on the European scene as a counter-weight to the Habsburg-led Roman Catholic forces. He was acutely aware of the influence of Gondomar and his party at the English Court,[71] and with this spur he tried to create an equally efficient set of English diplomatic representatives. The best method was to channel as much money as possible into the hands of these professionals and rely on their talents to do the rest. All things considered, Naunton did not do badly. Despite his reputation for being somewhat slow in taking care of business,[72] he very nearly corrected, in a year and a half,[73] a situation that had existed since the death of Salisbury almost nine years before.

Looking at Sir Robert's performance as supervisor of the anti-Spanish diplomats, one cannot help but be impressed by its overall

[70]See Aston's salary, 20 July 1621, PRO, E/403/1728.

[71]Naunton to Trumbull, Whitehall, 13 November 1620, Berkshire Record Office, Trumbull MS. 33, no. 43.

[72]Carleton to Nethersole, The Hague, 9/19 October 1620, PRO, SP/84/97, fos. 133-4.

[73]PRO, SP/14/111, no. 26.

success. In the first instance he was handicapped by lack of specific information, leading some diplomats to look down upon him. Nonetheless, through conscientious handling of his job and by looking after his charges' interests, Naunton overcame his difficulties and gradually gained the diplomats' respect and even their friendship.

The Secret Service

Clandestine activities on behalf of the state were not an invention of the Jacobean government. During Elizabeth I's reign, Burghley, Walsingham and Cecil were all noted for their skill in this field. Intelligence gathering continued in James's reign, and the Secretaries of State became more involved than ever before.

Under Elizabeth, the intelligence networks were largely personal, privately operated systems. Naunton himself was part of one when he worked for Essex. It was the great men of the kingdom who gathered secret information for the queen, not by virtue of any special office they held, but because they were great and important men. (Walsingham was, perhaps, an exception to this rule.) Diversification did not mean a significant loss of quality, and Naunton, for one, had nothing but praise for the Elizabethan system.[74]

With Salisbury acting as a bridge, the Tudor system carried into the Stuart era, but his death signalled a change. It was no longer the great men of the kingdom who supplied their monarch with intelligence information, but the Secretaries of State, who acted by virtue of their office. The secret service was in the process of being nationalized, and the private entrepreneur played a secondary role.[75] The type of work done by the reformed secret service, however, remained much the same. The domestic side concerned counter-espionage against foreign embassies, Roman Catholics, and other religious groups considered dangerous to the state. The direction of this work was almost invariably in Naunton's own hands.[76] The overseas aspects of the secret service ranged from simply maintaining informants where the English government had no regular agents, to complicated plots for infiltrating foreign governments. The management of these continental operations was split between the secretary and the ambassadors. Naunton did maintain personal contact with some of the people in

[74]R. Naunton, *Fragmenta Regalia, sub* Burghley, Walsingham and Cecil.

[75]This is not to say that men such as Buckingham did not keep their own sources of information, but they were used a good deal less for governmental purposes.

[76]6 July 1618, PRO, E/403/1724 is the first of the regular quarterly payments that Naunton received from the Exchequer for the secret service. The stipend was £700 per year.

the field,[77] but usually the English diplomats made the actual contact, even when the secretary designated the nature of the assignments.[78] The ambassadors also could and did carry out ideas on their own initiative. Lord Digby had very notable success in intercepting and decoding Gondomar's dispatches,[79] while Sir Henry Wotton worked out a similar plan involving the Jesuits' dispatches to Rome.[80]

The clandestine network under Naunton employed various types of agents whose quality was not uniform. On the top of the scale were the agents such as Herr Bilderbeck. He may have lacked diplomatic status, but he performed very much the same tasks as native English diplomatic agents. The fact that he also sent his newsletters to representatives of other countries in no way lessened his value to the English.[81] Next on the list were men such as Sir Thomas Wilson, Raleigh's inquisitor. They performed secret service work occasionally, but they had other duties — in Wilson's case, keeper of the state papers in the Tower — that occupied most of their time. At the bottom of the pile were the spies who made a full-time profession of finding out secrets and selling them to all comers. A good example of this type is William Sterill, who kept the Archduke Albert's Secretary of State, della Faille, as well as Naunton, supplied with information.[82]

Sir Robert's role in handling secret service matters was very much what one would expect from the secretary charged with the anti-Spanish and anti-Catholic side of government; he watched those he considered the enemy. When the new Venetian ambassador, Antonio Donato, was on his way to England with a troublesome priest named Gatti, Sir Robert warned the court.[83] Anything out of the ordinary concerning Roman Catholics tended to catch Naunton's attention. When one of the members of the Spanish embassy tried to stab a Romanist apostate, Sir Robert's suspicions were aroused because the Spaniard could speak English. Since a Spanish diplomat had assured Archbishop Abbot that only one member of the Spanish embassy's

[77]The correspondent, Bilderbeck, is one instance of this sort of situation. See PRO, SP/81/14, fos. 305-6, 322-3 and 325-6, SP/81/15, fos. 147, 187-9 and 190-2 and SP/81/16, fos. 192-3, for letters to Winwood, Lake and Naunton, respectively.

[78]Naunton to Trumbull, Whitehall, 17 September 1619, Berkshire Record Office, Trumbull MS. 33, no. 21.

[79]Mattingly, *Renaissance Diplomacy*, pp. 248-9.

[80]Smith, *Wotton*, II, 147. Wotton also had a more ambitious scheme for sending Protestant missionaries into Northern Italy. *Ibid.*, pp. 148-51.

[81]Munich, Geheime Staats Archiv, Kasten Blau, 118/1 II, fos. 981-1048.

[82]Archives Générales, Brussels, PC 55, fos. 33 and 55; Naunton to Trumbull, Whitehall, 16 April 1620, Berkshire Record Office, Trumbull MS. 33, no. 37.

[83]Naunton to Buckingham, Whitehall, 2 October 1618, Bodley Fortescue MS. Add. D110, fo. 77.

staff had a fluent knowledge of the language, there was cause for suspicion. The would-be slayer was not that man.[84]

As a result of repeated incidents such as those described, Naunton also kept a watchful eye on the French and Spanish embassies where English Roman Catholics tended to gather,[85] and carrying out this task he was not beyond violating the niceties of diplomatic etiquette by sending a spy inside the embassies to see what was going on.[86] Naunton's counter-espionage activities turned his sensitivity into something close to an obsession, for treachery and malice were always closely linked in his mind with the Papists:

> Stanly, the priest, shiftes from place to place here in towne, but I dowbt Father Patrick, the Scotishman, is hanging about the Court. My Lord Colvin saith his Majestie forgott to inquier at him of him, which I remember with the more care, because of an anxious apprehension I have of their mortal and hateful mallice against his Majesties sacred person as the maller and confounder of theyr batell, against whose malligancie we cannot be too jelously watchfull. For my own part I must protest it in season and out of season *quiciquid [sic] id est, timeo. . . .*[87]

Because of his zeal, Naunton built something of a reputation as a priest-hunter and guardian of the Protestant faith. Even after his dismissal, people continued to refer matters to him concerning priests and Papists.[88] What is more, many of the books dedicated to Sir Robert were of an anti-Romanist nature, or were written by people who were outstanding anti-Romanists.[89]

The information gathered on the dissidents was not meant for the secretary's personal use, but for the king. The difficulty was in transmitting it securely. At first, Naunton transcribed and handed everything to the king personally. Even after Sir Robert had hired his own assistants, he preferred this process. The most highly sensitive information he would only pass to James verbally.[90] It would not be

---

[84]Naunton to Buckingham, undated but probably April or May 1619, BL Harl. 1581, fo. 113.

[85]Discussed further below, pp. 63-5.

[86]Naunton to Buckingham, Whitehall, 2 April 1619, BL Harl. 1581, fo. 103.

[87]Naunton to Buckingham, Whitehall, 14 December 1618, *Fortescue Papers*, pp. 74-5.

[88]J. Tendring to Naunton, June 1624, PRO, SP/14/168, no. 437.

[89]F. B. Williams, *Index of Dedications and Commendatory Verses* (London, 1962), p. 135 and *DNB sub* Goodwin, George and Taylor, Thomas.

[90]Naunton to Trumbull, Whitehall, 4 October 1618, Berkshire Record Office, Trumbull MS. 33, no. 8; Naunton to Carleton, Whitehall, 21 December 1620, PRO, SP/84/98, fo. 96 and Lando to the Doge and Senate, 26 February 1621 (new style), *CSP, Ven., 1619-21*, pp. 574-5.

surprising if the memory of Antonio Perez and the problems that developed with keeping his information confidential caused Naunton to take such extra-special care.[91]

However much attention Naunton might pay to the execution of his work as supervisor of the secret service network, there were projects that taxed both his talents and his patience, for he never had total control. One of these concerned a talkative and persuasive Dutchman named Godfrey Boote. He had been trying for some years to ingratiate himself with the English,[92] and it finally appeared as though he had succeeded. The Dutchman managed to sell several courtiers (probably Buckingham was among them) on the idea that he should go back to the Dutch Republic and convince a large number of herring fishermen to come over to England.[93] As the Dutch and the English were engaged in a seemingly endless battle over fishing rights, Boote's project added the element of nationalism to profit, giving it attractions not only for courtiers but for the king as well.

Whatever Sir Robert thought of the project itself, he made it quite plain that he did not trust Godfrey Boote. He told Carleton to check on whether Boote had served as a customs official for the Dutch and whether, as he claimed, he had been forced to leave the republic because he wrote a book against the Arminians. There was also some checking to do on the Dutchman's story that he had left the service of the Elector of Brandenburg for lack of pay. Naunton concluded his letter to Carleton with obvious scepticism:

> If his dexteritie in overseeinge the customes exceede not that other facultie in writinge of theological controversies, I doubt we shall make but an easy purchase of him. . . . For my owne part that which I have seene and observed in him makes me not over credulous of what I have not seene, but our hungry courteyors that live upon new projects have raised me some obloquies that I shewed no quicker zeale to cherish and intertein so publique a threasor as they neads make of this man. . . . [94]

As is clear from the commentary, the 'hungry courteyors' were not pleased with Naunton's opposition to their scheme. For once the secretary let his zeal get the better of him and went too far. The result

[91]For Naunton's problems in keeping Perez's reports secret see T. Birch, *Memoirs,* II, 259; E. Reynolds to A. Bacon, 22 January 1597, Lambeth Palace, Bacon Papers, MS 654, fo. 76 and *Ibid.,* MS 660, fo. 61.

[92]G. Boote to R. Winwood, Antwerp, 12 July 1612, Boughton House, Northants, Winwood's Original State Papers, VIII.

[93]Naunton to Carleton, Whitehall, 18 September 1618, PRO SP/84/86, fo. 74.

[94]*Ibid.*

was that he had to back down. Soon after writing to Sir Dudley in September 1618, he complained to Buckingham about being forced to apologize for his behaviour.[95]

Apology or no apology, Sir Robert continued his interest in Boote, and was rewarded for his perseverance with success. By November 1618 Carleton had found out that there was no wrong done to Boote in the Dutch Republic,[96] and then, gradually, the whole story began to unfold. It was true that the Dutchman had been a customs official, but he had taken on the profitable sideline of spying for the Spanish Netherlands. What is more, far from being an enemy of the Arminians, he was part of their faction. He had only escaped arrest in the wake of Prince Maurice's *coupe* against Oldenbarnevelt and his Arminian followers because he was considered of no real importance. As for his service with the Elector of Brandenburg, he was dismissed when his previous disreputable behaviour came to light.[97] Certainly Boote's past history was enough to damn him, but he proceeded to compound his felony:

> Since his [Boote's] going wee have detected that finding him self a litle more narrowly looked into here then he expected or well liked of, he hath combined with a French companion (now he hath made his best prise here) by the mediacion of Le Clerc, our late French agent here, to present and vent his services of millions to that yong kinge. . . .

Once James found out what was happening as far as he was concerned[98] the Dutchman was finished, and Sir Robert was quite pleased.[99]

Had Boote just vanished from the scene there and then, this unsavoury business would have come to a neat and tidy end, but he did not. For a start, he managed to have himself arrested and jailed by the Estates of Holland. The English then had the unpleasant task of bailing him out and getting hold of his papers, lest the talkative little Dutchman decided to buy his freedom by revealing the purpose of his mission.

[95]*Fortescue Papers,* p. 63.

[96]Carleton to Naunton, The Hague, 21 November 1618, PRO, SP/84/87, fo. 50.

[97]10 December 1618, *Ibid.*, fo. 139.

[98]Naunton to Carleton, Whitehall, 16 December, 1618, *ibid.*, fo. 150. This statement of Naunton's is confirmed by a Dutch report, though the Dutch were not quite so certain about their information, Messrs, Goch, Dussen and Liens to the States General, 2 February 1619, BL Add. 17677 I, fo. 383.

[99]Naunton to Carleton, Whitehall, 21 December 1618, PRO, SP/84/87, fo. 172.

As might be expected, Naunton was put in charge of the rescue operation, and he directed Carleton to see what could be done. A little discreet probing by the ambassador revealed that the Dutch thought that Boote was involved in the Raleigh affair, or, more specifically the French attempt to aid in his escape,[100] but if they knew anything about his current project for England, they were not concerned with making an issue of it.

The affair proceeded to drag on through 1619. It took several interesting twists before it finally came to an end, and one of the more amusing ones involved Boote's wife. Quite unexpectedly, after a visit from her, Sir Robert solicited Carleton to do all he could for the Dutchman.[101] Since Boote had used her as his agent in dealing with Winwood some years previous,[102] one can only presume that her charm had not faded much in the intervening period, and her husband had not developed any scruples about making use of it.

By the end of 1619 Naunton was finally able to inform Carleton that James was finished once and for all with Godfrey Boote.[103] The gentleman, however, did not think so; he reappeared again in 1624 as Godfrey de Bolt and tried once more, unsuccessfully, to squeeze some money out of England.[104]

With respect to Naunton, except for some backsliding when Boote's wife intervened, he comes out looking rather well. He showed a willingness to speak out in the face of opposition, even when the ranks of that opposition included Buckingham. He exhibited persistence in continuing his attempts to prove Boote a fraud, even after he had been burned with the affair. All in all, he demonstrated that he was anything but the 'poor tool' of the favourite, as at least one author characterized him.[105]

Besides being a useful guide to Naunton's talents, the Boote affair provides an important link with a character who was as disreputable as the Dutchman and who was one of the key individuals involved in bringing the secretary's career to an abrupt halt. The man was François de Vertou who usually called himself Monsieur de La Forêt.[106] He was an official of the French embassy in London who joined company

---

[100]Carleton to Naunton, The Hague, 31 December 1618,*ibid*., fo. 204.

[101]Naunton to Carleton, Whitehall, 4 March 1619, PRO SP/84/89, fo. 5.

[102]See above, p. 48.

[103]Naunton to Carleton, Whitehall, 16 December 1619, PRO SP/84/93, fo. 192.

[104]Calvert to Conway, Canon Row, 14 November 1624, *CSPD, 1623-5,* p. 378.

[105]E. Edwards, *The Life of Sir Walter Raleigh,* (London, 1868), I, 705-6.

[106]BL, Add. 17677 I, fo. 383.

with Boote just before James attempted to dismiss the Dutchman. Like Boote, La Forêt also became implicated in the attempt to free Raleigh, and as a result he was called before the Privy Council; the Frenchman revealed nothing,[107] but nonetheless found it expedient to leave England.

The departure convinced Naunton that there was more to reveal, and when the opportunity arose, he made an effort to find out just what that was:

> I have encouraged Mr. Hall the best I could to prosecute the service who promised me to have made La Forest drunke, and so to have a copie of all his lettres at Gravesend, but he tells me that La Forest's wife was there and could not be parted from him to give place to that project. This night will see what he can do here . . . [108]

Apparently Sir Robert was fated to have other people's wives thwart his plans. What is significant is not so much the details of the attempt to lay hold of La Forêt and his papers but rather the distrust of the man that must have preceded its conception.

For nearly a year La Forêt and Naunton did not cross each other's path. The French embassy was closed down in the aftermath of Raleigh's attempted escape, and La Forêt was reassigned to the agent in the Spanish Netherlands. In October 1619, however, he made another appearance, this time as the quasi-official emissary for a group of Algerian pirates who were soliciting James for a pardon.

Before La Forêt left Brussels, he had a conversation with the British agent, William Trumbull, which was relayed to Naunton. In the course of the discussion the Frenchman said that, 'your Honour [Naunton] is his great patron and hath promised him a good turn'.[109] From what had previously occurred, one is forced to draw the conclusion that the man was either highly imaginative or the secretary had found a way to make use of this indiscreet gentleman in his own intelligence operations.

Co-option by Naunton is a distinct possibility for several reasons. La Forêt had been selling information to Gondomar while he was in England.[110] During the summer of 1619 when he returned to London

---

[107]Harlow, *Raleigh's Last Voyage*, pp. 289-90, citing Bodley, Carte 112, fo. 272 ff.

[108]*Fortescue Papers*, pp. 71-2.

[109]Trumbull to Naunton, Brussels, 23 October 1619, *Cabala, . . . Mysteries of State . . .*, (1691) 3rd edition, p. 353. The dispatch is misdated as 1618, but internal evidence strongly suggests the later date.

[110]Mattingly, *Renaissance Diplomacy*, p. 247.

52

on temporary assignment, he began sending it to della Faille, the Secretary of State for the Spanish Netherlands.[111] His behaviour certainly indicates that the Frenchman had few if any patriotic scruples, so there is no reason that he could not have decided to add England to his remittance list. In actual fact the question here is not really if La Forêt began working for Naunton but rather when. By April 1620 the secretary was definitely using this French triple agent as a messenger.[112] Back in the summer of 1619, however, Sir Robert had alerted Trumbull because; 'I heare Creswell and de la Forest ar both there expected much by Van Male [the Spanish Netherland's agent in London]. You may do well to hearken after them.'[113] The interpretation of this sentence depends much on the word 'hearken'. If it means 'go and talk to' then Sir Robert probably was already using La Forêt. It is much more likely that he meant 'watch out for'. His grouping with Creswell, an English Jesuit considered dangerous by James, may well indicate that in the early summer of 1619 La Forêt was still too suspect to be used as an agent. Thus any good turn the Frenchman expected from Naunton later that summer was probably the product of wishful thinking.

One can only make a guess as to how much later the secretary finally employed La Forêt. The negotiations about the pirates took place in October 1619, at which time the two men must have spoken with one another. The Frenchman returned to England on permanent assignment to the reopened French embassy in January 1620, and it was probably at this time that he and Sir Robert established a definite working arrangement. The employer-employee relationship between them should in no way indicate that they trusted each other. Naunton remained perpetually suspicious of this man who served many masters, and though he used him as an informant and messenger,[114] he was altert to La Forêt's inclination to tamper with the dispatches.[115] Their relationship was not such that either could afford to rely on the other's innate goodness.

La Forêt was only a minor part of the English secret service system, yet he is of such importance to Sir Robert's career, that it

[111]La Forêt to della Faille, London, 4/14 May 1619, Archivès Générales, Brussels, PC. 55, fo. 180.

[112]Naunton to Trumbull, Whitehall, 23 July 1619, Berkshire Record Office, Trumbull MS. 33, no. 18.

[113]Ibid.

[114]PRO, SP/77/14, fo. 158.

[115]Naunton to Trumbull, 16 April 1620, Berkshire Record Office, Trumbull MS. 33, no. 37.

would be impossible to understand the peculiar circumstances of the secretary's suspension without understanding the relationship between these two men. On Naunton's part the best characterization is one word: caution. In viewing Sir Robert's disgrace, this description will take on particular importance.

With respect to Naunton's role in the secret service as a whole, he played a key role and did it with his usual quiet competence. On the domestic side he was able to gather information about the groups that most concerned him: the Roman Catholics and the foreign diplomats. The reports were then passed to the king for his own use. There is no surviving case in which the secretary acted on his information without first receiving royal approval. Secretary Walsingham may have contrived Mary, Queen of Scots's death; Secretary Naunton had more modest accomplishments.

On the foreign scene, though Sir Robert had general supervision of the secret service, he was almost entirely dependent upon the efforts of the English ambassadors and agents in his charge. He evidently made no attempt to keep a coherent group of agents in other countries. In this respect there is something of a decline in the effective power of the Secretary of State when compared with the Elizabethan period. There was also another weakening of the office because of the pro-and anti-Spanish divisions. It was, in a sense, bad enough that Naunton had to depend on the ambassadors to supervise the agents, but he could not even use all the ambassadors. He only had access to the anti-Spanish ambassadors' reports, and it was thus only their agents that fed him information. The pro-Spaniards' sources that an ambassador such as Digby managed were closed to Sir Robert.

There were some exceptions such as Trumbull in Brussels, but his primary job could be viewed as a kind of extension of the domestic anti-Catholic concerns since he was watching Roman Catholics from the British Isles (though he did report on such things as General Spinola's troop movements as well). There was also one attempt by Naunton to send a spy into Spain, but the man was apparently to report to Cottington and had only been recruited by the secretary.[116]

The purpose of operating the secret service in a divided manner was closely related to James's nourishing of the pro- and anti-Spanish factions. It kept him as the only person in the kingdom with all the information. Men such as Naunton could never be entirely sure about

---

[116]J. Sanchez to J. Ciriza, London, 19 January 1619 (new style), PRO 31/12/21 from Arch. de Simancas — EL 2599, fo. 47.

what the countries beyond his jurisdiction had planned and thus found it difficult to bring pressure to bear on the king. James was then left with the maximum amount of freedom to act as he saw fit. In addition, because the ambassadors and agents were, by and large, operating in countries with which they had some sympathy, the people with whom they dealt were far more likely to feel at ease and let some worthwhile information slip. This procedure at times may have reduced Naunton to the role of bureaucrat or even messenger, but it certainly strengthened the position of the monarch, both internally and externally.

The foreign ambassadors

Given the way James had divided his government, it would be reasonable to assume that the foreign diplomats who resided in England would be dealt with in a manner befitting this scheme. On the whole this assumption is accurate. Naunton was expected to deal with the Venetian, French, Dutch and Protestant German diplomats, while Calvert handled the Spanish, Austrian and Spanish Netherlands representatives. What complicated the picture were conflicting tempera- ments and nationalities. In the case of Sir Robert there was particular difficulty because his militant Protestantism was mixed with a strong tinge of xenophobia.

Given the nature of the Venetian Republic, the potential for conflict between secretary and ambassador should have been at a minimum. Though of course Romanists, the Venetians were well known both for their antipathy toward Rome and its ruler and for their fear of Spanish dominance of northern Italy and the Adriatic. In addition, though it no longer could claim that singular pride of place as Europe's finest school for diplomats, for a country its size, Venice certainly had one of the best diplomatic services then in existence. All of these factors should have given the Venetians a common bond with Naunton, or at least made their contacts amicable. Eventually they did, but matters did not start out that way.

The problem was not so much with Sir Robert, but rather with one of the Venetian ambassadors, Antonio Donato. He was a young man who came to England after serving as ambassador to Savoy. Even before he arrived in October 1618, Naunton had reason to suspect that there would be trouble. For as mentioned earlier, the Venentian was accompanied by a priest named Allessandro Gatti who had been in England previously and had made a bad name for himself.[117]

---

[117]Naunton to Buckingham, 2 October 1618, Bodley, Fortescue MS. Add. D110, fo. 77.

Naunton's suspicion of trouble proved fully justified when Donato took a strong dislike to him. The young man felt that the secretary was ignorant of foreign affairs, and he looked down on the Englishman because he bought his office and used it for selfish reasons, at least so he said.[118] As it turned out, especially for one taking such a condescending attitude, Donato's own intelligence and purity were not such as to inspire confidence.

At the end of December 1618, the Venetian described Sir Thomas Lake as having charge of foreign affairs in England.[119] Since Lake had ceased functioning as Secretary of State some six months previously, one can only wonder at Donato's lack of perception. Ironically enough, the ambassador's real problem proved to be an irresistable attraction for other people's money. The Duke of Savoy accused him of embezzling 40,000 crowns of Venetian 'foreign aid' sent to Savoy. By April 1619 the Senate decided upon Donato's recall to face these charges.[120]

The decision should have put an end to the matter, at least as far as Naunton was concerned. Unfortunately, it was only the beginning. Donato was convicted of embezzlement and imprisoned, but in the summer of 1619 he escaped and fled to England.[121] Naunton was also fated to have problems with obnoxious characters who would not disappear as well as with other men's wives.

The Venetian's reappearance in London created a variety of difficulties. His popularity with many members of the English court and his rights under English law meant that he could not be arbitrarily deported.[122] Yet the Venetians were quite adamant that something had to be done, and Savoy was also concerned that the embezzler should not escape without punishment.[123] Under the circumstances James felt that he had little option but to take action. He began by making the council ban Donato from the court as well as forbidding him from coming within five miles of London,[124] and somewhat surprisingly it was intended more than just making a token gesture. So in June 1620, when the young Venetian was foolish enough to approach as close as

[118]CSP, Ven., 1617-19, p. 440.

[119]26 December 1618, (new style), ibid., p. 405.

[120]Wotton to Naunton, Venice, 26 April 1619, H. Wotton, Letters and Dispatches to James I and his Ministers, ed. G. Tomline, (London, 1850), pp. 118-19.

[121]Smith, Wotton, p. 173.

[122]CSP, Ven., 1619-21, p. 197.

[123]Wake to Naunton, Turin, 20/30 September 1619, BL Add, MS. 18641, fos. 97-8.

[124]BL Lans. 162, fo. 206.

Lambeth, James became angry and increased the distance he had to stay from the capital.[125] Donato could stand no more, and a month later he applied for passports so that he could leave England.[126]

Naunton's role was his usual one of intermediary. Even before the council acted, he warned Donato that he had better lead a more retired life because both the Venetians and Savoyards were trying to persuade the king to banish him.[127] After the council had acted Donato went to Naunton to discuss the matter before he left London.[128] All things considered, Sir Robert stayed reasonably calm about the matter. He realized that the king was in a difficult position, but felt that he had managed to cut himself a path down the middle of the road.[129] If the French ambassador is to be believed, there was, however, one incident that somewhat qualifies the picture of the quiet, competent bureaucrat that Naunton had acquired. When Donato raised the question of Franco-Venetian relations in his last talk with Naunton, the secretary's temper flared.[130] Perhaps Sir Robert could afford the luxury of letting go at a man who had given him considerable trouble and for whom he had no great liking; nevertheless, it was not good policy to let the world know that he could be goaded into an angry outburst.

Whatever the problems with Donato may have been, Naunton's relations with the next Venetian ambassador, Girolamo Lando, were a model of cordiality. Lando himself summed them up best when he said:

> The Secretary Naunton, who seems to grow more and more friendly to the Republic, told me that his Majesty wished to give the greatest possible tokens to your Serenity of his incomparable disposition towards the interest of the Republic.

Events continually conspired to strengthen the friendship. For a start[131] there was convenience; with James away on progress for so many months out of the year, it was simply easier for Lando to dispatch his business with Sir Robert rather than wait until the king returned. Obviously, any ambassador would prefer to deal with the

[125]CSP, Ven., 1619-21, p. 285.

[126]Ibid., p. 310.

[127]Ibid., p. 45.

[128]Ibid., p. 126.

[129]Naunton to Buckingham, Whitehall, 13 January 1620, Fortescue Papers, pp. 114-5.

[130]Tillières to Puysieux, London, 20 June 1620, (new style), PRO/31/3/53, fo. 122.

[131]CSP Ven., 1619-21, p. 254.

king as much as possible for it increased his prestige among the other members of the diplomatic community. Yet the Venetian was a realist and knew that he might lose opportunities if he did not act on them when they arose.[132]

Much more important than convenience was unity of interest. The group that Naunton represented, the one alien to Spanish designs, was the faction to which Lando was bound to be attracted. The Spanish threat to Venetian dominance of the Adriatic, not to mention the danger of Hispanic domination of the whole Italian peninsula, would naturally draw the Venetian to the English anti-Spaniards. If these people were also staunch Protestants who were hostile to the Roman Catholic faith, Lando had to be practical and realize that one could not always choose one's allies. Besides there was no love lost between the Serene Republic and the papacy.

This combination of expediency and community of interest showed itself in several ways, but perhaps the best example occurred in the autumn of 1620 when the Spanish in Milan helped to engineer the revolt of the Roman Catholic Grisons in Switzerland. The action led to Spanish control over the strategically important Valtelline pass, and thus assured Spain's ability to send troops from the south to the north of Europe. Their movement endangered both Venetian lands in northern Italy and Frederick's Palatinate holdings along the Rhine. Lando and Naunton were quick to perceive the importance of joint action:

> However, I have not slackened in my solicitude and in conformity with the promises made me by the king they have issued orders to encourage the Grisons and Swiss, as I have availed myself in particular of the goodwill of the Secretary Naunton, who has proved an excellent spur and an executor at the same time. He it was who obtained two commissions from his Majesty, and on receiving them he carried them into effect without delay, in answering Mr. Wake at Turin and recommending the letter to the master of the posts here . . . .[133]

The Venentian ambassador's confidence in Sir Robert was such that he assured the Doge and Senate that the best course of action was to pass all information on to the secretary, and not to bother James for audiences.[134]

The bond of trust between Lando and Naunton placed the

[132]*Ibid.*, pp. 390-1.

[133]Lando to the Doge and Senate, 2 October 1620, (new style), *ibid.*, pp. 420-1.

[134]*Ibid.*, p. 421.

58

secretary in a position to pass information to the Venetian with assurance that it would be well received:

> One day recently the Secretary Naunton, with that confidence which he observes with me out of his friendship for your Excellencies and his anxieties about the current affairs of the world, told me that . . . .[135]

Relationships such as Naunton's and Lando's demonstrate the strengths of James's system of divided government. Because of the empathy between his ministers and those of other nations, he could not only receive information that they would keep secret from their enemies, but he could pass on information with the knowledge that the source would not be viewed with undue suspicion.

Whatever the apparent advantages to the king, there is an important question about Sir Robert's dealings with the Venetians. Did his close link with Lando ever draw him into a position where he was inadvertently or otherwise disloyal to his master? If it did, it is a telling criticism of both James's choice of ministers and, by implication, of the whole system of divided government. There were times when Lando certainly thought Naunton had fallen in with his wishes to such an extent that he overstepped the king's directions. In one instance, James asked Naunton not to make a direct reply to a letter from Wake in Turin, but rather to simply praise the ambassador's diligence in sending news. The Venetian claimed he was able to talk Sir Robert into adding something more substantial by way of commentary to encourage Wake to continue his work.[136]

Although Naunton's actions here can be interpreted several ways, they are enough to give pause. A close examination of the existing information indicates that, when it came to major matters (which the encouragement of an ambassador certainly was not) Sir Robert was steadfast enough. When it was in England's best interests to do so, he was perfectly capable of keeping secrets from his friends as well as his enemies. This trait comes through clearly with respect to Savoy's desire to annex Genoa, a long-standing project of the Savoyard duke.[137] The Venetians would not have been pleased by such an action; they wanted Savoy for a friend, not a competitor. James was well aware that, if the Serene Republic ever got wind of the scheme, they would break with their ally. For the sake of counter-balancing

[135]*Ibid.*, p. 474.

[136]*Ibid.*, p. 465.

[137]Wake to Naunton, Turin, 8 January 1620/ 28 December 1619, BL Add. 18641, fo. 133.

Spain in Italy, the king did not wish such a split, and Naunton was apparently instructed to keep the matter to himself.

For his part, Lando knew that some kind of plot existed against Genoa, and he knew that Wake was keeping Naunton abreast of the matter, but he was never able to find out any details. Since Sir Robert was the only one (aside from the king) who could inform him of what was happening, the Venentian was left in the dark.

Perhaps if the correspondence of the Barons Achtichus and Christopher Dona, the Palatinate ambassadors to England, had survived, one would be forced to reconsider how loyal Naunton was to his king. Yet, as the facts now stand, though Sir Robert was on as good terms with the Venetian ambassador as any foreign diplomat in England, there is no evidence to indicate that he betrayed his master. Given the standards of the time, this conclusion certainly speaks well for the secretary.

After the Palatines and the Venetians, it would seem that a person of Naunton's religious and political persuasions would be drawn quite strongly to the Dutch. Sir Robert's predecessor, Winwood, definitely was. Yet strangely enough such was not the case. The problem was, when it came to the Dutch Republic (much to Naunton's confusion), religion and nationalism did not complement each other.

If England and the Dutch Republic had had a different geographic relationship to each other, or if their peoples had been interested in dissimilar industries and areas of the world, there would have been no problem. Unfortunately, both nations had strong maritime inclinations with pretensions to naval supremacy in the Channel and the North Sea, and both had a decided interest in the East Indies. For a while it was possible to claim that it was the Arminians among the Dutch who were the troublemakers and that staunch Calvinists led by Maurice of Orange would behave differently. But after the Orangist party staged its *coup* in 1618, arrested Oldenbarnevelt and ousted the Arminians, the problems remained.

The mission sent over by the Estates General in the winter of 1618-19 brought home clearly this unfortunate truth. As mentioned earlier, James had high hopes that the mission would settle all the outstanding differences between the two countries and was infuriated to discover that the commissioners had arrived without sufficient powers to negotiate a treaty.[138] As a result, the king was publicly sharp with the Dutchmen, and nearly sent them home.

[138]This was mentioned above in the section, *English Ambassadors and Agents.*

Had Winwood still been in office, the chances are that he would have acted as mediator and tried to soothe the king's anger. Naunton, on the contrary, was quite pleased with the rough reception the commissioners received, and he was particularly gleeful about Lord Chancellor Bacon's opening speech to them,[139] 'I conceive they have not bene used to heare such freedome of speache unless it were among them selves where they find them selves absolute.'[140] Whatever Naunton's personal feelings might have been and despite his being excused from the Privy Council committee charged with the Dutch negotiations,[141] he nonetheless found himself forced into his accustomed role as go-between. When James had a message concerning the fishing dispute, the secretary brought it;[142] when there were complaints needing attention, he handled them.[143] In spite of Naunton's basically antipathetic attitude, the personal relations between him and the commissioners were good. One can only presume that the secretary successfully masked his true feelings. Indeed he was so convincing that when the commissioners arrived home, they assured Naunton, through Carleton, that he would receive something tangible for his troubles.[144]

It was the matter of tangible reward that lay behind the next run-in that the secretary had with the Hollanders. In the summer of 1619, not long after the commissioners returned home, several Dutch merchants were fined and imprisoned by Star Chamber for illegally exporting gold coins from England.[145] Numerous requests were made of Naunton to intercede for these men, but all to no avail. Sir Noel de Caron, the long-time Dutch resident ambassador in England, pleaded with him;[146] Sir Dudley Carleton acted as an agent for a group that was willing to bribe him.[147] Through all these pressures Sir Robert remained apologetic[148] but firm. All he would do was echo the king's

---

[139]Naunton to Carleton, Whitehall, 21 December 1618, PRO SP/84/87, fo. 172.

[140]22 December 1618, *ibid.*, fo. 174.

[141]Naunton to Carleton, Whitehall, 3 January 1619, PRO SP/84/88, fo. 7a.

[142]Goch, Dussen and Liens to the States General, 9 February 1619, (new style), BL Add. 17677 I, fo. 387.

[143]London, March 1619, *ibid.*, fo. 393.

[144]Carleton to Naunton, The Hague, 21 August 1619, PRO SP/84/91, fo. 178.

[145]Naunton to Carleton, Whitehall, 23 October 1619, PRO SP/84/92, fo. 190.

[146]Caron to Naunton, undated, PRO SP/84/93, fo. 244.

[147]Carleton to Naunton, The Hague, 11 June 1620, PRO SP/84/95, fo. 222.

[148]P. Lengele to H. Danckaert, 16 May 1620 (new style), London, BL Add. 17677 K, fo. 49.

sentiments that the Dutch had no right to question the proceedings of English justice.[149]

Such steadfast incorruptibility should have done credit to even the late Victorian civil service. Regrettably, the motivation for these determined actions had nothing to do with incorruptibility, quite the contrary. The fines these merchants were to pay had been promised to Naunton,[150] and no combination of pleading and inadequate bribes could shake the secretary loose from his booty.

Even leaving the issue of monetary gain aside, considering the strength of Sir Robert's feelings against the Dutch, it is amazing that he could do any business at all with them. In August 1619, when he heard that Sir Thomas Dale's fleet in the East Indies had inflicted a heavy (but all too rare) defeat on the Dutch East India Company's ships, he was heartily pleased.[151] When writing to Carleton in June 1620 after another of those interminable delays in arranging for negotiations, Naunton was so upset about the Hollanders' behaviour that he managed to slip the adjectives 'boorish,' 'insolent,' 'treacherous' and 'savage' into one single sentence describing it.[152]

Somehow, despite everything, Sir Robert's relationship with the Dutch never deteriorated to the point of uselessness. In part, the reason lay in his ability to get along well with the Dutch agents and diplomats with whom he came into contact. There is no record either in his or their reports (or the reports of other diplomats) that their relationship was anything but cordial. Yet the most significant bond was their fear of Spain. Whatever the commercial differences were between England and the Protestant Lowlands, and however much they might wrangle him, Naunton never thought these problems were the dominant issue of his day. The limitation of Habsburg power was, and the secretary was willing to go a long way to keep the Dutch on their best behaviour, for fear that James might just forget about his troublesome republican co-religionists and form a firm alliance with monarchical Spain.[155]

At a different time, either a decade earlier or later, Naunton's

[149]Naunton to Carleton, Whitehall, 19 February 1620, PRO SP/84/94, fo. 158.

[150]M. Prestwich, *Cranfield, Politics and Profits under the Early Stuarts,* (Oxford, 1966), p. 269.

[151]Naunton to Buckingham, Whitehall, 30 August 1619, Bodley Fortescue Add, D110, fo. 172.

[152]Naunton to Carleton, Greenwich, 26 June 1620, PRO SP/84/95, fo. 301.

[153]*Ibid.*

relationship with the French ambassador might also have been salvaged by a common antagonism towards Spain. But from the ouster of Queen Maria de Medici's favourties, the Concinis, in 1617 until Richelieu's undoubted dominance in the 1630s, France was going through a period of internal chaos that caused her to let her foreign policy drift. The result was that Sir Robert could not depend on a common enemy (nor as it turned out on a close personal relationship) to shore up his dealings with the French. In addition, given the backlog of suspicion and distrust that the secretary had harboured towards Frenchmen since his work for the earl of Essex, little good could have been expected from Naunton's work with the French diplomatic agents.

Things got off to a bad start in 1618 when Le Clerc, the first French agent with whom Sir Robert dealt, became involved in the Raleigh affair and was expelled from England. Once diplomatic contacts were restored in 1619, the French sent over the Comte de Tillières. He shared many of the opinions of those close to the Queen Mother. Richelieu aside, her faction mainly contained people who were ardent Roman Catholics and who were not necessarily hostile to Spain. As for Tillières, there was great confusion in his mind on the requirements of his religion and the necessities of everyday politics. While highly sensitive to Gondomar's position with the English king and envious of his influence, the Frenchman could never quite bring himself to stomach an alliance with the 'puritans', as he called men such as Archbishop Abbot and Naunton. In fact, by Tillières's own admission he never lost an opportunity to give the puritans in general and Sir Robert in particular a bad turn.[154]

His confused attitude of envy for the Spaniards and dislike of the anti-Spanish faction led the ambassador into one scrape after another. In March 1620, there was a tilting display to which both the French and the Spanish ambassadors were invited.[155] Not only did James have to arrange the seating carefully, but he had to agree not to speak with Gondomar under any circumstances. Even so, Tillières believed that French honour was not satisfied and made difficulties about attending.[156]

Just how far the Frenchman's honour led him is further illustrated by his behaviour when dealing with the English secretaries. James

[154]Tillières to Puysieux, Leytonstone, 11 July 1620 (new style), PRO/31/3/54, fo. 131.

[155]Naunton to Herbert, Whitehall, 23 March 1620, PRO/30/53/2, fo. 121.

[156]*Ibid.*, & *Ibid.*, 24 March 1620, fo. 123.

usually sent Naunton to deal with Tillières. As Sir Robert was the senior secretary and a member of the anti-Spanish faction, this method of doing business made good sense. Gondomar, however, dealt with Calvert, and the Frenchman rapidly took offence at his differing treatment.[157] He was under the impression that the Spaniard always received the best and failed to perceive that politics and practicality played at least as important a part in diplomacy as honour did. Thus, in this very hierarchical age there is the strange picture of an ambassador feeling insulted because he had to deal with the senior secretary.

Tillières's sensitivity and frustration at his position led him into further ludicrous behaviour. Because of his envy of Gondomar's relationship with James, the Frenchman was willing to accept almost anything the Spaniard said about Anglo-Spanish relations. It tended to support his theory that James and the English accorded him second-class status, and the upshot was that Gondomar was able to plant information in Tillières's reports. In one instance the Spaniard played on his French counter-part's Romanism and convinced him that James was about to launch an anti-Catholic crusade on the continent.[158]

With Tillières feeling so terribly put upon, it was only a matter of time before he and Naunton ran foul of each other. The clash came in the autumn of 1620 over the issue of religion. Tillières's French almoner had gone on leave, and the comte felt it was necessary to find a temporary replacement. He decided on an English priest named Chamberlaine. When the priest made the mistake of leaving the embassy to administer the sacraments to English Romanists, he was arrested.[159] Naunton was soon informed of the arrest and went to question Chamberlaine. Upon discovering that the man was on the staff of the French embassy, the secretary reported that the priest was comfortably lodged and the record of his examinatin then referred to the king.[160] Once Tillières discovered what had become of his almoner, comfortably housed or otherwise, he began loudly protesting about Sir Robert's actions.

Shortly thereafter James asked Buckingham to write to Tillières. The favourite explained that Chamberlaine had been expelled from

[157]Tillières to Puysieux, 19 September 1620 (new style), PRO 31/3/54 from Bibliothèque Nationale, Paris, Fonds français, no. 15988, fol. 513.

[158]See 14 October 1620, *ibid.*, fos. 525-6. Here Tillières gives what is clearly Gondomar's version of an interview with James.

[159]*Ibid.*, fo. 513.

[160]Naunton to Herbert, Whitehall, 28 November 1620, PRO/30/53/3, fo. 181.

England twice before, and, since he had broken faith and returned, Naunton was justified in laying hold of the man. Nonetheless, Buckingham agreed to release Chamberlaine once again if Tillières would promise that the cleric would leave England and never return.[161]

The issue was too promising for the ambassador simply to agree to Buckingham's proposal. Here was an obvious opportunity both to embarrass Naunton and to obtain leave to deal with Calvert. So Tillières let loose a constant stream of complaints letting James know what he thought of his senior secretary and telling the court in France what a terrible man this puritan was. (In the course of these vitriolic attacks Naunton achieved the distinction of no longer being considered the mere 'enemy of France' but advanced to the role of 'enemy of nature.')[162]

Buckingham was once more sent to the rescue. By using all the charm he could bring to bear, which must have been considerable, he managed to soothe the Frenchman's hurt feelings over Sir Robert's behaviour.[163] Most important of all, in November 1620 Tillières obtained permission to deal with Calvert.[164]

Under the right circumstances there was a fair amount that the French diplomatic agent in England and Naunton could have agreed upon. A man with a benevolent attitude towards the Huguenots and a fear of Spanish domination of Europe would have been just the right sort of person to overcome Sir Robert's dislike of the French. Yet with a man such as Tillières, who was sensitive about honour, devoted to the Roman Catholic faith and confused about his attitude towards Spain, there was never any real chance for rapport. James had no option but to use Calvert to deal with the Frenchman, or there would have been scarcely any diplomatic relations between the two countries.

Given Naunton's difficulties with his 'friends' among the diplomatic community, it should not be difficult to imagine what his relationship was with the Spaniards and their allies. James, realizing that there would be problems, did attempt to keep these people apart from his staunchly protestant secretary, but his effort did not meet with constant success. By coincidence, in the autumn of 1620, at the time when Sir

[161] Buckingham to Tillières, 7 September 1620, PRO/31/3/54.

[162] Tillières to Puysieux, London, 8 November 1620 (new style), *ibid*.

[163] 14 November 1620 (new style). *ibid*.

[164] 20 November 1620 (new style). *ibid*.

Robert was having his difficulties with Tillières, he also clashed with Van Male, the archduke's agent from the Spanish Netherlands. The problem developed when Van Male encouraged a native-born Spanish Netherlander named Ferrin, who had been a long-time London resident, to have his fourth child baptized by a Roman Catholic priest. The man's other three children had been baptized in the Anglican Church, and the church wardens of his parish were on the scene quickly to make good this 'wrong'. Van Male wrote these parish officials a letter stating that they had better leave the citizens of the archduke's provinces alone if they knew what was good for them. The letter was a particularly foolish move because Ferrin and Naunton both lived in the same parish, St Martin's-in-the-Fields, and the secretary was bound to find out about it.

When James was informed of the state of affairs, he became furious. The agent had clearly overstepped his bounds in threatening the church wardens, and Naunton was ordered to warn him about his behaviour. If Van Male seemed penitent, the matter would go no further, but if he was truculent and persisted in causing trouble, then James planned to protest to the archduke.[165] Had only the baptism been involved, the king might well have winked at the whole affair. But when Van Male tried to interfere with church officials performing their duty, James had no choice but to act.

In the best of circumstances, which these certainly were not, the archduke's agent was a difficult man with whom to deal.[166] Here he showed himself at his very worst. First he tried to bribe the Clerk of the Privy Council, then he caused a scene at a council meeting; finally in Whitehall, he angered Naunton to such an extent that the fifty-seven year old bureaucrat nearly struck the archduke's agent.[167] In mitigation, it should be said that Van Male strongly believed he was saving the young child's soul from eternal damnation, thus justifying any action. Sir Robert, on the other hand, saw the affair as a dangerous precedent; if he had let it pass, it would have been a step towards the toleration that the Romanists claimed was soon expected.[168] Though the matter was eventually settled and Van Male reinstated in James's good graces (much to Naunton's sorrow),[169] it had repercus-

---

[165]Naunton to Trumbull, Whitehall, 26 August 1620, Berkshire Record Office Trumbull MS. 33, no. 41.

[166]C.H. Carter, *Secret Diplomacy of the Habsburgs, 1598-1625* (London, 1964), pp. 134-5.

[167]Naunton to Trumbull, Whitehall, 26 August 1620, Berkshire Record Office Trumbull MS. 33. no. 41.

[168]*Ibid.*

[169]13 November 1620, *ibid.,* no. 43.

66

sions that no one could have foreseen. For besides protesting to Albert that everything Sir Robert said was a lie,[170] the agent also called in his chief ally at the English court, Gondomar.[171]

The best one could expect from Naunton's relationship with the Spanish ambassador is that it would remain a distant one. Although for his own reasons James would occasionally order his secretary to go to Gondomar,[172] they were largely kept apart by the Spaniard's presence on the king's progresses. Van Male's complaints, however, brought Sir Robert and his politics directly to the ambassador's attention. The result was a heated discussion in which Gondomar tried to get James to admit that Sir Robert had acted without the king's knowledge. James would not rise to the bait and insisted that his secretary did nothing of moment without his permission.[173] In view of subsequent developments this statement is worth remembering.

On the whole, Sir Robert's performance as an intermediary with foreign diplomats is not particularly impressive. With the exception of Lando, Dona and the various Dutch representatives, the secretary simply did not get on well with the foreign diplomats in England.[174] It is true that there were often mitigating circumstances. His role as anti-Spanish secretary and chief priest-hunter did not predispose any of the Spaniards or their friends to look favourably upon him. What is more, the personalities of Tillières and Donato were such as to make any secretary's job a difficult one. Yet whatever the surrounding circumstances, the results were that Naunton managed to earn the active dislike of most foreign diplomats in England. There is a good chance that he provoked their displeasure by what they considered rudeness[175] and ill-temper. It is interesting that even among Naunton's English opponents, there was never any complaint about this sort of behaviour. One can only conclude that dealing with foreigners was Naunton's particular weak point, and it would not be surprising if the experience in Essex' service was in large measure responsible for this state of affairs.

[170]Van Male to della Faille, 11 September 1620 (new style), Archivès Générales. Brussels PC 56, fo. 328.

[171]18 September 1620 (new style), *ibid.*

[172]Gondomar to Philip III, London, 22 May 1620 (new style), PRO/31/12/21 from Bibl. de Palacio Est. G plut. 8.

[173]Lando to the Doge and Senate, 11 October 1620, (new style), *CSP, Ven., 1619-21*, p. 432.

[174]PRO, PRO/31/3/54 from Bibliothèque Nationale, Paris, Fonds français, No. 15985, fo. 478.

[175]*Ibid.*

Strange as it may seem, a secretary who lacked the diplomatic graces had advantages for James. For Naunton acted as a lightning rod that drew criticism away from the king and then permitted him to play the soother of the foreigners' hurt feelings. There is no way of knowing whether the king had the plan in mind when he made his secretarial appointment, but it certainly was one of the results of Sir Robert's tenure in office.

Whether the antagonism ultimately hurt Naunton, is an entirely different question. Owing to a peculiar combination of circumstances that developed during the autumn of 1620 (when there was the greatest trouble with the diplomatic corps), serious damage was done. By alienating so many of the foreign diplomats, especially Gondomar, Sir Robert was setting himself up as a potential target, a sacrificial lamb. He filled the role sooner than anyone could have predicted.

3

SECRETARY OF STATE: DISGRACE AND REHABILITATION

Suspension

During the first month of 1621, Secretary Naunton's political career came to a sudden halt: 'There is an accident fallen out heere unexpected two dayes since,' wrote a minor court official named Thomas Locke,[1] 'The same day the king went from hence which was the 17th of this [present], Mr. Secretary Naunton was by direction from the king commanded to his chamber and his place suspended.'[2]

Although the writer did not realize it, 'unexpected' was the key word in explaining Naunton's suspension. A series of unforeseen events, largely beyond Sir Robert's control, cut short his career as Secretary of State. More importantly, his suspension played a major role in altering the way James ran his government. An understanding of what happened begins with the charges brought against Sir Robert and the circumstances surrounding the suspension. In fact, the charges can only be surmised because they were never formally stated. So far as one can tell, they centred upon Naunton's efforts to convince the French that, if they were willing to provide a large enough dowry for Princess Henrietta Maria, she could become the bride of Prince Charles.[3] As for the surrounding circumstances, the disgrace followed immediately in the wake of an extraordinary embassy of Maréchal de Cadenet, the brother of the duc de Luynes (Louis XIII's favourite). Cadenet's party of noblemen and court hangers-on had left a progress that Louis had made to Calais,[4] and, on the suggestion advanced some months before by Sir Edward Herbert, the maréchal had come to England.[5]

Although there had been a great deal of speculation about the mission's real purposes,[6] Cadenet's letters of introduction did not give

---

[1] *APC, 1618-19,* p. 23.

[2] 19 January 1621, PRO SP/14/119. no. 35.

[3] G. Goodman, *The Court of King James the First,* ed. J. Brewer (London, 1839), II, 227-8.

[4] Herbert to Naunton, Paris, 8/18 December 1620, PRO/30/53/3, fo. 193.

[5] 2 March 1620, PRO/30/53/2, fos. 91-2.

[6] See BL, Stowe 176, fos. 175-6 for a Huguenot point of view, BL, Add. 36445, fo. 3 for the opinion of an Englishman interested in the success of the Spanish match and PRO, SP/14/119, no. 24 for John Chamberlain's opinion.

him the power to negotiate anything but merely to explain and question. The French government's attitudes towards the Huguenots and the situation in Germany were the chief matters mentioned in the instructions. The marriage received passing and largely negative mention.[7] This nebulous state of affairs encouraged both sides to do some probing of one another's intentions on various matters.[8] The topics ranged as far afield as the Scots guards whom Louis employed, to the more internationally significant troubles among the Grisons of the Valtelline. Yet despite the wide range of subject matter, a French match did not have a prominent part in the discussions. According to Van Male's information, James said that he could not consider a French match until the pope had decided on whether or not he would issue a dispensation for a Spanish one.[9] There the matter rested.

Perhaps it would be more accurate to say that a French match did not have a prominent part in the discussions between the two principals. For some time between the 12th and 14th of January 1621, Naunton met with that many-mastered official of the French embassy in London, La Forêt,[10] and 'by way of discourse'[11] made his ill-fated proposal concerning the French match. In a remarkably short time Gondomar heard a slightly exaggerated version of Naunton's statement. By the evening of 16 January, the ambassador had convinced James that the secretary required punishment,[12] and the necessary action was taken.

So far the matter seems straightforward enough, but shortly there were hints that there was more involved in the episode than the punishing of an indiscreet official. Others were implicated. Archbishop Abbot, Baron Dona, Thomas Murray (Prince Charles's secretary), and Doncaster were all connected. Rumours began to circulate that they had conspired with Naunton over Bohemia,[13] or that they were up to some underhand business with the Huguenots at La Rochelle.

[7]PRO/31/3/54, fos. 145-8.

[8]Naunton to Herbert, Charing Cross, 14 January 1621, PRO/30/53/4, fos. 14-15.

[9]C. H. Carter, *Secret Diplomacy*, p. 195.

[10]This is the date on the dispatch that La Forêt took to Herbert. See PRO/30/53/4. fo. 11.

[11]These were La Forêt's own words. PRO/30/53/4, fo. 32.

[12]Gondomar to Philip III, 10 February 1621 (new style), PRO/31/12/21 from Arch. de Simancas — EL 2602, fo. 18.

[13]19-20 January 1621, London, *CSPD, 1619-23*, p. 215; *Ibid*., 2 February 1621, 218; Tillières to Puysieux, London, 29 January 1621 (new style), PRO/31/3/54, fo. 154.

Murray was imprisoned;[14] Abbot and Doncaster were reprimanded;[15] Dona was at first reprimanded but after further difficulty, left the country.[16] Before the summer was over, further blows were struck. The archbishop was in trouble again, supposedly because of a hunting accident, and the earl of Southampton was imprisoned for his behaviour in the 1621 Parliament. What had occurred was the virtual overthrow of the major members of the anti-Spanish faction.

The reasons for the suspension of Naunton and the decimation of the anti-Spanish party lie enmeshed in the diplomatic situation in Europe and the English political scene. Both areas had been dominated by Frederick's acceptance of the Bohemian throne and, since the middle of September 1620, the Marquis of Spinola's invasion of Frederick's homelands in the Palatinate. The two events roused the Protestants and their allies on both sides of the Channel to a frenzy of activity. A good deal of their action was directed towards James in an effort to convince him to do something for his son-in-law.

Though some have questioned the English king's willingness to aid Frederick,[17] royal intentions do not really seem to be the issue. Where James differed from his more militant Protestant subjects was in the type of aid that could and should be extended. The king wanted Frederick and Elizabeth to regain their lost lands in the Palatinate just as much as their most militant supporters. James's motivation was, however, in some respects a little unusual for his day. He was more concerned with peace than the victory of militant Protestantism over the papal anti-Christ. He was also conscious of the dishonour of his daughter being married to a penniless 'elected' king, and he was unenthusiastic about the prospect of having these two quixotic wanderers shown up in England one day to become figureheads of an ultra-Protestant war party.[18]

With all these considerations in mind, and given James's prejudices and inclinations, it should not be entirely surprising that he never abandoned the hope that he could negotiate his and the Palatines's way out of their difficulties. Throughout the many twists and turns in the situation in the next few years this thought remained the key to the king's behaviour.

[14] A. Valaresso to the Doge and Senate, 26 August 1622 *CSP, Ven., 1621-3,* p. 398.

[15] PRO 31/3/54, fos. 154 and 158.

[16] For Dona's attempts to excuse his faults see PRO SP/81/20, fo. 156.

[17] *Germany and England,* I, preface & D. H. Willson, *James VI and I* (London, 1956), pp. 357-9, 408, 411, 412 & 414.

[18] *CSP Ven, 1619-21,* p. 436. This is a letter which was written in 1620, probably in June or July, judging from the context, from Gondomar to a Spanish official.

From a domestic point of view, James was simply being realistic. First and foremost, despite the efforts of the Treasury Commission, the king had scarcely enough money to meet his everyday expenses.[19] Though there is no question that James lacked sense about economic matters, he did seem to realize that wars were expensive propositions which the ordinary resources of the crown could not bear. He must also have known that, if he became involved in a war before there was adequate financing, he would eventually have to call a parliament to extricate him from his difficulties. This action would put him at the mercy of such a parliament. It was not a position he would relish. The king's more militant subjects were thinking in terms of a parliament as early as 1619,[20] but a year later there was still a decided lack of royal enthusiasm for the subject.

The financial situation was one of the key reasons that James tried so hard to talk his way out of the mess into which Frederick had got them both. Though talk had its price (the five extraordinary embassies for peace had cost £69,485),[21] yet a war would be infinitely more expensive. In the 1621 Parliament Calvert asked for £500,000 for a military effort. This sum was considered very modest. Shortly thereafter the Council of War estimated that to field an army of 25,000 foot, 500 horse and 20 pieces of artillery would cost £207,736 plus an additional £76,046-17/8 per month to keep it in the field.[22]

Circumstance, however, contrived to make James much less able to resist the call of war and its associated financial burdens. By the end of September 1620, he realized that talk alone would no longer ensure peace. Spinola and his army were in the Lower Palatinate and showed promise of eventually conquering the whole province. Their success caused the pressure from the anti-Spanish faction to mount to such a degree that James complained that he was surrounded by 300 Winwoods.[23] There seemed little choice but to start the wheels slowly turning in order to relieve some of the pressure. The process was undertaken by attempting to raise revenues from extraordinary sources. The funds raised could either be sent directly to Frederick, or, if all else failed, could be used to finance an effective English army

[19] R. H. Tawney, *Business and Politics under James I* (Cambridge, 1958), p. 142 n. 1. Tawney's whole book is based on the thesis that James was deeply in debt and needed drastic reforms to correct the situation.

[20] See Bodley Tanner 74, fo. 221.

[21] HMC, *4th Report*, p. 281.

[22] F. C. Dietz, *English Public Finance, 1558-1641*, (New York, London, 1932), p. 188.

[23] D. H. Willson, *Privy Councillors*, p. 18.

for the recovery of the Palatinate. (General Horace Vere's troop of 4,000 English volunteers, who were already in Germany, were facing five times their numbers and were able to do little more than hold a fortified town.)

In order to obtain the money needed, James decided to call for a voluntary contribution from the aristocracy, clergy and municipal corporations. Simultaneously the subject of a parliament received increasing public attention.[24] It is interesting that the king embarked on both measures at the same time, for despite appearances to the contrary, this combination provided a means for a counter-attack against the anti-Spanish party. James relied upon the awareness of those who were asked for a voluntary contribution; they would know a parliament would mean a mandatory subsidy as well for the same purpose. This fact would tend to confine giving to the most militant Protestants. The result was that the king had an opportunity to postpone or even cancel the parliament on the grounds that the small contribution to the voluntary fund showed that, when it came to practical matters of finance, the country was unwilling to support the war. Naunton was so upset by this turn of events that only a month after the programme started, he was afraid it would collapse.[25]

James could afford to do all this tactical manoeuvring because the military campaigning season was nearly over, and despite Spinola's advances, at least part of the Lower and all of the Upper Palatinate were in Frederick's hands along with Bohemia, Silesia and Moravia. Whatever legal justification there was for the Prince Palatine's possession of these latter three provinces, practically speaking they represented his best bargaining chip with their former owner, the Emperor Ferdinand. He might be willing to take them back in return for a guarantee of the security of the hereditary Palatinate lands.

The impression that there was still time to jockey for position was enhanced by reports indicating that the troops opposing Frederick in Bohemia were not in very good physical condition.[26] With any luck at all there would be no real need for succour before the 1621 campaigning season began again in May, at the earliest.

On top of all this good news, the voluntary contribution and the talk about calling parliament served a double purpose. It not only put the

[24]Naunton to Nethersole, Whitehall, 2 October 1620, PRO SP/81/19, fo. 14.

[25]Naunton to Trumbull, Whitehall, 13 November 1620, Berkshire Record Office Trumbull MS. 33, no. 42.

[26]Nethersole to Naunton, Prague, 1 October 1620, PRO SP/81/19, fo. 3 & *Ibid.*, 16 October 1620, fo. 111.

anti-Spanish faction at a tactical disadvantage when it pressed for a war, but it also frightened the Habsburgs and their allies with the prospect of the English having the funds to join in the battle on an effective scale. Though the effects were seemingly contradictory, the result was that both sides were more willing to listen to James's peace proposals than they might otherwise have been.

It was Frederick's disastrous and wholly unexpected defeat in the battle of White Mountain on 8 November 1620 (new style) that irreversibly altered all these calculations. This devastating military loss had the side effect of withering the Prince Palatine's negotiating position as though it were an early flower faced with a belated frost. For no matter how his father-in-law may have felt about the moral question of the Prince Palatine occupying the Bohemian throne, it was now recognized by all concerned that there were no longer any bargaining points between Frederick and the Emperor Ferdinand; the Habsburgs had taken all of the Palatine's cards away from him.

This train of events did not seem to alter the king's immediate intentions for raising money. The voluntary contributions trickled in, and he continued with plans to call a parliament. It is true that it was not until December that the news of the battle was confirmed in England, but even so matters went along much as before. The reason that James did not deviate from his plan was that, although Frederick may have run out of negotiable points, James still had one left: the Spanish match for Prince Charles. The disquiet that the collection of money caused in the Habsburg court was part of the English king's scheme for achieving the marriage. What he had to do now was heighten the disquiet as quickly as possible.

The English and Spanish had been dithering for several years over the possibility of matching Charles with a Spanish princess, but the recent events had made the marriage a matter of some urgency. A Spanish marriage contract with a proviso for either Frederick's or his eldest son's restoration to their hereditary German lands was the last hope of a peaceful settlement.[27] Yet the English king's being aware that the Spanish marriage had now taken on a new importance did not mean that he was going to let others know it. He was far too wily a diplomat to let the other side know that he had decided on the Spanish match. With James's mind working in the manner of a late Baroque musician, he automatically sought a counterpoint, an anti-Spanish counterpoint. By this device the king hoped to force the Spaniards to play the piece his way and to do so at a rapid tempo.

[27]C. V. Wedgwood, *The Thirty Years War* (London, 1950), 5th edn. pp. 159-60; C. Oman, *Elizabeth of Bohemia* (London, 1938), p. 282.

Given the divided nature of the English government with its pro- and anti-Spanish factions functioning at the highest levels, the situation was ready made for such a programme. What is more there was no real problem about the Spaniards accepting the sincerity of the king's actions. Previous examples of anti-Spanish digressions such as Raleigh's last voyage to South America (and more recently Captain North's to the same area) made them seem all too believable. Further, just in case the Spanish had been reading the French ambassador's mail, for some time he had been reporting to his government about feelers concerning a possible French match for the Prince of Wales.[28]

What James did was intensify the anti-Spanish activity. The collection of the voluntary contribution and the continuation of the plans to call parliament were part of it, for they pointed up his potential readiness to use military force to restore Frederick. But more importantly he tried to convince everyone that he had finished hinting and was now seriously considering a French match.[29] All these actions were designed to fill the Spanish with feelings of insecurity and to hurry their efforts to procure a dispensation from Rome for the proposed marriage with the heretic English prince.

Perhaps the biggest help in this line of attack came from the extra- ordinary embassy of Maréchal Cadenet in January 1621. James surrounded the mission with as much secrecy as possible. Even Tillières was excluded from the discussions with the maréchal. It is difficult to believe that a man as wise in the ways of diplomacy as James was not fully aware that rumours would start flying about an impending French marriage negotiation.[30] His scheme worked exceedingly well because he had Van Male convinced that the English had finally decided to throw over the Spanish match in favour of a French one.[31]

Naunton had an active interest in all these proceedings. As already indicated, almost from the moment Frederick had considered accepting the Bohemian throne, Sir Robert was one of his most ardent supporters. The misfortunes the prince suffered at the hands of the Habsburg and Bavarian armies had not in the slightest weakened the secretary's support. What he now tried to do was be certain that others shared his opinions.

[28]Tillières to Puysieux, 3 February 1620 (new style), PRO/31/3/53, fo. 70; 18 September 1620, (new style), PRO/31/3/54, fo. 142 & *Ibid.*, 28 September 1620 (new style).

[29]22 and 27 December 1620 PRO/31/3/54.

[30]Naunton to Carleton, 2 January 1621, PRO SP/84/99, fo. 4 & *CSP, Ven., 1620-1*, pp. 534-5.

[31]Carter, *Secret Diplomacy*, p. 184.

As for the ambassadors with whom Naunton dealt, Doncaster had, of course, favoured the Palatine's claims from the first.[32] Sir Edward Herbert and Carleton were both warned about doing too much for the prince,[33] so they certainly were no problem. Though Trumbull and Wotton ne,er did anything overt to help the Winter King, their sentiments were never in doubt.[34] Finally, Wake and Nethersole did whatever they could for Frederick while managing to stay within the bounds James had set.[35] Since these men were, after all, the anti-Spanish ambassadors, one could scarcely expect anything different from them.

Of much more importance was winning over a large number of privy councillors,[36] for such an accomplishment ultimately gave Sir Robert his real chance for action. Though it would be overstating the case to say that Naunton was the leader of the anti-Spanish faction who marshalled his forces for an attack on the king's neutral position, the secretary was spokesman for both the councillors and the ambassadors. With nearly all of them of one mind, it was only natural that Sir Robert's voice began to sound a little more authoritative to James.

It was also natural that, having once won the king's co-operation, Naunton should play a major part in implementing the anti-Spanish programme. In fact he had an important administrative role in directing the collection of the voluntary contribution.[37] He was also influential in bringing about the meeting of the 1621 parliament, and indeed, if the Venetian ambassador is correct, it was Naunton who bore the major part of the burden of keeping the king to his original intentions of calling it into session.[38] If this activity was not enough, it was Sir Robert who moved James to form a Council of War,[39] and

[32]*England and Germany,* I, 206-7.

[33]Naunton to Herbert, 8 November 1619, PRO/30/53/1, fo. 191 & Naunton to Carleton, 16 December 1619, PRO SP/84/93, fo. 192.

[34]Trumbull to Naunton, Brussels, 20 January 1620, PRO SP/77/14, fo. 9: in this dispatch Trumbull refers to Frederick as king of Bohemia, an almost sure sign of his support. Wotton's Protestantism placed him in the Palatines' camp. See Smith, *Wotton,* II, 147-8.

[35]Wake to Naunton, 13/23 December 1620, PRO SP/92/7, fo. 264 Nethersole's appointment as secretary to the Palatines, while he also acted as James's ambassador to the Princes of the Union, automatically made him a partisan of the Palatines. Several years later his partisanship got him into trouble with Charles I. See *DNB sub* Nethersole, Sir Francis.

[36]Willson, *Privy Councillors,* pp. 147-8.

[37]Naunton to Calvert, Charing Cross, 13 December 1620, PRO, SP/14/118, no. 25.

[38]Lando to the Doge and Senate, 11 June 1621, (new style), *CSP, Ven., 1621-3,* p.64.

[39]8 January 1621, (new style), *CSP, Ven., 1619-21,* pp. 516-17.

then formalized the idea by proposing the resolution at the Privy Council.[40]

This event brings the story of Naunton's suspension nearly full circle, for it was only a few days after the appointment of the Council of War that the king suspended him. To all appearances, he was at the height of his power and influence within the government. So far as any outsider could see, he had turned his position of spokesman and intermediary into one of importance and now had the initiative in the king's councils.

Yet the secretary's new-found position of influence turned out to have very little substance to it. The ultimate reason for this situation and his downfall was that the anti-Spanish programme was only a conterpoint, not the main theme. It was a device to force the Spanish into action, but it was never anything more than a device. When it failed to produce the desired results, it was abandoned and Sir Robert with it.

Such a conclusion, nevertheless, does not really explain why Naunton and the anti-Spanish counterpoint were cast aside short of achieving a Spanish match. On examining the events, four possibilities present themselves: Naunton could have gone too far on his own; foreign ambassadors could have laid a trap for him; his superiors in the English government could have wanted him out of the way, or some fortuitous combination of events could have brought him to grief. Though all these possibilities have some element of truth in them, it was primarily the last that explains most fully what happened.

From what has already been observed about Naunton, the possibility that he acted on his own cannot be dismissed out of hand. The man who was capable of plotting to imprison a French messenger on the trumped-up charge of being a Roman Catholic priest,[41] or of sending people to spy on the supposedly privileged foreign embassies[42] would certainly not be deterred by moral scruples from deciding that the end justified the means. Clearly, when it came to anything to hurt the Spanish, one wonders whether Sir Robert had any reservations at all. These observations, however, need qualification. Whatever plotting Naunton had done in the past had been done with official approval. All through his career as secretary he had built up a

[40]Naunton to Carleton, Whitehall, 2 January 1621, PRO, SP/84/99, fo. 4.

[41]Discussed above, pp. 51-2.

[42]*Ibid.*

reputation for being cautious and doing nothing without warrant from higher authority.[43] Sir Robert made circumspection and care the keynotes of his actions. If he had decided to over-extend himself in this one case, it is inconceivable that he would have chosen a man so eminently untrustworthy as La Forêt to be a party to the action.

There is the possibility, of course, that the Frenchman might have done something that would have caused Naunton to drop his guard. It is true that he had promised Sir Robert to take a dispatch back to Paris and to inform Sir Edward Herbert about the activities of a certain Monsieur Boislorée, one of Naunton's spies on the verge of defecting to the French. If, as seems likely, it was La Forêt who supplied Sir Robert with the information on Boislorée's disloyalty, then it is possible that the secretary might have been inclined to trust his French informant a little further than usual. Yet the probability remains remote that Naunton would have started pouring state secrets into the ear of someone whom he knew had such catholic loyalties.[44] It also should be kept in mind that as Secretary of State, Sir Robert would have automatically had access to people within the French extraordinary embassy who were much better suited for such confidences than a courier who doubled as a spy. Given all these considerations about La Forêt and Naunton, one is driven to the conclusion that the secretary must have been ordered to spread a rumour about the French match.

This line of reasoning is given substance by Lando's and Caron's dispatches. They were the two diplomats in England with whom Naunton was on the best terms, and both of them reported the rumour concerning the French match. Lando does not cite his source, but Caron states quite plainly that he got his information from Naunton. It is also interesting to note that both the Venetian and the Dutchman posted their dispatches containing the rumour at almost exactly the same time as Sir Robert had sent La Forêt to France as his messenger.[45] The combination of Naunton's cautious nature and of a double agent plus two anti-Spanish ambassadors simultaneously reporting the same information certainly gives reasonable assurance that orders were issued to spread the rumour. Sir Robert was not acting on his own initiative.

[43]Locke to Carleton, 5 February 1621, *CSPD, 1619-23*, p. 220.

[44]See Naunton to Herbert, Whitehall, 12 January 1621, PRO/30/53/4, fo. 11. For Boislorée as an agent of Naunton's see Bodley, Fortescue MS., Add. D110, fo. 91, and for Boislorée's defection see Boislorée to Puysieux, 18 December 1620, (new style) from Bibliothèque Nationale, Paris, fonds français, No. 15988, fo. 548.

[45]Lando to the Doge and Senate, 22 January 1621, (new style), *CSP, Ven., 1619-21*, pp. 534-5 and Caron to Estates General, South Lambeth, BL Add. 17677 K. fos. 93-4.

If Naunton was ordered to spread these stories, he might well have been the victim of a preconceived plot. If there was such a plot, the French are certainly possible candidates for having hatched it. La Forêt was, after all, supposedly in their employ. Stretching all the way back to Sir Robert's part in the Raleigh affair, the French government had reasons for wanting him out of the way. Furthermore some of the French ministers could have wanted to please the Spanish. As late as the autumn of 1620 Isaac Wake was reporting from Turin that the pro-Spanish element in the French government was so powerful, it might gain control.[46] On a more immediate level, of course, Naunton and Tillières were anything but the best of friends. Thus the elements were all there on the French side to do Naunton an injury.

Despite the undoubted hostility, it is difficult to believe that the French would have concocted a plot to dispose of Sir Robert that was so basically foreign to their interests. If they had wanted the man removed, it would have been much better for them if he had been caught by a French agent while negotiating a match with some Protestant country. This way there would be no suspicion that they had encouraged Naunton's advances in order to interfere with Anglo-Spanish relations. For if either James or Gondomar had thought that Sir Robert had been led on by the French, his disgrace might have brought them closer together. Even a French pro-Spaniard could never have wanted that result. In fact, even Tillières overcame his initial elation at Naunton's removal and gave way to genuine discomfort that his former foe had gone down over the question of a French match.[47]

If Sir Robert was not laid low by a French plot, one could look closer to home. There is one school of thought which contends that Buckingham virtually ran the English government during the last years of James's reign. Therefore any pro-Spanish move would have needed his consent. Yet there is no convincing evidence that Buckingham did dominate either foreign or domestic policy making in 1619 or 1620.[48] It was not until his return from Spain with Prince

---

[46] Wake to Naunton, Turin, 28 October/8 November 1620, PRO SP/92/7, fo. 226.

[47] Tillières to Puysieux, 13 February 1621, (new style), PRO/31/3/54, fo. 156.

[48] As late as March 1620 Gondomar considered Buckingham merely to be a good-looking young man of twenty-five with a penchant for interfering. Lando, viewing matters from the opposite side of the political spectrum, thought the favourite was a weathercock who always took his lead from the king, but who tried to give the impression that all favours came from him. If Buckingham fooled these two, everyone's hats must go off to him: he outwitted two professionals who should have known better. PRO/31/12/21 from Arch. de Simancas, EL 2600, fo. 63 and Lando to the Doge and Senate, 8 October 1620, (new style), CSP, Ven., 1619-21, p. 430.

Charles in 1623 that he played a clear and decidedly aggressive role in this area. Yet his lack of complete control does not preclude plotting, and the favourite had some reason to do just that. In 1620 he had no love for some of Naunton's anti-Spaniards.

In the summer of 1620 one of the chief reasons for his dislike concerned Frederick's ambassador, Baron Achtichus Dona. The baron decided to choose General Horace Vere to lead the small volunteer relief force for the Palatinate. The choice offended the favourite. Buckingham had promised Sir Edward Cecil the post, and, like the spoiled child he sometimes was, upon the discovery of his plan's frustration, the favourite reportedly threatened to have a defenestration of his own with Dona as the victim.[49] It is true that some days later he regained his composure sufficiently to prevent Cecil from running Dona through with a sword,[50] but the offence was not quickly forgotten. In October 1620, when James began his anti-Spanish programme, Buckingham was still cool enough towards the baron to necessitate a formal reconciliation.[51] Despite these attempts at improving appearances, the favourite's relationship with the Palatines remained strained. Perhaps the real problem was that they preferred to use other English contacts.[52] It was not uncommon for them to use Pembroke's dependents as their channel of communication, and Buckingham was never one to take such a snub with good grace.

But if it is possible to show that the favourite had his grievances with the anti-Spanish faction, it is not possible to show that he harboured any ill-feelings towards Naunton. Though there is no evidence of any genuine friendship between the favourite and the secretary, there is evidence that the former was willing to be helpful. He did, after all, make a politic defence of Naunton when Tillières was up in arms about the arrest of the priest Chamberlaine.[53] Over and above this action, Buckingham was well known for his loyalty to his relatives, no matter what their politics or religion. It is difficult to envisage him making a special exception for Sir Robert.

One final commentary on Buckingham's political attitudes should be made. Whatever he thought of the Palatines personally, he was not entirely negative to their cause. Even before James began his

[49]Tillières to Puysieux, 3 July 1620 (new style), PRO/31/3/54, fo. 127^V.

[50]Naunton to Carleton, received 16/26 July 1620, PRO SP/84/96, fo. 30.

[51]CSP, Ven., 1619-21, p. 430.

[52]Lando to the Doge and Senate, 25 September 1620, (new style), ibid., p. 418.

[53]Discussed below, pp. 63-4.

anti-Spanish programme, Tillières had heard that Buckingham had been reproached by two leading members of the pro-Spanish faction, Arundel and Digby, for his lack of enthusiasm for the Spanish match.[54] If Buckingham had gone over wholeheartedly to the pro-Spanish faction by January 1621, it was the best kept secret in the English court. Not even Gondomar reported it.

If the favourite is abandoned as the cause of Sir Robert's disgrace, the next logical step is the king. Ultimately, of course, it was the king who suspended his secretary, but his action does not necessarily mean that he had plotted to do so. Perhaps Gondomar provides the best clue to both his and James's role in Naunton's disgrace. In his 10 February 1621 (new style) dispatch Gondomar stated:

> Secretary Naunton is the greatest enemy of Spain, of the House of Austria and of Catholicism and all those who are badly disposed against Spain meet at his house. Naunton has sent word to Marquis [sic] Cadenet not to mistrust the French marriage, for King James had told him to insist on it, and he might offer a good dowry, for the Spanish marriage would never be fulfilled. Gondomar knows that Naunton has taken measures against the Catholics without the king's orders; he is pensioned by Venice and Holland. Gondomar was well aware of the necessity of stopping this evil and determined to see the king and Buckingham on the 26th of January [new style]. *He spoke for five hours to them* [my italics] urging them to put a remedy to this. Digby went that same evening to his house to tell him the king was determined to arrest Naunton, and deprive him of his secretaryship, likewise to remove the Archbishop of Canterbury from the Council, and that Baron de Dohna should no longer be allowed to mix in court affairs. All these things induce the populace to be against King James and against Spain; Digby was told by King James to ask Gondomar if he wanted more to be done, or in another form. Gondomar approved this, and the next day Naunton was arrested, and his post taken from him. Orders were given to the Elector's envoy not to interfere in English affairs, and the King spoke to the Archbishop in such a way as to alarm him. . . .

> The only secretary who is left is Sir George Calvert, and he is friendly to Spain, and has therefore many enemies.[55]

[54] 8 September 1620, (new style), PRO/31/3/54.

[55] PRO/31/12/21 from Arch. de Simancas — EL 2602, fo. 18. This is a translation of a minute of the information in the original dispatch. See PRO/31/12/24, fo. 46. Though these minutes are sometimes misleading, this one appears to have the essence of the original. See C.H. Carter, 'Gondomar: Ambassador to James I', *Historical Journal* 7, no. 2, 199.

Gondomar's dispatch must put to rest any thought that it was the king who planned in advance to trap Naunton in order to demonstrate his good faith to the Spanish. If this had been the case, James would almost certainly have called the ambassador in to announce his decision to suspend the secretary. The whole effect is destroyed if it seemed an unwilling favour. Yet Gondomar indicates that he approached James and then spent five hours convincing him that Sir Robert had to go.[56] Even if there had been a carefully contrived sham, it is not likely that so much time would have been spent in the meeting. A polite show of doubt, perhaps, but not a day-long meeting which left the matter still undecided. In all likelihood sending Digby later that night was more than a face-saving gesture. Even after five hours, James still did not know what to do.

The Spanish ambassador does not say specifically what he said to the king to cause such indecision, but the best contemporary theories were that he threatened to break off the negotiations for the Spanish match[57] and warned that Frederick's restoration in the Palatinate was hopeless unless the king did what was required of him.[58] If these speculations are correct, then James had to choose between either disavowing a minister of state as a gesture of good faith, or facing delay or even cancellation of the Spanish marriage and with it, the peaceful settlement of Frederick's plight. Although Gondomar could not make top level decisions on his own, he was, however, one of the chief advocates of the match at the Spanish court. His negative judgment would at the very least have delayed matters until the situation was re-evaluated. Delay was of course what James did not want. The whole anti-Spanish counterpoint had been devised just to speed the marriage of Charles to the Infanta. When it failed, there was nothing left to do but abandon it and Naunton as well.

The Spanish ambassador's part in this affair leaves him as the least likely candidate for having plotted Sir Robert's disgrace. He was not only the prime mover of the king, but was also in a position to have engineered La Forêt's meeting with Naunton in the hope of provoking the secretary into saying something indiscreet. Gondomar's motivation for this move is plain enough, but whether he was able to plan it all out in advance is not nearly so clear.

---

[56] Though Tillières may have had the story from the Spaniard, it is nonetheless interesting that he, too, uses this figure of five hours. Tillières to Puysieux, London, 29 January 1621, (new style), PRO/31/3/54, fo. 155.

[57] *Ibid.*, fo. 154

[58] Lando to the Doge and Senate, 21 September 1622, (new style), *CSP, Ven., 1621-3*, pp. 442-3.

Granting Gondomar's undoubted talents, entrapping Naunton by using La Forêt was just too difficult a project. Even if he had sent La Forêt to Sir Robert, even if he had provided him with the information concerning Boislorée, he still would have had no way of knowing that any useful information would be passed to his agent. Gondomar might have tried the project as a gamble, but with someone as unreliable as La Forêt on the mission, there was no telling what he might do. Gondomar would have been much more likely to use one of the French noblemen in the Cadenet suite for such a design. There were plenty of them available who were either of Spanish sympathies or in need of money (or both). Naunton was far more likely to drop his guard for a respected aristocrat than for an embassy clerk he did not trust.

Having disposed of all the potential plotters, it only remains to construct a coherent pattern of motivations and events for those involved in Naunton's disgrace. Of particular interest here is an understanding of just what James expected from the rumour he made Naunton spread and how he expected the Spanish to react to it.

It seems clear that the rumour of a French match was meant as the appropriate echo of the Cadenet mission. The echo, however, was meant to come from the European side of the Channel. That was why La Forêt received the information just before he left for France and why Lando and Caron were told the story at almost exactly the same time, for that was when the maréchal was leaving. This device was the seventeenth-century equivalent of what sometimes appears in the twentieth-century press: 'This reporter has learned today from sources close to the government that . . .'. In short, it was a fairly modest rumour designed to be blown out of proportion by the time it surfaced.

Viewing the rumour as an echo of the Cadenet mission gives a new perspective to the information that Van Male obtained about the ambassador's interview with James. He learned that the king had said that he was 'engaged with Spain and was unable to hear any other proposal until he knew what resolution the pope would take regarding the granting of a dispensation'.[59] The statement was another of the king's double-edged weapons. It put the French off in the correct manner while not closing the door completely. If the information leaked to the Spaniards, it contained the veiled threat that they had better get the pope to grant the dispensation or the English would look elsewhere. The approach taken coincides very well with what it appears

[59]Carter, *Secret Diplomacy,* p. 195.

that Naunton's rumour was designed to do: panic the Spanish into action before it was too late.

It was La Forêt who was responsible for throwing all these calculations out of kilter. What he did of course was to run immediately to Gondomar with his information, and that allowed the ambassador to confront James with it too soon for the plan to work. There was no way to know in advance that the news would surface so quickly; it was simply an unexpected accident.

The result was that, having been caught off balance, the king went into a panic. Calvert claimed he had never seen James 'apprehend anything so passionately'.[60] The king was apparently desperate to save the Spanish match and went so far as to write to Louis XIII personally to put a stop to any thoughts he might have had that Naunton's statement was anything more than unofficial.[61] It is worth noting that in the previous October Gondomar had reportedly threatened to break off marriage negotiations and James had not become especially anxious.[62] It was the unexpectedness of the whole affair and the changed nature of the diplomatic scene that must have caused the king to collapse before the Spanish ambassador's onslaught.

As was true of Queen Elizabeth I, one is never quite certain when James put on an act and when he genuinely felt emotions. To some extent, the king was probably acting in order both to play for time and to convince Gondomar that the Spanish match did mean something to him. In both respects, he was successful with the result that he gave Gondomar the minimum concessions possible: Naunton was suspended and warnings were issued to the other anti-Spanish ministers. This action was a good deal less than the initial proposal of dismissing both the secretary and the archbishop from the royal service. Sir Robert's suspension is also an important indicator of James's thinking. He had not permanently abandoned the idea of a divided government. The suspension gave him room to manoeuvre because he was still in a position to reinstate or threaten to reinstate his secretary.

What the king managed to salvage should not, however, detract from Gondomar's achievement. Gondomar was lucky in several ways, not the least of which was in the prorogation of parliament until after his meeting with James.[63] Yet he was quick enough and intelligent

[60]Calvert to Herbert, 19 January 1621, PRO/30/53/4, fo. 18.

[61]Boswell to Calvert, Paris, 30 January 1621, *Ibid.*, fo. 37.

[62]Bibliothèque Nationale, Tillières to Puysieux, 14 October 1620, (new style), Bibliothèque Nationale, fonds français, no. 15988, fo. 524.

[63]J. F. Larkin & P. Hughes, *Stuart Royal Proclamations* (Oxford, 1973), I. 497.

enough to force the abandonment of one of the touchstones of royal policy. The apparent balance between the pro- and anti-Spanish factions had been destroyed, and it had happened just as Thomas Locke had written, because of 'an accident fallen out heere unexpected'.

Into the pit and out again — 1621-24

Whatever Naunton's limitations might have been, an unwillingness to look after his own best interests was not one of them. He was not going to accept disgrace without a fight. If he had any one special talent, it was keeping his balance when the political ground beneath his feet shifted. He did it when Essex fell from favour, and again when Salisbury died. Here for the last time in his political career, he kept his balance. He accomplished this feat by virtue of his own talents and by virtue of some timely assistance from what can only be described as his guardian angel.

Once Sir Robert was suspended, his first problem was to see to it that his position did not deteriorate even further. Such a situation conceivably could have occurred if parliament decided to enter into his case. For besides being one of the prime movers of the 1621 Parliament, Naunton was also a member for Cambridge University. His suspension and house arrest occurred only days before the first session began; thus the secretary was unable to take up his seat. The Commons took a dim view of having its members arrested and could have made Sir Robert's case a matter of privilege.

If Naunton had been content to become the object of such a proceeding, any hope of regaining the king's favour would have been lost. The suspended secretary was well aware of the problem and wrote to assure Buckingham that everything was being taken care of:

> My sweet lord, I most humbly thank you for your care of me, intimated by Mr. Packer touching the parliament house; in which, though I have not yet refused to serve, because I should have made myself uncapable to answer the obligation I have to do his Majesty service there when he shall be pleased to accept thereof, yet I do not hold myself bound to admit of their choice that elected me, being now none of that body till I shall receive assuranced of his Majesty's gracious approbation. I have entreated some of my friends to oppose that motion, if any such should be made, for my calling thither, and am resolved they shall send me to what prison they will, yea, and pull me to pieces too, before I will be fetched out of my house with my own consent, till my sovereign dear master shall enlarge me. . . .[64]

[64]G. Goodman, *James the First,* II, 226-7, citing Bodley Tanner 73, fo. 97.

Sir Robert was true to his word. He asked Sir Samuel Sandys, another M.P. and the brother of his good friend Sir Edwin Sandys, to ask parliament not to call him to the House without the king's consent.[65] Fortunately for Naunton, the Commons had other things on its mind and did not choose to make an issue of his absence. He never did take his seat, nor was an election held to replace him.

Despite Sir Robert's success in avoiding parliament he remained in disgrace. Therefore most of the people in government and court circles with whom he dealt could not afford to associate with him. After a pause to be certain that the information they had received about his status was true, most of them had no other choice but to abandon him.

The English diplomats, upon whom Sir Robert had lavished so much attention, were no different from any other group of political appointees; they began to move away from the suspended secretary. Carleton started treading carefully within a couple of weeks of Sir Robert's fall: 'My dispatch by this bearer I adresse aswell to your honor [Calvert] as Mr. Secretary Nanton heareing of some disgrace befallen him, and not knowing whether or noe he hath overcome it, which I hartely wysh he may for the interest I hadd in his favor. . .'[66]

To give Sir Dudley full credit, it is obvious that he had come to depend on Naunton and was loath to see him in trouble., Though self-interest was in large measure responsible for the ambassador's feelings, some few days after the above dispatch was written, he indicated to Sir Francis Nethersole that his sentiments about Sir Robert may have at least been mixed with some degree of respect:

> One I send you hereinclosed from thence [the court], which will tell you of Secretarie Nauntons disgrace and likelyhood to overcome it of which I am unfainedly glad, knowing him to be a man of much integritie and though I finde myself amongst others voyced to his place I protest I had rather be shutt owt of preferment whilst I live then enter at such a gap. . . .[67]

The situation with Sir Edward Herbert went much the same way. Upon hearing that there was some difficulty, Sir Edward's secretary hastened to assure Naunton of his master's certainty that the king's anger would pass quickly.[68] A week later, however, after Herbert had no

---

[65] 6 February 1621, John Pym's diary, Notestein *et al., Commons Debates of 1621* (New Haven, 1935), IV, 18.

[66] Carleton to Calvert, The Hague, 9 February 1621, PRO SP/84/99, fo. 146.

[67] Carleton to [Nethersole] The Hague, 12 February 1621, *ibid.*, fo. 151.

[68] Boswell to Naunton, Paris, 30 January 1621, PRO/30/53/4, fo. 32.

doubt received further information, he had a letter written to Calvert asking him to redirect dispatches if Sir Robert was not supposed to receive them.[69] Though the commentary is lacking in the other diplomat's dispatches, it is fairly safe to assume that those who were in Naunton's charge reacted in much the same way. There might have been one exception, William Trumbull. Even after Sir Robert was obviously going to be dismissed, the agent continued to write for information and advice.[70]

What happened to Naunton was, of course, exactly what had happened to Sir Thomas Lake two years before and what was going to happen to Sir George Calvert after Buckingham and Charles returned from Spain; he became isolated. In Sir Robert's case, almost all the diplomats had stopped writing him by the end of February or the beginning of March 1621. The Privy Council was immediately taken from his supervision, and, though he remained a member, there is no record that he even attended a meeting until after he was appointed Master of the Wards three years later.

The representatives of foreign powers who had dealt with Naunton reacted in much the same way as the English diplomats had done. Their pleasure at having to do so varied according to whether their country favoured a Spanish match and how they personally got along with Sir Robert. The Venetian ambassador was, as one might expect, among the most upset, and, as he explained it, he had good reason:

> The said letters [from Spanish interests] are not communicated to other ministers or to the Council, unless on some point upon which his Majesty does not incline to give them satisfaction, and the letters which arrive from Spain usually get into the hands of this man or of the said two or three, and are scarcely seen by the others, a very great distinction being made between minister and minister in this particular, while on the other hand the affairs of every other part are frequently dealt with too openly and publicly. Thus by passing also through the hands of the partisans of Spain, they are dragged out at length and thwarted. . . . There was a very convenient way to his Majesty's ear through the Secretary Naunton, by whom some business was transacted with the knowledge of the king and himself alone. Now this is closed and as the Spaniards easily succeed in capturing the ministers of this country who specially serve the king in their Court, so the

[69]Boswell to [Calvert], Paris, 8 February 1621, PRO SP/78/69, fo. 51.

[70]Trumbull to Naunton, Brussels, 16 December 1622, Berkshire Record Office Trumbull MS. 33, no. 46.

English ambassador at present in Spain is greatly dependent
upon them and seems to write only for their great advantage. . .[71]

What Lando is demonstrating here is the effects of the breakdown of
the system of divided government. Unfortunately for the Venetian it
broke down in such a way that the pro-Spanish faction remained in
control, and he had to suffer for it.

Despite the disgrace, the Venetians remembered the good turns
that Sir Robert had done them, and in hopes that he might again prove
useful, they did what they could, in a discreet way, to keep in contact
with him. After Lando left England in 1622, the new ambassador,
Alvise Valaresso, quietly sent word to Naunton that, although the
representative had changed, the sentiment the Venetians felt towards
him remained the same.[72] An experienced ambassador would be well
aware of the sudden changes that often occurred on the political scene.
If Sir Robert had unexpectedly fallen, he might also unexpectedly
rise, and it was best to maintain cordial relations with him.

Naunton's friends, despite the hazards involved, did their best
to help lift his suspension. Doncaster was noted for being particularly
devoted.[73] Sir Robert's foresight in courting him so assiduously back
in 1619 looked as though it might finally pay off, for, apart from
Buckingham, Doncaster could have done Sir Robert the most good
with James.[74] In this case, however, Doncaster was under the
handicap of being tarred with the same brush as Naunton, and there
was a limit as to how importunate he could be, without feeling the chill
of royal displeasure. Whatever usefulness Doncaster did have for
Naunton came to an end in the summer of 1621 when the viscount was
sent as an extraordinary ambassador this time to France, and thus lost
direct access to the king.

Despite several rumours that Naunton was on the verge of
reinstatement,[75] the efforts of Doncaster and the others were to no
avail. As long as James could not bring back Sir Robert without
causing serious harm to his relations with Spain, there was no hope of
his restoration. The Spanish match negotiations continued for the

[71]G. Lando to the Doge and Senate, 12 March 1621, (new style), *CSP, Ven., 1619-21*, p. 598.

[72]A Valaresso to the Doge and Senate, 15 July 1622, (new style), *ibid., 1621-3*, p. 372

[73]*Ibid.*, p. 339.

[74]Discussed above, pp. 24-9.

[75]Locke to [Carleton], 16 February 1621, *CSPD, 1619-23*, p. 224 & HMC, *Mar Supplement*, p. 106.

whole of 1621, and with Naunton saddled with the burden of being the symbol of the anti-Spanish policy there was no way for his status to alter.

Strangely enough it was precisely because of his symbolic value that Sir Robert remained suspended and was not dismissed. Whenever James wanted to frighten the Spanish a little or goad them into action, he said something complimentary about Naunton.[76] In October 1621 Sir Robert was sent on an errand to Caron,[77] and again in May 1622, he was permitted to write to Carleton on some trifling affair.[78] This procedure usually sparked off rumours of Sir Robert's impending return to favour,[79] and it would be surprising if such a reaction was not exactly what the king had had in mind. Indeed, James succeeded so well in building up his suspended secretary's importance that as late as October 1622 Valaresso wrote that it was almost a prerequisite for a successful parliament to restore Naunton to favour.[80]

Yet Sir Robert's state of limbo could not last indefinitely if for no other reason than that Calvert was doing the work of two people. Even without consideration of Sir George's work load, there were too many people hungry for office to permit someone as seriously damaged as Sir Robert to retain his place for long. The first attempt to oust Naunton permanently from office came in the autumn of 1621 at a time when there was a general shake-up in the government and only a couple of months after the secretary had been given some limited freedom from house arrest.[81] Several people were supposed to leave office at this time including Sir Fulk Greville, the Chancellor of the Exchequer, and Viscount Mandeville, the Lord Treasurer. Sir Richard Weston, sometime roving ambassador and naval commissioner, became chancellor and Sir Lionel Cranfield, Master of the Wards, naval commissioner and resident financial wizard, became treasurer. Though these replacements may very well have been an effort to find men who could cope with the king's shaky finances (as both were eminently suited for their posts), it is also notable that they were considered quite favourable to the Spanish match, whereas their precedessors had not been.

[76]Chamberlain, *Letters*, II, 399.

[77]Naunton to Carleton, Charing Cross, 5 May 1622, PRO, SP/84/106, fo. 169.

[78]Chamberlain, *Letters*, II, 399.

[79]G. Lando to the Doge and Senate, 11 June 1621, (new style), *CSP, Ven., 1621-3*, p. 69.

[80]A. Valaresso to the Doge and Senate, 14 October 1622, (new style),*ibid.*, p. 476.

[81]29 July 1621, *APC, 1621-3*, p. 29.

With posts at such a high level changing hands it was the obvious time to dispose of Naunton. Indeed, matters went so far in this direction that it appeared that all that remained was to swear in his intended successor, Sir John Suckling, Lionel Cranfield's brother-in-law.[82] Yet for reasons that apparently escaped the notice of contemporaries, the change did not come about. If there was a time to dispose of a controversial minister, it must surely have been in the midst of a wholesale change-over. Perhaps as the failure of Digby's peace mission to Austria beame clear to James, he drew back from making his final, symbolic gesture towards appeasing the Habsburgs.

In the very next year a successful assault was made on Sir Robert's post. In October 1622, after previous discussion with Naunton, Buckingham began to question Cranfield (now earl of Middlesex) about what could be done for the outgoing secretary.[83] A lack of generosity with the crown's money had never been one of Buckingham's problems; in this case, he was thinking in terms of £500 a year worth of land. Middlesex, on the other hand, had not become Lord Treasurer because of his talent for giving away royal assets. He did not oppose the proposal outright, but he did manage to delay matters until a better opportunity presented itself.[84]

The delay in fixing Sir Robert's departure from office was not in the least unwelcome to him. Though he had probably abandoned all hope that he could retain his post, there was another pressing consideration on his mind. In 1622 he was fifty-nine years old, and his wife was pregnant with what he rightly believed would be the last child born to him. He had lost a son the previous year because of his wife's distress about his political difficulties and the social implications that went with them.[85] Naunton's heir was now a two year old daughter, and he wanted desperately to have a son. This unborn child seemed his last hope. Taking advantage of the pause Sir Robert wrote to Buckingham and asked permission to retain his office until the child was born, at which time he promised he would willingly turn over the post to his successor.[86] Whether it was the obvious sincerity of Naunton's pleas or because there were still details to work out for his replacement's assumption of the office, the request was granted. It is interesting that Buckingham must have been just a bit suspicious of

[82]Calvert to Doncaster, 15 October 1621, BL Eg. 2594, fo. 133.

[83]Buckingham to Middlesex, Royston, 9 October 1622, Kent Record Office, Sackville MS., M.39, fo. 20.

[84]14 November 1621, *Ibid.*, MS. 7580 and Prestwich, *Cranfield,* p. 363.

[85]Chamberlain, *Letters,* II, 399.

[86]Naunton to Buckingham, Charing Cross, 23 September 1622, BL Harl. 1581, fo. 115.

his cousin, because he tried to get Sir Robert to write a letter of resignation.[87] It is also possible that the favourite wanted the letter in order to obtain some kind of leverage with James. Buckingham and the king may not have been seeing matters in the same light about this time.

Despite all the manoeuvring, the inevitable finally happened. Naunton's hoped-for son (tactfully named James) arrived early in January 1623. By the tenth of that month Buckingham had stood godfather to the infant,[88] and by the fourteenth, almost five years to the day after Sir Robert had taken office, he left it to his successor, Sir Edward Conway.[89] Conway was a professional soldier who had served for many years in the Dutch Republic. He was thus of anti-Spanish sympathies, but he had no pretensions to being a politician, (or a scribe for that matter; his handwriting was among the worst in Jacobean England). Nonetheless, if James wanted once more to reverse his path and follow an anti-Spanish policy, he had a secretary who could help him.

Naunton was not left completely empty-handed when he lost his office. He had the promise of a pension and of a suitable place when one became available.[90] It took a great deal of effort and no small amount of luck to make good on both promises.

With respect to the first matter, the pension, it is necessary to know how much Naunton earned as Secretary of State in order to evaluate it properly. The office had several regular or official sources of income attached to it. These included the diet, the salary, the secret service money and the dividends from the signet office, the petty bag and the hanaper.[91] The sums of money earned by these sources individually have been dealt with by others,[92] and of more immediate concern here is the total. It is fortunate that there is a contemporary estimate of the total made by Secretary Calvert at a time when he was negotiating with Sir Dudley Carleton for the sale of his place to the ambassador. Figuring 'the diet, the wages, intelligence money and other things ordinary and certaine,' Calvert thought the office was worth £2,000 a year.[93]

[87]Ibid., & Naunton to Buckingham, Charing Cross, 4 November 1622, G. Goodman, James the First, II, 241-4, citing Tanner MS. 73, fo. 215, (Now Tanner MS. 73, fo. 254.)

[88]Arthur, Lord Chicester to Carleton, Holborn, 10 January 1623, CSPD, 1619-23, p. 481.

[89]Ibid.

[90]25 January 1623, Chamberlain, Letters, II, 474.

[91]D. Coke, The Last Elizabethan, Sir John Coke (London 1937), pp. 137 & 178-9.

[92]Ibid., and F.M.G. Evans, The Principal Secretary, pp. 194-221.

[93]Dudley Carleton junior to Sir D. Carleton, London, 3 May 1624, PRO SP/14/164. no. 7.

These regular sources of income, however, represented only a fraction of the financial story. Gifts, either of money or goods, were the most common irregular sources of income. In 1619 Carleton assured the secretary that the Dutch commissioners from the Estates General would 'acknowledge' the latter's help in their late embassy to England.[94] When the Dutch merchants faced the Star Chamber fines for illegally exporting gold, they, too, promised to show their 'thankfulness' to Naunton for any help he might give.[95]

Though gifts were undoubtedly numerous, foreign governments probably supplied the bulk of Sir Robert's irregular income. Gondomar maintained that Naunton received both a Dutch and a Venetian pension,[96] and given what is known about the secretary's relations with the representatives of these two countries, the allegation is probably not unfounded. Though there is no contemporary comment, the Palatines could be safely added to the list as well. Gondomar thought another Secretary of State, Sir Thomas Lake, was worth a pension of 2,000 ducados a year[97] (about £400).[98] If the Dutch, Venetians and Palatines were paying Naunton, he was certainly receiving at least that much from each. Too much less would have been considered an insult to his dignity as a Secretary of State.

To gifts and pensions, one could add another category called privilege. While Sir Robert was secretary, James leased him certain lands in the counties of Suffolk and Carmarthen, the latter of which he passed on to his heirs in his will.[99] When the Dutch merchants were fined in Star Chamber, Naunton and Lord Chancellor Bacon were to split their £10,000 fine.[100] It is unlikely that such opportunities would have fallen Sir Robert's way unless he held high office.

All these figures are not sufficiently specific to permit an accurate estimate of the secretary's irregular income. However, one modern scholar who had delved into this area suggests a figure of approxi-

---

[94]Carleton to Naunton, The Hague, 21 August 1619, PRO SP/84/91, fo. 178.

[95]Carleton to Naunton, The Hague, 11 June 1620, PRO SP/84/95, fo. 222.

[96]Gondomar to Philip III, London, 10 February 1621, (new style), PRO/31/12/21 from Arch. de Simancas, EL 2602, fo. 18.

[97]*Documentos Ineditos*, II, 178.

[98]A ducaton was worth approximately one English crown (five shillings); W. C. Hazlit, *The Coinage of the European Continent* (London, 1893), p. 197.

[99]Appendix D., and PRO, C/66/2209, no. 15.

[100]Prestwich, *Cranfield*, p. 269.

mately £2,000 net income from a gross of between £4,800 and £6,000.[101] The difference between the net and the gross is accounted for by scribes' salaries and other departmental expenses. Though a good guide in many respects, on the surface, at least, these figures seem something of an exaggeration for Naunton's expenses. He only employed two scribes and he does not appear to have laid out much money for secret service expenses. On the other hand, £4,800 seems closer to the truth of his gross intake than £6,000; Sir Robert simply was not skilled enough in finance to make the most of his office. By a process of elimination, £3,000 or perhaps £4,000 a year would be the most realistic estimate of Naunton's net income.

It fell to Conway to act as mediator in obtaining a pension that was commensurate with the position and income that had been lost. He began in February 1623 by once again approaching the Lord Treasurer, Middlesex, on the matter.[102]

Sir Robert was concerned with making his request for a pension as acceptable as possible. He was also aware that the crown's finances were not in good condition. He was therefore willing to postpone the immediate expense to the king, provided that the pension took the form of a fee farm grant in reversion for his newborn son.[103]

Armed with this concession and hoping to strengthen his hand with Middlesex, Conway took up the whole question with the king. For understandable reasons, James was a little uneasy about his former secretary. He did not want to act without Buckingham's advice and begged Sir Robert to be patient until the favourite's return from Spain, at which time the king would see to everything.[104]

The Lord Treasurer saw his opportunity to win a victory for economy in government by attempting to eliminate or at least cut back the former secretary's pension before Buckingham returned. He wrote to Conway to explain that the first proposal had been for a pension of £1,000 a year, the second for £500 a year in improved lands, i.e., lands with a seventeenth-century value, worth £7,500 at fifteen years' purchase. The third proposal was for £500 a year in unimproved lands, i.e., lands with a medieval or old rent value, that were worth £20,000 at forty years purchase. After quoting these figures,

[101]G.E. Aylmer, *The King's Servants* (New York, 1961), p. 204.
[102]Conway to Lord Treasurer, Royston, 18 February 1623, *CSPD 1619-23*, p. 493.
[103]Naunton to Conway, Charing Cross, 22 February 1623, HMC,*Cowper*, I. 130.
[104]Conway to Naunton, 1 March 1623, PRO SP/14/139, no. 9.

Middlesex ended with thinly veiled sarcasm: 'Whether this may stande with his Majesty's service or it be his graciouse meaning to quadruple this value of his first intention, I must humblie leave to his own princely wisdome'.[105]

It would be pointless to follow the twists and turns taken in these pension negotiations, but some interesting matters did arise in the process. One was that Naunton's scribe, George Verney, proved himself an excellent go-between. In at least two instances he used his initiative to obtain as much as possible for his master. He went so far in one case as to provide Conway with a list of land available should Middlesex claim that the king had none to give out.[106] Conway was quite impressed with Verney and told Sir Robert so.[107] From this time on both Verney and the other scribe, Thomas Lord, came to play a significant role in Naunton's public career.

The second point is that, despite Buckingham's known wishes, Middlesex was quite capable of cutting Sir Robert's pension down to size. The final agreement for the pension was that Naunton would get £1,000 yearly for life with the stipulation that, when and if £500 per year in improved lands became available, Naunton or his heirs would have a claim on them.[108]

In answer to the original inquiry concerning how the pension compared to Sir Robert's earnings as Secretary of State, it represented between one quarter and one third the annual value. Such a figure is not unreasonable, considering the services he rendered the crown and is, if anything, slightly on the low side for the times. Even Calvert, who also left the secretariat under something of a cloud, managed to sell his post at a handsome profit, obtain a peerage (even if it was only an Irish one), and tracts of land in Ireland and North America.[109]

Despite the amount of energy Naunton devoted to it, the pension was, in large measure, of secondary interest to him. What he wanted most of all was a new office worthy of his talents and status. With Buckingham's and Charles's return from Spain, he did not have long to wait. The romantic quest that 'Steenie' and 'Baby Charles' had undertaken in 1623 for the hand of the Infanta had failed, and both men

[105]Middlesex to Conway, 7 March 1623, Whitehall PRO, SP/14/139, no. 52.

[106]Verney to Conway [9 June 1623], PRO SP/14/146, no. 42.

[107]Conway to Naunton, 1 August 1624, [Apthorpe], PRO SP/14/171, no. 4.

[108]8 July 1623, PRO SP/38/12.

[109]DNB *sub* Calvert, Sir George.

returned home in no mood to negotiate any further over a Spanish match. Indeed they had some warlike plans for their former hosts. Naunton's reaction to the return of the two discontented young men was one of unbounded enthusiasm. He could not restrain himself from expressing 'an intire congratulation of this happie and holy day, the happiest that mine eyes have seene, since that of his Majesties moist [sic] joyful entrance into this kingdome. No other words can fully expresse my hart's Jublie for this happiness, as those of that glorious Angel "GLORIE BE to GOD in the highest, on earth peace, good will toward men" '.[110] Though peace and good will were not exactly what Sir Robert's cousin and the prince had in mind, his seemingly impious analogy was not as ill-founded as it might seem. His saviour had indeed come.

The first step on Buckingham's and Charles's anti-Spanish programme was a parliament, for there would be no war with Spain without money. It was their hope to convince the various borough patrons to return MPs who were favourable to their new war policy. The programme, however, was not likely to find favour with James who had devoted his whole reign to the pursuit of peace.

It was with this conflict in the background that Naunton found himself elected an MP for Cambridge University in the 1624 Parliament. On the face of it, his election at royal behest seems most peculiar. Yet on closer examination the move made sense. Sir Robert's election had appeal to both the prince and the king. He was surely identified firmly enough with the anti-Spanish group and was, indeed, one of their martyrs. On the other hand, during the whole period of his disgrace Naunton had remained loyal to the king. He could have done a great deal of damage in the 1621 Parliament by teaming up with that other slighted privy councillor, Sir Edward Coke, but he did not do so. James therefore had no objection to instructing the Lord Keeper Williams, who had Cambridge connections, to see about getting Naunton his old seat for the University.[111]

At this first sign of favour Sir Robert sought more. He wrote to Buckingham that it would be unseemly for him to appear in parliament as less a man that when he was last there. He further maintained that it would be advisable to remove the last vestiges of restraint that had been placed on him at the time of his disgrace, or it would seem that parliament was responsible for removing them.[112] He need not have

[110]*Fortescue Papers,* pp. 192-3.

[111]Naunton to Buckingham, Charing Cross, 14 January 1624. PRO SP/14/158, no. 30.

[112]*Ibid.*

worried either about the embarrassment to himself or to the king. So far as the diaries and the Commons Journal indicate, Naunton made no appearance at the 1624 Parliament.[113] One can only speculate as to why he once again failed to appear in the House. Perhaps James feared the temptation to join the anti-Spanish crusade would be too great. Ultimately, the king was unwilling to take such a chance. Why the Commons did not protest remains a mystery.

Whether Sir Robert was there or not, the 1624 Parliament did produce one useful result for him; it successfully impeached the Earl of Middlesex. He was the one major officeholder most vehemently against war with Spain. It was this vehemence that ultimately caused him to lose the support of those who mattered.

In order to prevent war, Middlesex told Charles that he should marry the Spanish Infanta regardless of his princely sensibilities.[114] He had even been involved with his brother-in-law, Arthur Brett, in an attempt to supplant Buckingham in the king's favour.[115] The upshot was that Middlesex was convicted by his peers of various crimes, fined £50,000, and dismissed from his offices.[116]

This action left two of the nation's most lucrative and prestigious offices available. It did not take long for the competition to develop. Lord Zouch, Viscount Mandeville, Sir Edward Leach, and Sir Benjamin Rudyerd were just a few of the people named as possibilities for either Master of the Wards or Lord Treasurer. In addition, there was Naunton.[117] The usual talk that these offices would be sold to the highest bidder was reported,[118] but in the last analysis the choices depended much more heavily on other factors.

Buckingham was one of them. He had decided that it was time for his cousin to be reinstated as a government minister.[119] Once again, George Verney appeared on the scene as Naunton's agent[120] and did

[113]M. Rex. *University Representation in England, 1604-1690* (London, 1954), appendix, and *Commons Journal*, I, *sub* 1624 Parliament and manuscripts of Yale Diary Project.

[114]M. Prestwich. *Cranfield*, p. 426.

[115]S. R. Gardiner. *History of England*, V, 229.

[116]*Ibid.*, p. 231.

[117]Nethersole to Carleton. London, 3 July 1624, PRO SP/14/169, no. 14.

[118]*Ibid.*, and Chamberlain to [Carleton]. London, 3 July 1624. *CSPD. 1623-5*, p. 292.

[119]Conway to Naunton, 1 August 1624 [Apthorpe]. PRO SP/14/171, no. 4.

[120]Nethersole to Carleton, London, 14 August 1624, PRO SP/14/171, no. 49.

his usual competent job.[121] Competence was needed, for bringing James around was a slow process. He was undoubtedly reluctant to see the reappearance of a disgraced minister in his government. Naunton's failure to take his seat in the 1624 Parliament is evidence of this attitude. Yet despite such a major handicap, by 30 September 1624, all objections had been smoothed over, and, after the king had conferred with Buckingham for two hours at Wallingford House, 'Sir Robert Naunton was sent for, who is now Master of Wards; and hath had a great deale of joye wished him of his frends'.[122]

The appointment was made for much the same reasons that Naunton was placed in the 1624 Parliament; he pleased both sides and offended no one. From the king's point of view, ever since Salisbury's death, the mastership had been occupied by a series of men who were either innocuous personally or who held little prestige or political power in their own right. Even Middlesex ultimately had no political constituency. This procedure was just another aspect of the policy noted earlier with respect to the secretariat. It was James's way of seeing to it that no minister grew strong enough to rival the king. With Naunton in office, he would have nothing to fear.

On the other side, Buckingham had promised his cousin a better post than his secretaryship, and the mastership of the wards was definitely that; both in terms of prestige and profit it was clearly a move up. There was also every reason to believe that Sir Robert would not try to threaten Buckingham's interests in any way, nor would he be uncooperative in the approaching war against the Habsburgs. All in all, considering the conflict between the heir to the throne and the favourite on one side and the king on the other, Naunton was about as effective a compromise candidate as could be found.

Sir Robert ability to retain his self-control and to step carefully had played a major role in his successful return to office. By doing so, he performed a unique feat; he was the only disgraced Jacobean minister to return to a higher office than the one he left. Nonetheless, whatever pride Naunton may have taken in this accomplishment must have been tempered by the knowledge that a major share of the credit belonged to the force that had played such an important role in his suspension from the secretariat: luck.

[121]PRO SP/14/171, no. 4.

[122]Dud   Carleton junior to John Chamberlain, London, 30 September 1624, PRO SP/14/1   no. 70.

4

MASTER OF THE COURT OF WARDS

Granting of wardships

Stated as concisely as possible, the Court of Wards was concerned with selling the wardships of minor heirs who inherited lands that were held of the king in knight's service or some other superior feudal tenure. In practice, the bulk of the gentry could be subject to this court. As for Naunton, his role in the administration of the Court of Wards was split between granting wardships and adjudicating disputes concerning the royal wards and their property. With respect to wardship grants, Naunton followed a set of royal instructions issued in December 1618.[1] These directives concerned two sets of circumstances. In the first instance, if friends, relatives or executors of the deceased royal landholder came forward within a month of his death, they would have the first chance to buy the wardship and lease of the ward's lands.[2] They would also have preferential treatment in that they had to take an oath that, to their knowledge, no gift or bribe was offered to any official of the Court of Wards.[3] This procedure was the carrot, and for the sake of the king's revenue, it was hoped that all would bite.[4] The stick was brought out for those who tried to conceal the wardship, protract the proceedings beyond what the court considered a reasonable time, or failed to meet the payments for the wardship. In those cases, others were openly invited to bid for what was classified as a concealed or neglected wardship. These outsiders were not bound to take the oath on bribery, and they were to have a suitable (though unspecified) reward for their services so that they would be encouraged to repeat them at some future date.[5] These circumstances did not necessarily mean that the relations of the ward had lost the minor in question permanently, but it did mean that they either would have to bid against an experienced wardship hunter who was familiar with the ways of the court, or they would have to buy the wardship from this individual at a greatly inflated price. Just what the

[1] M. J. Hawkins, *Sales of Wards in Somerset, 1603-1641* (London, 1965), p. xix & note 2.

[2] *Instructions to the Master and Counsaile of the Wards* (London, 1610), p. 4.

[3] *Ibid.*, pp. 13-14.

[4] For the background to this approach see J. Hurstfield, *The Queen's Wards,* ch. 15, esp. pp. 311-4.

[5] *Instructions* (1610), p. 14.

98

latter process could mean is demonstrated by the case of Miles Bussey's daughters. Through what was technically a neglect (that is, a failure through oversight), to sue for the wardship within a month's time, Bussey's widow lost custody of her three daughters to George Verney and Thomas Lord, Naunton's secretaries. Using Sir John Bale, a former sheriff of Leicestershire,[6] as their agent (or possibly buying from him later), Verney and Lord bought the wardship of the three Bussey girls from the court for £6 3s. 8d.[7] They demanded £100 each for the girls if the mother wanted to buy them back.[8] Here was a handsome profit indeed.

Generally speaking, Naunton's court was supposed to deal as fairly as possible (and as cheaply as the king's profits permitted) with relations of the ward who came forward to claim the wardship within a month's time. In practice, these people were charged the yearly value of the ward's lands as shown on the feodary certificates,[9] or perhaps somewhat less. If the relations were foolish enough to ignore the opportunity offered them by the grace period, they then were faced with the prospect of high expenses and no end of trouble if one of the wardship hunters discovered their deception.

During the first four years of Sir Robert's tenure as master, 1624-8, the main bulk of the business was done with the relatives of the wards. A relatively small proportion, a maximum of 20 per cent, was done with people who had no apparent relationship to their wards. For comparison's sake, it should be noted that 35 per cent was the figure for apparently unrelated people in the last three years of Cranfield's administration as master.[10]

[6]*Official Lists of Sheriffs* (London, 1898), p. 75.

[7]PRO, Wards 9/163, fo. 2ᵛ.

[8]Minute of the petition of the widow of Miles Bussey, PRO, SP/16/126, no. 77.

[9]Feodaries were officials of the court who were placed in each county. There was also an escheator who was responsible to the Chancery. These men also did a valuation of the lands called the inquisition post mortem, but their figures had ceased to have any real significance. Hawkins, *Sale of Wards*, p. xxiii.

[10]These percentages are based on the information found in the books of grants of wardship: PRO, Wards 9/162, 207 & 163 and are supplemented by information found in the 'feodary surveys' (Wards 5) which are really surveys, certificates and schedules. A person was considered as connected with a ward if he or she was so called in the document, if he or she bought in conjunction with someone who was so called, if the surname of the purchaser and the ward were the same, or if a man and woman bought a ward jointly which usually meant that a mother and stepfather were buying. Nonetheless, the percentage figures quoted are probably high for those not connected with the ward because some of the executors did not fit into any of the above-named categories.

This set of conditions means that there was no concerted programme of hidden wardship hunting during the early part of Naunton's tenure. Besides the percentage figures, there is further evidence to support this assertion. The names of the purchasers seldom appear more than once, and it is difficult to conceive of any attempt to hunt hidden wardships that did not involve the same group of people over and over again. It is possible, of course, that there was a team of wardship hunters who used such a wide variety of agents that it would not be possible to detect their activities through the records of the Court of Wards. But such a possibility seems quite remote because of the high correlation, in the 1624-7 period, between the price of the wardships and the feodary valuations of the wards' lands. Stated in mathematical terms, a correlation of 1.00 is perfect. During the 1624-7 time span, the feodary survey and the wardship price had a correlation of 0.98. In Cranfield's last years, when the hidden wardship hunters were active, the correlation was only 0.59. Since those who sought out wardships were supposed to receive special consideration for their services, any activity on their part was bound to reduce the correlation. The only other alternative was that some vast group of men operated purely out of good will towards the Court of Wards and neither expected nor received any reward for their services. Given the context of early seventeenth-century society such behaviour hardly seems likely.

It is true that some of the hidden wardship hunters from Cranfield's period put in an occasional appearance during Naunton's early years. Lewis Sheffield, who bought several wards while Cranfield was master,[11] did buy during the 1624-7 period. In at least one case, however, Sheffield bought the son of a ward he had previously owned,[12] and there is no indication that he was receiving favoured treatment in this purchase. Probably he had been named guardian in the father's will.

Given the potential for profit that was involved in searching out wardships, it seems strange that the Court of Wards under Naunton refrained from doing so in his early years as master. Yet there were good reasons for restraint. The agitation in parliament during Cranfield's impeachment was at least in part beause of his management of the Court of Wards.[13] Whether the charges against Cranfield were justified or not, some measure of discontent was inevitable because

[11] PRO, Wards 9/162, fos. 417^v, 424 & 427^v.

[12] PRO, Wards 9/207, fo. 91 & Wards 9/162, fo. 391^v.

[13] M. Prestwich, *Cranfield*, pp. 441, 450-1.

generally he was not using the feodary certificates as a guide when dealing with relations of the wards.[14] The correlation for sales to mothers was only 0.64. It therefore made good sense for the new Master of the Court of Wards not to press too hard. The advent of Charles on the throne in 1625 made no difference to the running of the court in this respect. He likewise did not wish trouble here.[15]

This even-handed management of the court did not last forever. In the early months of 1628, certain people connected with Sir Robert began to show an interest in searching out hidden wardships. Emanuel Downing, a close friend of Naunton's and a lawyer who practised before the Court of Wards, bought a hidden wardship in April 1628,[16] and sold it in May.[17] That same month Roger Twyford, who knew the master of the court well enough for a member of his family to borrow several hundred pounds from him,[18] bought a neglected wardship.[19] In July Twyford obtained an order from the court to take possession of the lands of another recently acquired ward. It is interesting to note that in the second case it was the ward's step-father who was holding the lands,[20] indicating that there were relatives available. All this activity occurred before Buckingham's death in August 1628. There was even more activity after Buckingham died. The following February Thomas Lord purchased a hidden wardship.[21] Almott Clench, the Essex feodary, did the same in November,[22] as did Edward Byshe, the Surrey feodary, the following month.[23]

The appearance of these men and their activities is closely related to Naunton's status at court and, to a lesser extent, with Buckingham. This time span was the beginning of the period when Sir Robert was drifting away from the mainstream of political and religious thinking of the court. He was very close to being in disfavour and found himself with time on his hands and some wounded pride to mend.[24] By playing

---

[14]See appendix C, esp. the introduction.

[15]Yale Diary Project from BL, Add. 48091, fo. 9ᵛ.

[16]PRO, Wards 9/163, fo. 1ᵛ.

[17]Easter Term, 4 Charles, 19 May 1628, PRO Wards 9/543, p. 99.

[18]See appendix D.

[19]Easter Term, 4 Charles, 20 May 1628, PRO Wards 9/543, p. 108.

[20]Post Term, 4 Charles, 4 July 1628, PRO *ibid.*, p. 355.

[21]PRO, Wards 9/163, fol. 10ᵛ.

[22]*Ibid.*, fo. 7.

[23]*Ibid.*, fo. 9ᵛ.

[24]Discussed further below, pp. 118-20.

the dispenser of patronage and favours, he could gain back some of his lost prestige in the eyes of his subordinates if not his superiors. There was, needless to say, profit involved, and one cannot exclude such an attraction as a possible source of inspiration as well. Yet given Sir Robert's meagre financial talents, he probably gave in to importunate friends and connections and did not direct them in their search for hidden wardships. His two secretaries, especially Verney, had already shown themselves as clever young men, and this project has their stamp on it.

Buckingham's death in August 1628, whatever its political implications for Naunton, permitted him a second, more intense, flurry of wardship hunting. With the virtual monopolizer of royal patronage gone, and no one powerful enough to take his place, Sir Robert could use the patronage he possessed in any way he saw fit. Parliament was still a worry, but after the 1629 session, even that prospect faded from view.

Whatever the political dangers, there was no doubt that the revenues of the Court of Wards were falling. In the fiscal year ending Michaelmas 1627, new wardships, the court's major source of income, amounted to £23,650 (in round figures).[25] In 1628, the first year that Naunton's connections come on the scene, new wardships accounted for only £17,000,[26] and in 1629, the first complete year after Buckingham's death, the new wardships had declined to £13,670.[27] The absolute depths came in 1630 when, though net profits had risen slightly over the last year, new wardships were down to £12,200.[28] In three years the court's major source of income had declined by nearly half.

As one might expect, there was not one single factor responsible for this state of affairs, but rather a combination. The attitude of the gentry must have played a part. A large number of them differed with the king on a variety of issues, not the least of which was the royal method of raising taxes, which had been the subject of two of the three resolutions read out in that final, riotous session of the 1628-29 Parliament.[29] It would therefore not have been at all surprising if there had been a taxpayers' strike against the Court of Wards similar to that against ship money a few years later.

[25] PRO, Wards 9/417, fo. 146[v].

[26] *Ibid.*, fo. 214.

[27] *Ibid.*, fo. 288.

[28] PRO, Wards 9/422, fo. 50[v].

[29] S. R. Gardiner, *History of England,* VII, 75.

Justification for such action could have been found beyond political interests in one of those ill-considered moves for which Charles is so well known. Elizabeth Bennet, the widow of Richard Bennet, went through all the proper procedures for obtaining the wardship of her son, Symon, during the Easter term of 1628. She was on the point of paying the fine for the wardship when a messenger delivered a note to Naunton from Buckingham and the earl of Holland stating that the king wished all proceedings stayed until his further pleasure was known. Such a directive was not in the least pleasing to the officials of the Court of Wards, and they asked Naunton to see the king about the matter. In their protest, the members of the court pointed out to Charles that, since Mrs. Bennet had come forward on her own and confessed her son was subject to wardship, any royal interference with the procedure of the Court of Wards would probably discourage other people from following a like course.[30] Unfortunately, this good advice was cast aside, for when the court sat again the following Michaelmas term, Sir Walter Pye, the Attorney of the Court of Wards, was forced to declare that the grant made by the king of the wardship of Symon Bennet to someone besides the mother (one Walter Steward), though unusual, was in fact legal. As a face-saving device, the court said it would not recognize Steward's grant unless he gave the usual covenants for educating the ward and for ordering his affairs. Needless to say, the gentleman complied, and the wardship went to him.[31] One further concession was wrung out of Steward; rather than have the ward immediately turned over to the two men to whom he had sold the wardship, he agreed to leave the child with its mother because of the boy's 'tender years'.[32]

Though there is no definite evidence that word of the Bennet wardship spread, the possibility is certainly a real one. Quite naturally, in that case, anyone holding land liable for wardship would have been reluctant to declare his liability. Wardship was unpleasant enough without having one's heir stolen by a court favourite.

Over and above the attitude of the country gentlemen, there is some chance that the members of the Court of Wards itself might have had their own reasons for letting matters slide. Royal interference undoubtedly had a demoralizing effect. There was also the question of

[30]Post Term, 4 Charles, 8 July 1628, PRO Wards 9/543, p. 370.

[31]Michaelmas, 4 Charles 21 November 1628, *Ibid.*, p. 613.

[32]Post Term, 4 Charles, 5 January 1629, *Ibid.*, p. 706 and Hilary, 4 Charles, 24 January 1629, *Ibid.*, p. 720.

how sympathetic the members of the Court of Wards were to royal policy as a whole. Naunton surely was growing rapidly apart from his sovereign's policies.[33] To the extent that they disliked Arminianism, so were Sir Myles Fleetwood, the Receiver General, and Sir Benjamin Rudyerd, the Surveyor.[34] Though there does not seem to have been an active protest by these men, royal displeasure with their attitudes might have convinced them to stay away from the capital and the court for a little longer than usual. One's country manor is infinitely more comforting than the stony stare of a king.

Even leaving aside potential political problems, there is some evidence that the court was not at all times diligent. In the summer of 1626 a commission was set up under the Lord Treasurer, the earl of Marlborough, and Buckingham to investigate the state of the king's revenue. The commission decided that the Court of Wards was slack in getting the appropriate individuals to sue out their liveries.[35] If they were lax in this aspect of the court's operations, one must wonder how well they performed its other functions.

Chance is the final factor that must be included when discussing the decline of the wardship revenues. The years of decline were unquestionably years of poor harvests and increased illness across the country. One could therefore presume that under the circumstances a larger number of people liable for wardships would die and that a disproportionate number would be less affluent. Yet an examination of the available data indicates that there was amazingly little variation in the percentage of high, medium and low priced wardships in the court. For example, from 1621 to 1637, through Cranfield's, Naunton's, and Cottington's tenures as master, high priced wardships (those of £500 and above) represented around 10% of the total for each of the years considered. If chance was against the court during the years when its profits declined, it distributed its effects quite evenly over all the various price ranges of wardships.

Whatever the balance of factors might have been for the declining wardship profits, it was clear that something had to be done about the problem. The decision was made to turn loose the hidden wardship hunters in earnest. Naunton must have played an active part in this proposed action, for many of the hunters were associated with him. Verney and Lord were involved. There was also William Lambe, an

[33]Discussed below, pp. 119-22.

[34]G. E. Aylmer, *The King's Servants,* pp. 353-4.

[35]Michaelmas, 2 Charles,PRO Wards 9/95, fo. 495ᵛ.

escheator and later feodary, and Ralph Briscoe, escheator for Middlesex and Kent in 1630 and 1631.[36] Randall Briscoe, probably a relative of Ralph's, and Roger Twyford, were also wardship hunters during the 1630-4 period. From here the circle widens to include men such as Thomas Owen, who, like Twyford, was a Welsh resident of the capital. He lived in St. Martins-in-the-Fields, Naunton's parish. Owen joined Lord in the purchase of one wardship as well as buying others for himself.[37] Also connected with Lord's and Owen's purchase was Anthony Barry, an old wardship hunter from Cranfield's time and before.[38] Barry, in turn, sometimes used Thomas Short, a yeoman of Waybred, Suffolk, not far from Barry's home in Sileham, as an agent and associate in his purchases.[39]

That these people were connected to each other and the court's officers is readily shown by tracing some of their histories. John Juce of St. Albans, Wood Street, which is not far from Fetter Lane (where William Lambe lived), acted as guarantor for a wardship purchased by Sir Myles Fleetwood.[40] Two of the Yorkshire feodaries, John Goodhand and Thomas Danby, bought wardships.[41] Goodhand was helped by Thomas Owen in one case,[42] and he was associated with John Juce in another.[43] Interestingly enough, when Goodhand came to London, he resided in Fetter Lane.[44]

There were other people active besides the members of this inner clique. Matthew Vesey bought several wardships in Durham,[45] and Isaac Gearing did the same in Wiltshire.[46] Thomas Hill, on the other hand, preferred to confine his activities to the home counties.[47]

It took about a year for the wardship hunters to affect the court's revenues. In the fiscal year of Michaelmas 1629 to Michaelmas 1630, of at least one hundred wardships bought, the wardship hunters

[36] PRO, Wards 9/275, fo. 28[v].

[37] PRO, Wards 9/163, fos. 27 and 49[v].

[38] Purchase of Thomas Pretyman, junior, PRO Wards 5/40 & Wards 9/162, fo. 396.

[39] PRO Wards 9/163, fo. 47[v].

[40] Ibid., fo. 24.

[41] Ibid., fos. 26[v] & 45[v].

[42] Post Term, 6 Charles, 16 February 1631, PRO Wards 9/544, 866.

[43] Michaelmas, 7 Charles, 28 November 1631, PRO Wards 9/545, 780.

[44] Trinity, 2 Charles, 30 June 1626, PRO Wards 9/95, fo. 430.

[45] PRO Wards 9/163, fos. 52 and 56[v].

[46] Ibid., fo. 38[v].

[47] Ibid., fos. 44, 50[v] and 66[v].

and other speculators such as courtiers accounted for about 13 per cent of the total sales. The following fiscal year, this group was responsible for approximately the same percentage of sales, but the sales themselves had increased to at least one hundred and twenty wardships. What is more important, the profits of these new wardships rose to £22,200.[48] This level of profits went down only slightly the following year,[49] although the sales had declined to the 1629-30 level. In 1632-3 both were on the rise again with new wardship profits up to £24,300,[50] and sales at a level of no less than one hundred and forty-one. The use of these wardship hunters was thus a success, and with their stimulating new wardship sales, the other revenues of the court began to rise as well. The money collected for liveries and associated expenses showed a marked upward trend in both the fiscal years 1630-31 and 1632-33.

Despite the success of the wardship hunters, they could be something of a mixed blessing to royal finances. Since they were entitled to some kind of consideration for their efforts, the court charged them lower prices than anyone else. Correlating the feodary land valuations with the price of the wards indicates just how low. For the period 1628-35 the correlation for wardship hunters was 0.46. For mothers who acted as purchasers during the same period the correlation was 0.88. Thus if the wardship hunters were allowed to account for too high a number of wards, especially when there were friends and relations available as purchasers, the king's profits would suffer.

The same was not true for the individual members of the court. They had a great deal to gain from keeping the wardship hunters coming in large numbers. After all, these people did not have to take the oath concerning bribes and gifts to officials of the Court of Wards. There is no doubt that there were those of the court who took full advantage of the situation. For Naunton's part, even a man as closely connected with him as John Winthrop, the future Massachusetts governor and sometime practising lawyer in the Court of Wards, found it expedient to offer a gift.[51] With regard to the other members of the court, it is, perhaps, sufficient to note that the lowly clerk, Hugh Audley, died 'infinitely rich', and had a book written

[48] PRO Wards 9/422, fo. 132.

[49] *Ibid.*, fo. 222^v.

[50] *Ibid.*, fo. 312^v.

[51] L. Downing to J. Winthrop, London, March 1628, *Winthrop Papers* (Boston, 1929), I, 380. For Winthrop's connection with Naunton see below, pp. 117-18.

about him called *The Great Audley or the Way to be Rich.*[52] Yet so far as the records of the Court of Wards indicate, the officers contrived to stay within the letter and sometimes even the spirit of the law while they went on their way accumulating riches. In so far as Naunton was active in the court, it is to his credit that included among its records are examples of the failures as well as the successes of the hidden wardship hunters. From an examination of the record, it would appear that these men were as much subject to the law as any other potential purchaser.

There are several examples of wardship hunters' failures in the Court of Wards. One who seemed to have more than his share of ill luck, perhaps because he was so well disliked by his contemporaries,[53] was the Yorkshire feodary, John Goodhand. He tried to obtain one wardship only to have the young gentleman in question produce letters patent showing that the tenure of his lands did not make him eligible for wardship.[54] Even when Goodhand met with success, he needed every bit of help he could get. He succeeded in gaining possession of another wardship only after a long drawn out legal battle lasting several years. If the decree granting the wardship is accurate, then Goodhand needed the assistance of a near relative of the ward, the failure of the guardians to pay the full fine of the wardship, cruelty to the ward and misuse of his lands by the step-father to finally win his case.[55]

Despite the apparent altruism involved in the last of these Goodhand cases, it should not be assumed that the wardship hunters were all fine, public-spirited men who always played by the rules and let virtue be its own reward. There were too many people engaged in hunting wardships and too much money involved for a total lack of abuses. It is, however, to the court's credit that, under Naunton, it did make some effort to keep the more blatant misdemeanours in check.

A case involving Anthony Barry and Thomas Short perhaps best illustrates both the way in which Naunton and the court operated and what they could do to control the activities of the wardship hunters. Through a series of complicated events one Thomas Story became

[52]*Students Admitted to the Inner Temple, 1547-1660,* (1887), p. 163. Also see *The Way to be Rich According to the Practice of the Great Audley* (London, 1662), Section VI.

[53]*Diary of Sir Henry Slingsby,* ed. D. Parsons (London, 1836), pp. 16-18.

[54]Hilary, 6 Charles, 26 January 1631, PRO Wards 9/544, p. 719.

[55]*Ibid.,* 618 & 718; Hilary, 10 Charles, PRO Wards 9/99, fos. 454-6. For the step-father's side, see F. Guevara to Sir W. Pye, 3 June 1629, Cowkewell, *CSPD, Addenda, 1626-49,* p. 729.

subject to wardship proceedings. Anthony Barry was the one who had uncovered the case, and when Story's two uncles, who were executors of the ward's late father, discovered what was happening, they approached Barry. After some negotiating it was agreed to let Barry continue with his plans to buy the wardship with the uncles now paying part of the legal costs. It was further agreed that for 100 marks (one mark = 2/3 of £1) the uncles could buy back their nephew's wardship. After the bargain had been struck, Barry combined with Thomas Short, and it was in the latter's name (for reasons that were not made clear) that the wardship was carried forward. During the process, the two prospective purchasers were approached by the ward's maternal grandmother and uncle, Margaret and Symon Harris, and some of their friends, who also wanted to buy the wardship from Barry. Evidently they came close to doing so. That is when the uncles brought the case to the Court of Wards to protect their interests.

When appearing before the court, Barry testified that he had enlisted the aid of Randall Briscoe and George Verney to help procure the Story wardship. Actually, they agreed to split the profits three ways. It was not long after this deal had been struck that the uncles approached Barry and their arrangement was made. The uncles, in pursuance of this agreement, then spent an undetermined amount on legal costs. They also forwarded £20 to Verney, and Barry received £40 as part of the 100 marks promised. Whether the first £20 was part of the deal or a separate gift was not mentioned, but it seems likely that it was in the original arrangement. How or whether Barry divided the other £40 is also not divulged. After all the money had been paid out, the Harrises appeared on the scene. According to Barry's testimony, he told them that he already had an agreement with the uncles. He claimed further that the only reason he had not legally signed over the wardship to the uncles was that Naunton had ordered a stay in the proceedings.

In contrast to the seeming openness of Barry's testimony, Short adopted the role of misused dupe. He testified that initially he did not even know that his name had been used. All he said he wanted now was recompense for his time and travel and freedom from any financial liability in the case. Having heard all the evidence the court ordered the original agreement with the uncles to be honoured and Barry and Short to receive in full all money due them.[56]

This case is revealing on several key aspects of the Court of Wards' operation under Naunton. In the first instance, it is worth

[56]Hilary, 10 Charles, PRO Wards 9/99, fos. 440-440ᵛ [sic].

noting just what a bargain the hidden wardship hunters received. Barry and Short were to be paid £20 for the Story wardship.[57] The uncles paid them an additional 100 marks or just triple the actual wardship fine. One is led to suspect that the value of the wardships that the crown lost when the hidden wardship hunters moved in was large indeed. The use of Verney and Briscoe is also significant. Neither of them were actually officials of the Court of Wards, so it was no violation of anyone's oath to give them a gift or bribe. Yet it is clear that these men had Naunton's ear, or a wily old hand like Barry would never have bothered with them. Sir Robert's share of the take from these men, if any, remains uncertain. Surely in cases such as this where the oath did not apply he must have received something. One can only wonder if on other cases that fell under the oath, the letter of the law was not circumvented by seeing to it that the Master of the Court of Wards' secretary received some handsome encouragement to help speed matters along.

Despite any lingering suspicions, in the Story wardship the court acted quite fairly. Granted that the Masters of Request, or possibly Chancery, might have enforced the agreement between the uncles and Barry, the Court of Wards was under no obligation to do so; its instructions made no mention of this type of situation. Nonetheless, the spirit of these directives clearly stated that relatives or executors should obtain the wardship, and the Court of Wards under Naunton ruled accordingly in this case. Had the court been thoroughly corrupt, it might well have dragged matters out, taking money from all sides until they became disgusted and took the matter to another court. Evidently even in an age where the opportunities were large they kept some restraint on their greed.

Naunton's role in maintaining such restraint is rather cloudy. All decisions were made, according to the official record, by the Master and Council of the Court of Wards. There is no record of how much say each of the parties had, or even whether they were present. There is thus no way of telling whether Sir Robert asserted himself or was dominated by the other members of the court. Contemporaries had no such doubts about Naunton's role. They were certain that he was dominated by the others, especially the attorney, Sir Walter Pye. It was Sir Robert's performance as a judge of disputes involving the royal wards that justified contemporary opinion.

An indifferent judge

Two negative factors dominated Naunton's role as a judge in the

[57] PRO Wards 9/163, fo. 47ᵛ.

Court of Wards. First and foremost, he had no legal training either as a civilian or a common lawyer. It is true that he was admitted to Lincoln's Inn,[58] but he did not gain admission until November 1616, after he had become Surveyor of the Court of Wards.[59] In all likelihood, he was only an honorary member and never received any legal instruction.

His lack of legal training was exaggerated by insufficient experience with the everyday running of the court. To be more precise, Naunton had less actual working time on Court of Wards cases than the other members of the council. The attorney, Pye, the receiver-general, Fleetwood, and the surveyor, Rudyerd, were all with the court when Cranfield was the master, and they remained with it for varying periods of time after Naunton was replaced by Cottington. What is more, the tradition of the Court of Wards had been for the attorney of the court to control and, to a certain extent, to dominate its business.[60] There is every reason to believe that this tradition was followed by Pye while Sir Robert was master.

Finally, the whole situation was exaggerated by Naunton's concern with other areas of royal government during the first three or four years of his tenure as master.[61] Although there is no evidence to indicate that Sir Robert was continuously away during these years, his other projects had to take time away from the court's business, and the other members of the council must have been accustomed to working without him.

In looking for evidence about what kind of judge Naunton was, as with the wardship grants a good place to start is his treatment of the wardship hunters. They were the most controversial group and thus most likely to be involved in conflict. Interestingly enough, an examination of their cases reveals much the same pattern as with wardship purchasing: according to the official records, sometimes they won and sometimes they did not. The determining factor seemed to be the instructions issued to the court.

Isaac Gearing of Wiltshire was a wardship hunter who won several cases in the Court of Wards. As a rule he was the defendant, but this fact may have worked in his favour. Naunton and the court were well aware that it was easy to make accusations of a scandalous

---

[58]*Lincoln's Inn Admissions Register: 1420-1779,* (1896), I, 175.

[59]*Ibid.*

[60]Goodman, *James the First,* I, 310, cited in R. H. Tawney, *Business and Politics,* p. 183.

[61]Discussed below, pp. 114-17.

nature and quite expensive to disprove them. In one case involving Gearing, the court ruled that unless the plaintiff was willing to make his charges in specific terms, no matter how scandalous the general charges were, no ruling was possible.[62]

In another case, the court awarded Gearing 500 marks plus costs by the court from his ward, Arthur Crew, because the latter refused to marry the woman his guardian had chosen for him.[63] The decree recorded by the court explained that Crew was the owner of £300 worth of land in Gloucester which made him liable for wardship. The young man not only tried to deprive Gearing of the profits from this estate, but also refused to marry a gentlewoman who brought a dowry of £600, claiming that he would marry no woman bringing less than £1,000. Crew's reply was to deny knowledge of any estate in Gloucester and to claim owning only heavily mortgaged Wiltshire lands that did not make him liable for wardship.[64]

Part of the difficulty with this case was that, by the time it was settled, Crew was of legal age. Because his father had died so close to his twenty-first birthday he had apparently decided to chance discovery by wardship hunters. Thanks to Gearing, he lost his gamble. Another problem was that the amount of money at stake meant that Gearing would not give up without a fight. He only paid £20 for the wardship,[65] and the Gloucester lands alone were worth at least £300 per year. The refusal of the marriage netted him another £333 at the ward's expense. If Crew was bitter about the outcome, he had good reason.

Was the Court of Wards' seemingly harsh ruling in the Crew case an example of either the master's ineffectuality or the attorney's voraciousness? The answer is apparently not. Crew had undeniably tried to conceal his own wardship, and since he was unfortunate enough for Gearing to catch him, he had to accept the consequences. In legal terms, the refusal of the marriage was not justified either. Crew had to marry any woman offered by his guardian who would not disparage him, i.e., was not beneath his social class, or else pay the guardian the equivalent value of the dowry.[66] Crew's claim that he would accept no wife who brought a dowry of less than £1,000 was no

[62]Michaelmas, 9 Charles, 8 November 1633 PRO Wards 9/546, p. 570.

[63]23 November 1633 *Ibid.*, p. 670.

[64]Michaelmas, 9 Charles, PRO Wards 9/98, fos. 211^v-212^v.

[65]PRO, Wards 9/163, fo. 38^v.

[66]See J. Hurstfield, *Queen's Wards,* pp. 139-42 and M. J. Hawkins, *Sale of Wards,* p. xvi.

doubt an attempt to establish disparagement, but here he was hoist on his own petard. A man who denied owning £300 worth of land and who had, as he claimed, only heavily mortgaged lands, had no right to cry disparagement at a bride who brought £600 with her. Arthur Crew may have been treated harshly by Naunton and the Court of Wards (though even this assertion is questionable), but he was not treated illegally.

Yet the court and its master were capable of acting with equal harshness towards one of the wardship hunters. One has only to turn to John Goodhand, the Yorkshire feodary, for an example. He became involved with other defendants in a suit concerning the possession of lands claimed by the executors of a ward whom they did not own.[67] During the process of rather lengthy litigation, the other defendants dropped out of the case leaving only Goodhand. He was finally ordered to vacate certain premises, but was permitted to store his hay and grain in the barn on the disputed lands until thrashing and sale the following May.[68] Goodhand's stubbornness was, no doubt, one of the qualities that made him unpopular. In this case, he simply decided to ignore the court's order. The result was that another order was issued demanding payment of £200 a year rent on the property he illegally held.[69] When he ignored this order as well, the sheriff was instructed to dispossess him forcibly if need be.[70] Once again, it would appear that the court and Naunton followed their instructions.

There is, however, a two-fold difficulty with a firm conclusion at this point. First, all the evidence so far presented is based entirely on the official records of the court. One could hardly expect these records to throw an unfavourable light on the proceedings. At any time the king might appoint a royal commission to investigate the court, and if they were not careful this information could be used against the personnel. Second, these official papers do not really give any insight into Naunton's actions. He is still seen in conjunction with other members of the court, and there is no way to tell whether the decisions were made because of or in spite of him.

Fortunately some pieces of evidence survive that do throw light on the question. The most famous person to provide such evidence was Sir Anthony Ashley Cooper, 1st earl of Shaftesbury. He described

[67]Michaelmas, 7 Charles, 7 November 1621, PRO Wards 9/545, p. 656.

[68]Trinity, 9 Charles, 5 June 1633, PRO Wards 9/546, p. 225.

[69]Hilary, 9 Charles, 3 February 1634, *Ibid.*, p. 829.

[70]13 February 1634, *Ibid.*, p. 914.

Naunton as 'not the activest' of men and Pye as 'a corrupt man, who then swayed the court'.[71] In his memoirs Shaftesbury set down his case in detail. When he became a ward at age eleven, he contended that his lands were unjustly sold at an unreasonably low price to pay off his father's gambling debts. He further accused the court of appointing his father's creditors as commissioners for the sale of these lands. If his tale has villains, it also has heroes — Sir Daniel Norton and Edward Tooker, Shaftesbury's guardians, who resisted these shady practices and thus earned themselves a term in the Fleet. But most heroic of all was the young earl himself, who personally approached Attorney General Noy, a fellow West Countryman who had drawn up the original papers on the properties. He persuaded this royal appointee to stand against the wrath of the king's court and plead the case personally. Like all good melodramas, this one has a dramatic climax. At the very moment when Sir Francis Ashley, Shaftesbury's uncle and the chief villain of the piece, rose in the Court of Wards to refute Noy's arguments, he was struck dead,[72] thus enabling the earl ultimately to reclaim his lost estates.

The Dickensian flavour of Shaftesbury's story is just a bit too rich for it to be true. To begin with, the commissioners appointed to superintend the sale of his father's lands in 1631 did not include Sir Francis Ashley or any of the other chief claimants mentioned, but did include Thomas Hannam, one of the executors appointed by Sir John Cooper to look after his son. It is true that Hannam later backed out of his role as executor and guardian, but at the time of his appointment as commissioner, he had not yet done so.[73] In addition, though Shaftesbury made no mention of the fact, John Pym was one of the two people appointed by the court to help the commissioners value the lands. Pym was supposed to have a particular knowledge of the estate,[74] and thus was in a position to give an independent judgment. It also might be added that Pym had been the victim of an effort to rob him of his estate by a wicked uncle back in Elizabeth's reign,[75] and it is not inconceivable that he might have tried to protect this young gentleman from the same fate.

As for the value of the lands, there were £34,680 in debts that had

[71]PRO/30/24, Bdle. 17, no. 15, fo. 4.

[72]*Ibid.*, fos. 4-7.

[73]Michaelmas, 7 Charles, 16 November 1631 and 23 November 1631, PRO Wards 9/545, pp. 701 & 748.

[74]PRO, 18 November 1631, *Ibid.*, p. 717.

[75]Conrad Russell, 'The Wardship of John Pym', *English Historical Review,* 84, pp. 303-17.

to be cleared by the sale. Rather than protesting that the lands were being sold at too low a price, Norton and Tooker claimed that the lands were not worth enough to repay the debt, and if they were sold, their ward would be ruined. The lands in fact brought in £50,680 leaving the young Shaftesbury with £16,000 in cash plus an estate worth £40 a year in old rent value, and additional lands worth about £400 a year (presumably in improved rent value), coming to him after the death of his step-mother.[76]

As for using Noy to plead his case, Shaftesbury must have run into something of a problem. The drama-filled scene at the Court of Wards, in which the Attorney General appeared by the earl's own statement,[77] did not come until after Naunton was dead and Cottington took office.[78] Noy died on 9 August 1634, six months before Sir Robert's death.

Given all the inaccuracies, inconsistencies and outright fabrications in Shaftesbury's story it would be simple to discard his charges against Naunton. Yet the very extremity and wildness of the tale does lend credibility to the claim of Sir Robert's inactivity as a judge. It is hardly conceivable that, if the master of the court had made the slightest gesture either for or against Shaftesbury, his action would have passed with no comment. Indeed, it would probably have been blown up and magnified out of all proportion. Yet the sum total of the earl's remarks about Naunton was that he was not 'the activest of men'. Under the circumstances, the plea is quite believable.

It is not without significance that in another instance in which the injured party also had a strong sense of the rights of his own cause, inactivity was also the strongest charge brought against Sir Robert. One Nicholas Roberts accused the clerk of the court of forging the official record and accused the court's attorney of blatant bias.[79] Yet when it came to Naunton, all he would say was that he passively permitted these prejudicial acts to take place.[80]

The surrounding circumstances of Sir Robert's life tend to confirm his alleged inactivity. The charge began to appear after 1631, when he had both fallen from royal favour and was in poor health.[81] In

[76]Hilary, 7 Charles, 6 February 1632, PRO, Wards 9/545, pp. 922-4.

[77]PRO, PRO/30/24, Bdle. 17, no. 15, fos. 5-7.

[78]Hilary, 12 Charles, PRO Wards 9/100, fos. 67ᵛ-68.

[79]PRO, SP/16/535, no. 64.

[80]*Ibid.*

[81]Discussed further below, pp. 126-7.

addition, at about the same time, his relationship with his wife was deteriorating so badly that their disputes had become public knowledge.[82] Naunton had never been particularly forceful, and these factors, plus his lack of experience and legal training could very well have caused him to withdraw into his shell. As a result he only went through the motions of being a judge.

Sir Robert's sorry state does not mean that he was senile or unaware of the world about him. While these unfortunate events were occurring, he wrote his book, *Fragmenta Regalia*, which may have been written by an old, bitter and timid man, but was certainly not written by a senile one. Naunton's problem was that he lost the will to exert himself. He simply no longer cared about his task as judge in the Court of Wards, and left the job to others.

Naunton, in his prime, had been filled with zeal to utilize his office for specific ends. He had never relished just handling business for its own sake. He sought office to put through a programme: thwarting Spanish-Habsburg power abroad and abolishing Roman Catholic influence at home. When the loss of royal favour made these goals impossible, he found no solace in the seemingly meaningless execution of functions that he scarcely understood and to which others had become accustomed.

Politician in decline

What Sir Robert could not have known when he became Master of the Court of Wards in late 1624 was that the whole style of government would change in less than a decade. There would be a world of difference between the broad-based government of James I, which included members from as many factions as possible and the exclusive, limited government of his son, which contained representatives from as few as possible. The change did not work in Naunton's favour. Nonetheless, in 1624 he assumed his post with the good wishes of many people connected with the government. With Calvert playing an increasingly smaller role in the administration of business due to his involvement with the pro-Spanish party, the other secretary, still Sir Edward Conway, found that the burden of work was more than he could manage. The addition of a man who had acted as coordinator for the Privy Council and knew how things worked was a relief to all. There were even rumours in January 1625 that Sir Robert might take up his old post of Secretary of State.[83]

---

[82]*Letters and Dispatches of the Earl of Strafford*, ed. W. Knowler (London, 1739), I, 227.

[83]T. Locke to Sir D. Carleton, 15 January 1625, PRO SP/14/181, no. 74.

Actually, very little chance existed of Naunton re-entering the secretariat. The last time the mastership of the wards and a secretaryship were occupied by the same man, Salisbury held them. Though Sir Robert was not the potential threat to royal control over government that the earl had been, neither the king nor Buckingham were going to put that much temptation in anyone's path. Besides, with the number of people clamouring for posts, pluralism at that high a level was becoming a much more remote possibility.

Whatever limitations were put on Naunton's role in the executive, he surely had more freedom when it came to the legislative. Within six months of Naunton's reassumption of office, James was dead and the policy of peace with Spain died with him. Now, unquestionably, the aggressive anti-Spanish foreign policy of the new king and his favourite would be pursued with vigour, and this line of action meant money from parliament. Here was surely the opportunity for the right man to begin a major parliamentary career. The court and country did not seem far apart on policy goals; all they needed was someone to coordinate their aims. The circumstances looked ready-made for Sir Robert. Coordination was his strong point, and he now had credibility with the Commons as well. For if there was a man in the government who could be classified as a martyr to the Spaniard's influence in England, it was Naunton. If he could handle himself properly, capitalizing on this role, he could become one of the most influential men in the country.

Sir Robert had other advantages that could have helped him become the government leader in the Commons. One of these was the lack of competition. Calvert resigned his secretaryship, became Lord Baltimore not long after, and retired from politics. His successor, Sir Albertus Morton, was not even in England during the time parliament was in session. The other secretary, Sir Edward Conway, was not noted for his oratorical ability and was elevated to the House of Lords in the middle of the 1625 Parliament. The remaining crown servants, Sir Humphrey May, Chancellor of the Duchy of Lancaster, and Sir Julius Caesar, Master of the Rolls, both had long years of parliamentary experience, but lacked the prestige to lead the royal forces in the Commons. Sir Richard Weston was suspect as a man who leaned towards Rome. So there was Naunton. He had once been the Public Orator of Cambridge University (which again returned him as its M.P.); he was a literate man who was used to talking before the most important people in the realm. What is more, he had both the prestige and the sympathy for his voice to mean something to those who heard it.

Whatever the glowing possibilities might have been, Sir Robert achieved next to nothing. Part of the reason for his failure was undoubtedly the surrounding circumstances, but part was also his apparent reluctance to speak out. When parliament opened in the middle of June 1625, the plague was raging in London, and many of the MPs were nervous about contagion. To complicate matters further they became diverted onto the question of Arminianism. An issue of this sort held no attractions for Naunton, perhaps because he knew Charles's feelings on the subject better than most MPs. Yet his failure to speak out meant that he lost his chance for leadership. Had Sir Robert immediately made his sympathies on religion known, he might have been able to lead the Commons back to discussing the war with Spain. More importantly, he could have led them to discuss granting sufficient supply to fight the war effectively. When, nearly two weeks later, the issue of supply was raised in a thin House still fearful of the plague, it was Naunton's old friend, Sir John Coke, the naval commissioner, who raised it. He was ignored by the Commons.[84] His part, however, did not go unforgotten. When Sir Albertus Morton died later that year, it was Coke who became Secretary of State.

The parliament was finally adjourned on 11 July because of the danger of pestilence, and reconvened at Oxford on 1 August. This session lasted for only twelve days, and in it Naunton somewhat redeemed his previous silence by making the only speech before the House of Commons that his contemporaries ever saw fit to record. It is to Sir Robert's credit that the speech was a genuine reflection of his thinking on the reasons that parliament should support the royal war effort. He began by discussing not only the loss of men and money that would result from withholding supply but also the loss of reputation. He went on to mention how grateful the king would be for a gift freely given. He further added commentary about the goodness of the Prince and Princess Palatine and the danger to the Protestant religion if the Roman Catholic victories on the continent were consolidated. Finally, he did not fail to remind his listeners that parliaments had traditionally supported the king at war, and he hoped that this parliament would live up to that tradition.[85]

Naunton's speech was made on 10 August, and had no perceptible influence on the attitude of the Commons towards granting the king supply. Perhaps part of the reason for this was uncovered by one of the major figures in the opposition, Sir John Eliot:

[84] Harold Hulme, *The Life of Sir John Eliot* (New York, 1957), pp. 82-4. This section was written before the appearance of Conrad Russell's *Parliaments and English Politics 1621-1629*.

[85] *Debates in the House of Commons in 1625,* ed. S.R. Gardiner (Camden Society: Westminster, 1873), pp. 107-8.

> this message was seconded without anie interim of consideration
> first admitted by a long compos'd oration of the Master of the
> wards, Sir Robert Nanton, who, in his former times having
> beene publicke orator for that place, the Universitie, thought it
> his dutie then to render some demonstration of his skill, but
> found that the could rhetoricke of the Schools was not that
> moving eloquenc which does affect a parliament.[86]

Whatever the reasons for Naunton's ineffectuality, two days after his
speech Charles and Buckingham gave up hope of obtaining sufficient
supply from the 1625 Parliament and dissolved it.

Had the king and favourite been more fortunate in their naval war
against the Spanish, Naunton's next effort as a parliamentarian might
possibly have been more successful than his 1625 experience. The
Cadiz voyage, however, was an unmitigated disaster. Buckingham
had decided to repay his political debts to Sir Edward Cecil by making
him commander of the voyage,[87] and the man simply was not up to
the job. As it was, the fleet left late in the campaigning season
(October 1625), and limped back to England the following December
with all its human wreckage. With their habitual lack of political
acumen, the king and Buckingham issued writs for a new parliament
that same December, in the wake of the worst English naval and
military disaster in nearly a century.

The election, whatever it boded for the crown, presented an
unusual opportunity for Sir Robert. The social summit of any English
gentleman's ambition was to occupy the chief seat in the Commons
for his county. This place was generally reserved for someone from
the most prestigious family, either a member of an ancient knightly
house or the son of the most prominent peer. In Suffolk, Naunton's
home county, he detected an opportunity to carry off this great prize.

The method he chose is, in its way, as significant as the action
itself. He was aware that his role as a privy councillor and Master of
the Wards was much more of a hindrance than a help in presenting
himself to the county gentlemen who controlled the elections. So he
chose to play up the aspects of his career that the puritan-leaning
gentry would find appealing.

First, he chose John Winthrop as one of his agents. This noted
puritan and future governor of the Massachusetts Bay Colony was at

---

[86] Sir John Eliot, *Negotinum Posterum* (London, 1881), pp. 80-1.

[87] Buckingham's efforts to find Cecil a suitable military post are discussed above, pp.
78-9.

that time a practising lawyer in the Court of Wards. He probably wrote a series of letters to influential Suffolk figures. One that survived went to Sir Robert Crane of Bury St. Edmunds. Winthrop's appeal for support touched several areas. Of most importance, he listed Naunton's previous suffering for the 'Commonwealth,' which was supposed to far outweigh the disadvantage of being a privy councillor. Next, Winthrop pointed out that Sir Robert's high position with the court was not really a hindrance since he bore a deep affection for the county and was in an excellent position to watch out for the interests of local clothiers.[88] In short, the Master of the Court of Wards was being sold not as a royal appointee, but rather a transplanted county gentleman.

The appeal worked. Naunton was the only privy councillor returned for a county seat in the 1626 Parliament.[89] As events developed, Sir Robert probably wished he had been a good deal less ambitious. He was now in a completely untenable position. In 1625, with some good fortune and the right approach, it might have been possible for him to act as a bridge between court and country. In 1626 this posture was no longer feasible. The military disasters of the past few months required a scapegoat, and that was quite clearly going to be the Lord Admiral, Buckingham, Naunton's patron. A wiser, more politically astute king (and a more callous one) would have thrown the favourite to the snarling MPs and saved himself. Charles was incapable of doing so. Naunton was left with nowhere to turn. His loyalty to his patron and royal master in the Commons would have meant betrayal of the interests of those who elected him. The opposite course would have cut him off from all hope of royal favour.

As the attack on Buckingham was mounted by Sir John Eliot and the other members of the country party, Sir Robert desperately tried to walk a neutral path. Though he did report to the Commons on a conference with the Lords,[90] there is no record of him giving even one speech representing his own point of view during the whole of the 1626 Parliament. One wonders whether he even exspressed his opinions privately. Sir Robert did not, however, take the path one might have expected and avoid the Commons altogether. He attended regularly and found himself in the thick of things whether he liked it or not.

[88]Winthrop to Sir R. Crane, London, 14 January 1626, Bodley Tanner 72, fo. 69, printed in *Winthrop Papers*, I, 326.

[89]D.H. Willson, *Privy Councillors*, p. 73.

[90]Yale Diaries Project, 7 March 1626, Cambridge University MS. D.D. 12, 20, fo. 40.

His membership on various *ad hoc* committees of the House is evidence for this assertion. Some committee assignments were quite insignificant, such as the one for the sale of Barrington Manor in Derby by Vincent Low.[91] Others, however, were of a good deal more importance. Sir Robert was on both the committee that drew up the Remonstrance against Buckingham,[92] and the one that brought similar protests to the king.[93] The role he played on these committees is not known, but one cannot imagine Charles smiling warmly at his Master of the Wards, while the gentleman stood before the throne with a group of 'radical' MPs as they presented charges against the royal favourite that included the murder of James I. It is true that Naunton might have accepted these committee assignments so that he could give his patron warning of what was afoot. Indeed it would be surprising if he did not pass on information. Yet Sir Robert's problem may have been that he was expected to do more than just act as an informant, but his position as county member and the connection with the country party prevented any such action.

Given all that happened, it is not entirely surprising that Naunton was absent from the 1628 Parliament. He may have been afraid he could not hold his county seat and did not want the humiliation either of being turned out or of reappearing for a borough, for Naunton's behaviour probably pleased the county gentry no better than it had the king. To them, moderation in the cause of liberty was not considered a virtue. Yet it is difficult to believe that if Charles had been pleased with Sir Robert, he could not have found some way to soothe his servant's wounded feelings over losing his county seat (say with an Irish peerage) and procured a safe borough seat for him. It is true that Naunton had not exactly overawed the Commons with his oratorical ability, but he did know his way about the House and, in 1628, with yet another unsuccessful military adventure (this time to the Isle of Ré), even Charles must have realized that he needed all the help he could get.

The king's problem was that he was not at all sure just how much help Sir Robert would be. He was probably not unaware of how his Master of the Court of Wards gained election to the previous parliament, and this action raised questions about where his ultimate loyalties lay. The puritans and the parliamentary radicals were not the king's favourite people and, as a result, Sir Robert seemed to suffer by guilt through association. He was not only supported by John

[91]27 February, *Commons Journal*, I, 825.

[92]*Ibid.*, 8 June, p. 868.

[93]*Ibid.*, 5 April, p. 843.

Winthrop, but he had also recommended Sir Peter Heyman for the command of a company in Ireland.[94] Though Heyman was a relative of Naunton and entitled to favour from his cousin according to the etiquette of the time, the gentleman was also one of the key figures in the parliamentary opposition, and ultimately helped create the chaos at the end of the 1628 Parliament.[95]

None of these relationships should be taken as evidence of open hostility between Naunton and the court. On Sir Robert's side, he dutifully helped collect the forced loan of 1627[96] that caused the famous Five Knights Case. He even suggested a way of collecting the loan with a minimum of complaint, by rigorously enforcing the recusancy laws 'which will without all question give the people infinite content, and make them most willing to anything that shall be required, and God will bless the whole action.'[97] On Charles's side, he still had enough faith in Naunton to appoint him temporary Secretary of State while Secretary Coke was elsewhere and the debates on the Petition of Right raged in the 1628 Parliament. Both the king and Sir Robert may have had reservations about the other, but neither was prepared to make a decisive break.[98]

Although during the early months of 1628 this gap between Naunton and the court was not insurmountable, it became so in August 1628. That was when John Felton, a discontented lieutenant from the Ré expedition, killed Buckingham by plunging a knife into his chest. Besides being Naunton's patron and protector at court, Buckingham had acted as a shield for such men as Sir John Coke and Sir Dudley Carleton (now Viscount Dorchester), who were not necessarily enthusiastic about Charles's religious views, but who were competent administrators and valuable assets to the government. With this secure haven within the king's heart destroyed, it was necessary to find other means of protection.

Under certain circumstances, Sir Robert might have been able to act as his own protector. If he had used his early years as Master of the Court of Wards to build up a fortune or massive land holdings, he would have been a political power in his own right. With the great master of patronage gone, he might even have set up a faction of his

[94]*CSP*, Irish, 1615-25, p. 556.

[95]*DNB sub*, Heyman, Sir Peter.

[96]E. of Suffolk and Naunton to Buckingham, Blandford, 12 January 1627, *CSPD, 1627-8*, p. 16.

[97]*CSPD, Addenda, 1625-49*, p. 194.

[98]Naunton to Conway, Charing Cross, 21 May 1628, PRO SP/16/104, fo. 111.

own. Unfortunately, the lack of financial skill that had been notable while Naunton was Secretary of State does not appear to have lessened when he took on the more lucrative mastership. In fact, one modern-day historian classified Sir Robert among those servants of Charles who left a smaller estate at his death than might otherwise have been expected from one in such an eminent position.[99] As a result, Naunton had no hope of becoming his own patron.

Having failed to qualify personally, Sir Robert had to look elsewhere. Whether it was an atavistic urge or because he had kept the relationship alive, Naunton first turned to his potential saviour of nearly a decade before, Viscount Doncaster (now earl of Carlisle). Sir Robert's appeal went out almost exactly three months after Buckingham's death, and it has the ring of a genuine cry for help from a man who did not like the way the political scene was changing:

> My Lord, here is much good service to be done by such a servant of the state as your selfe, to God and his church, to the king and his whole kingdome, to your selfe and your true frends that misse you most. This is it [sic] I had to say. For the occurences in court I presume you have them all from many that ar more conversant there. . . .[100]

There is no evidence that this plea was ever heeded, but evidence exists that there was adequate reason for Naunton to be fearful. As the letter to Carlisle went out, indications are that Charles considered appointing Edward Nicholas (an admiralty commissioner and a future Secretary of State) to Sir Robert's place as Master of the Court of Wards.[101]

The signs of royal disfavour came tumbling one upon the other after this time. Though Naunton's name still appeared on the membership lists of the oversized commissions assigned to look into various matters of state,[102] his attendance at the business meetings of the Privy Council showed a marked decline. While appearing at nearly one hundred meetings in 1628,[103] he came to barely one third

[99] Aylmer, *The King's Servants*, p. 320.

[100] Naunton to Carlisle, Charing Cross, 23 November 1628, PRO SP/16/121, no. 44.

[101] D. Nicholas, *Mr Secretary Nicholas*, p. 68. Professor Aylmer is of the opinion that this offer was made as early as 1626. Although it is certainly conceivable that Charles might have contemplated something like this in the wake of the 1626 Parliament, it does not seem too likely that Buckingham would abandon his cousin except in the face of overwhelming evidence of his involvement in the impeachment. So far as I could discover, such was not the case.

[102] *CSPD, 1631-33*, p. 547.

[103] *APC, 1627-28* and *1628-29*, ff.

that number the following year.[104] By 1630, Naunton attended only two meetings during the first half of the year.[105] Such behaviour is a far cry from the man who once acted as deputy Secretary of State and was one of the crown's most active privy councillors.

Sir Robert was well aware of how far he had fallen, but eventually he almost resigned himself to it. In May 1631 he wrote to his old friend, Sir Francis Nethersole, that he had grown 'retired' both in respect to ill health and disfavour from unnamed higher powers at court.[106]

Given the factional structure as it emerged by the early 1630s, Naunton's inability to fit in is not surprising. The Laud-Wentworth alliance would have been viewed by Sir Robert with marked suspicion. Anyone such as the bishop who appeared to be 'soft' on Romanism could not have been to Naunton's liking. As for Wentworth, this former Cranfield protégé was known to favour good relations with Spain,[107] hardly the way to attract Sir Robert's favourable interest. What is perhaps of more importance, neither of them would have cared for a man with violent anti-Spanish or anti-Romanist leanings.[108] Sir Richard Weston (now Earl of Portland) was an even less likely candidate to aid Sir Robert. He was Lord Treasurer and had embarked on an economy drive that meant no foreign adventures.[109] His lack of interest in eliminating the Habsburg menace from the continent, coupled with the earl's tolerant attitude towards Catholicism would have made him incompatible with Naunton.[110] The only source of patronage left was the group around Queen Henrietta Maria. But on two counts, their youth and their Romanist inclinations, Naunton would have rejected them. Just as surely, a sour old puritan with a wife half his age would have attracted the scorn of these young Roman Catholics rather than their patronage.

It was this group about the queen who was responsible for Naunton's ultimate degradation at the Stuart court. Sir Robert had two step-children as a result of his marriage with Penelope Perrot Lower. The younger child was a boy, Thomas Postumus Lower, who was a ward of Sir Robert and his wife. The elder was a daughter, Dorothy, who had married Sir Morrice Drumond, a servant of

[104]*Ibid.*, *1628-29* and *1629-30*.

[105]*Ibid.*

[106]Naunton to Nethersole, Charing Cross, 27 May 1631, PRO SP/16/192, no. 57.

[107]D. Mathew, *The Age of Charles I* (London, 1951), pp. 84-6, and 90-2.

[108]C.V. Wedgwood, *Thomas Wentworth,* p. 70.

[109]S.R. Gardiner, *History of England,* VII, 166.

[110]Aylmer, *King's Servants,* p. 357.

Henriette Maria's. Living among the fast set about the queen, the Drumonds had managed to go bankrupt, and in order to make good their losses, the scheme was hatched for Lady Drumond's younger brother to come to their rescue. He was to turn over to them £3,000 from what he would receive as a dowry from his future, and as yet unchosen, bride. The rationale behind this action was that one John Lower claimed to have known that Sir William Lower, Penelope's first husband, had intended to bestow that amount on his daughter, but he died before he could carry out his plan.

This situation in itself was not tragic, merely expensive. Unfortunately the story does not end here. In order to assure themselves that Thomas Lower would in fact marry a bride with a £3,000 dowry, the Drumonds insisted that Naunton and his wife turn over the custody of the boy to neutral third parties (in this case, the earls of Pembroke and Carbury). These men would presumably make all the necessary arrangements for the boy's marriage when the proper time came. As one might expect in an age when people and property were inextricably bound together, the custody of the ward was accompanied by all the rights to the ward's lands. The whole situation was humiliating enough, but even more degrading was the manner in which the process was legalized. It was recorded by a decree dated 4 May 1632 and was registered in the Court of Wards.[111]

Even leaving aside the political repercussions of this fiasco, the personal ones were great enough for Naunton. His wife was the daughter of one of the most notorious termagants of the age, the countess of Northumberland, and whether from heredity or environment, more than a little of the wife's personality was derived from that source. Even on his deathbed Sir Robert saw fit to complain about the treatment to which his wife and her friends had subjected him over this affair.

Ineffectual complaints were all Naunton had left. He was in the completely untenable position of wishing to remain part of an administration that wanted no part of him and of trying to remain loyal to a king who had redefined the constituent parts of loyalty. Sir Robert's sad state exhibited itself in a variety of ways, but one of the most trying for him involved Sir Francis Nethersole who was acting as Elizabeth of Bohemia's agent in England. In May 1633 Nethersole approached Charles with a proposal for raising a voluntary contribution for a military expedition designed to reinstate Elizabeth and her son, the new Elector Palatine, in their hereditary lands along the

---

[111]Easter Term, 8 Charles, PRO Wards 9/98, fos. 12-13ᵛ.

Rhine. Nethersole had managed to gain the tentative support of a couple of London merchants and Lord Craven, who were willing to give financial backing to the scheme under the right circumstances. The king approved the idea, but before all the legal papers could be drawn, the plan mysteriously became public knowledge, and Lord Craven expressed his reluctance to cooperate further.

Understandably Nethersole became quite furious at this turn of events because Craven's withdrawal probably meant that the whole scheme would collapse. For some unexplained reason his anger was directed at George, Lord Goring, one of the queen's favourites, who Sir Francis presumed had reasons for wanting the voluntary contribution to fail. Goring, smarting under Nethersole's charges, counter-attacked, enlisted Henrietta Maria's aid and convinced first the council and ultimately the king that his sister's agent was the person at fault in this matter. Late in the summer of 1633 Charles confined Nethersole to his house for a period of time and eventually demanded a formal apology from him for his behaviour.[112]

The king was in Edinburgh while at least part of the business was taking place, and in June 1633, the Privy Council held three sessions on the Nethersole-Goring dispute. The result was a letter signed by the members of the council condemning Nethersole for his actions. There was, however, at least one signature missing from the letter: Naunton's.

Secretary Coke, who was with Charles in Scotland, was instructed to find out why. In reply to the secretary's inquiry, Sir Robert referred to his poor health (he claimed that his illness had caused him to miss two of the three council meetings), but he appealed to other factors as well. He stated that he was appalled by the rude reception Nethersole was given by the council and claimed that the man was constantly interrupted before he could speak his piece. He further voiced the suspicion that this whole business would somehow hurt the king, presumably by damaging the Protestant cause in Europe.[113]

Naunton's sympathy for Sir Francis is obvious. Goring's connection with the clique around the queen only reinforced his view, but he could not bring himself to say outright, that he disagreed with the council's decisions. What Sir Robert did was abstain from taking any action until he was forced to state an opinion.

This policy of withdrawal from public business did not mean that

[112]*DNB sub* Nethersole, Sir Francis.

[113]HMC *12th Report*, part 2, p. 22.

Naunton's mind was deteriorating, for his lack of activity applied only to his political affairs. There is internal evidence in his book, *Fragmenta Regalia,* that it was written during the 1630s when he was least in evidence in governmental matters. The *Fragmenta* is not only useful in demonstrating that Sir Robert was anything but senile, but it also gives an effective insight into his political philosophy: loyalty to the monarch and faith in the triumph of militant Protestantism both at home and abroad.

That Sir Robert was a firm believer in the institution of monarchy can be illustrated by a variety of comments he makes in the *Fragmenta.* The most important ones concern his efforts to show that the monarchy had God's direct sanction. What Naunton had in mind was a variant form of divine right that relied upon the principle of trial by ordeal. He said plainly that God had to be on Elizabeth I's side, or she would most certainly have failed in her endeavours.[114] He saw her surrounded by both internal and external enemies and yet triumphing over all of them. In his view her success was only possible with divine intervention.

Having made the case for the late queen, Naunton connected Charles to the Elizabethan monarchy. He said that the English in the 1630s were living under the same 'form and frame' of government as they had in Elizabeth's day, and that this type of government was the work of 'no human providence'.[115] Obviously, any man who opposed the existing government as it then stood was opposing divine will.

Buried beneath this firm belief in the divinity of the monarchy, and by implication the government it directed, was a vague suspicion that somehow things (or rather people) were just not the same as they had been in the days of Elizabeth. He was particularly upset by the behaviour of certain parliamentarians. He cited examples from both the 'Addled Parliament' of 1614[116] and the parliaments of the 1620s.[117] Yet, on the other hand, he could not avoid the unpleasant thought that Charles was no Elizabeth. He thus felt it necessary to include a plea in the *Fragmenta* for the king to call a parliament into session.[118] Both the crown and the parliament were part of Sir Robert's divine system of government, and the thought seemed to have entered his mind that the former, as well as the latter, could

[114]R. Naunton, *Fragmenta, sub* Cecil.

[115]*Ibid.,* and introduction.

[116]*Ibid.,* introduction.

[117]*Ibid.*

[118]*Ibid.*

disrupt God's system. The idea must have been deeply disturbing to the old man.

The real world had a way of impinging on Naunton's thoughts. The hungry courtiers of the Carolinian court would not leave an old man to his reveries so long as he occupied one of the most profitable posts in England. As early as December 1631 there were rumours that Lord Cottington, then Chancellor of the Exchequer and formerly an agent in Spain, would become Master of the Wards.[119] Yet it turned out that forcing this tired ancient from his office was no easy matter. In theory he may have held his post at the king's pleasure, but in practice he had virtual freehold rights to it. Unless there was a scandal, political, financial or personal, he would hold his office until he decided to release it.

The scandal, such as it was, did finally come in the summer of 1634. For some years Naunton had not been in good health. In September 1628 he had asked to be excused from the Privy Council for a while, at least in part because of eye trouble.[120] In 1631 he mentioned to Nethersole that he was lame,[121] but matters took a sudden turn for the worse in the summer of 1634. At that time, George Verney wrote to Sir John Coke that:

> His honour going to the Wells at Tunbridge hath rather been of prejudice than benefit to his health; he is hastening for Suffolk; his lower parts are of little assistance to him, his vital parts are yet good; little hope yet keeps [us] from despair.[122]

About a month later, in August, Emanuel Downing echoed Verney's sentiments when he wrote to Coke: 'I am going with his honour . . . into Suffolk, his native soil, in hope that will conduce to his gaining strength, who I thank God is rather mending than pairing.'[123]

By whatever means, Naunton managed to remain alive through the autumn and winter of 1634, but his decayed condition must have been evident to all: he was not sitting at the session of the Court of Wards.[124] Under ordinary circumstances, whether an official as prestigious as the Master of the Court of Wards appeared for his duties was a matter of indifference to most people; the court was

[119]William Murray to Sir H. Vane, 18 December 1631, *CSPD 1631-1633,* p. 205.

[120]Naunton to Conway, Charing Cross, 11 September 1628, PRO SP/16/116, no. 99.

[121]PRO SP/16/192, no. 57.

[122]Verney to Coke, Charing Cross, 28 July 1634, HMC, *Cowper,* II, 60.

[123]E. Downing to Sir J. Coke, 23 August 1634, *ibid.,* p. 64.

[124]*The Earl of Strafford's Letters and Dispatches,* I, 338.

perfectly capable of functioning without him. With Naunton's non-existent political standing, it was an entirely different story; the vultures quickly dived for the carcass.

Lord Cottington was the victor in this effort to pry Naunton loose from his office. He set his aim for the invalid master and out-manoeuvred several competitors on the way to his target.[125] Using the threat of a royal commission to investigate Sir Robert's health, Cottington finally forced the old man to resign.

It says much for Naunton's tenacity that, even on the verge of death and disgrace, he was able to write in a shaky but clear hand:

Scribled out of my sicke bed

Your Majestie hath been informed that my sicknes is and hath bene a great hinderance to your revenue in your Court of Wards whereof I wold to God you wold have taken a strickt accompt by the examination of your sworne officers there who understand it best. But I heare there is a new devised commission coming out to inquire of my estat of health and habilitie to serve you any longer in the place I have held thus long and that this course is advised upon I know not what pretended stoutnes in me who have incurred infinite displeasures and envies (under which I now groane) for standing out for your Majesties service that never had so litle sence of dutie and understanding to presume to wrastle with your Majestie otherwise then by humble prayer as Jacob wrastled with God himself and prevailed not to depart without a blissing. Sire, it hath bene the joy and comfort of my life hetherto (as God best knowes) that I have bene no improsperous servant to your royal father and your selfe neither will I ever desire to live to your disservice. Your Majestie was graciously pleased to accept of one extraordinary tryal of my duetiful conformitie to your good pleasure in the wardship of my wives sonne, for which you then vouchsafed me your princely thankes. Knew you the continual domestical martyrdomes which I have suffered ever since [which] have given me this sicknes and will give me death if your Majestie shall give credi[t to] thos causeles yea senceles and phrenetike clamors which she and her instruments [have] rayesed against me, your Majestie would commiserate my case more and comfort me that have so much need of comfort.

If your Highnes will not be pleased to except the tryal of my healths recoveries untill the next terme (which they that understand the course of that court best do know you may without prejudice or disprofit) Sir I am the humblest of your

[125] Aylmer, *The King's Servants,* pp. 114-17.

128

servants that can not lift up a thought against you, but am and
ever will be readie to tender up my patent at your command
without trobling any commissioners whatsoever. . . .[126]

Once before when Naunton was under the cloud of royal displeasure
he had managed to delay matters on what might be called personal
grounds.[127] He hoped that a similar formula would work here in
conjunction with his usual show of humility before the royal majesty.
But his career was over; Charles called back the patent and gave it to
Cottington in mid-March 1635. His life was over too; before the end
of the month, Sir Robert Naunton, privy councillor and Master of the
Wards, was dead.

126Naunton to the king, 5 March 1635, PRO SP/16/284, no. 23. ,
127Discussed above, pp. 89-90.

CONCLUSION

The monetary worth of Sir Robert Naunton is the obvious place to begin an evaluation of him and his governmental career. It is not possible to make a definitive statement here, especially if one looks at Naunton's career as a whole. All that can be said with any certainty is that Sir Robert earned a good deal more by accepting royal office than he would have had he remained a Suffolk gentleman.

With respect to the profits of specific offices, the mastership of the wards is especially difficult to estimate in terms of cash value. Part of the problem is that during Naunton's tenure as master, there is only one recorded example of his accepting a gift and, even then, the amount is unspecified. Undoubtedly the mastership was the most lucrative office Sir Robert held. He thought it was worth more than the secretaryship and most of his contemporaries shared his opinion. If previous estimates of the worth of the profits of the Secretary of State are accurate, then Naunton was earning something in excess of £4,000 per year as master, and it is not inconceivable that the total could have been double that amount. This rather broad range is about as close as one can come.

When discussing profit, qualifications are always necessary with regard to Sir Robert, for however much he made, the odds are that someone else would have made more. Sir Robert was the only master after 1614 who neither had nor received a peerage while in office. It would not be surprising if the lack of sufficient fortune to support such an honour was one reason why he never received it.

The absence of personal accumulation of wealth does not necessarily mean that Sir Robert was an honest man, in the present sense of the term. Though he was possibly concerned to see that no monetary sin prevented his soul from flying straight to heaven, he had no compunctions about accepting gifts from suitors, and the line between gifts and bribes was often hard to draw. Yet given the custom and common practice of the times, it is in no way unusual that he did so. What appears most likely is that he lacked the talent rather than the inclination, to reap greater rewards from his position. Yet when Naunton described himself in his final letter to the king as 'no improsperous servant' of the royal interest, he was probably not far from the truth. For in all likelihood the money that Naunton did not take for himself fell, at least in part, to the crown. In addition his inability to extract the maximum from the clients of the Court of Wards may have been a good public relations measure for both the crown and for Naunton. One suspects, however, that the greediness of his subordinates may have done much to cancel these benefits.

Money alone was not the major indicator of a man's worth in the society of Stuart England. Land was the real key, and here Naunton's position was not very impressive. Through the course of his life, he did manage to acquire at least four manors near Wickham Market in eastern Suffolk. According to Sir Robert's will, these holdings included Leatheringham, the former seat of his Wingfield relations, and the nearby manors of Kettleborough, Hoo and Branston. His father's old holdings near Alderton must have been sold sometime before 1635. This small group of manors was enough to give Sir Robert credibility as a county M.P., but did not endow him with the same kind of political influence in Suffolk as families such as the Bacons or the Barnardistons.

As for holdings in other counties, Naunton possessed only a scattering: his mother's dowerlands in Leicester and one manor in Essex. There was also some land in Wales, and it was here that Sir Robert had the greatest hopes for expansion. When he married Penelope Perrot Lower, he hoped not only for temporary possession of her son's Welsh properties, but also to reclaim the lands of her grandfather, Sir John Perrot. As Naunton points out in *Fragmenta Regalia,* Perrot's holdings in Wales were equal to that of many peers and, as a result, he had been one of the major political forces in Pembrokeshire. The legal complications and expenses of regaining these lands proved to be beyond Naunton's capabilities, and his hopes of becoming a leading landed magnate evaporated.

If the rewards in landholding proved small, there were other signs that Sir Robert's status in society had risen through the course of his career. The Nauntons, though old gentry, were not of the first rank in their county. Had they been otherwise, Sir Robert would not have been only the second member of his family to serve in parliament. In addition, it should be pointed out that whatever illustrious ancestry the Nauntons claimed was acquired fairly late in their history and came mainly through their connection with the Wingfields, who had links with many titled aristocrats.

Naunton undeniably improved on this situation. He was not only a member of parliament, but managed to finish his career in the highly prized and sought-after senior county seat for Suffolk. What is more, the marriage he arranged for his daughter with Paul, Viscount Bayning was a major step up from the social point of view. It is true that the Baynings were newly titled, having made their money in the

City and recently purchased in Essex and Suffolk. It is also true that the £4,000 dowry that Naunton provided for his daughter was not an unduly large one. (The earl of Strafford proposed to give each of his two daughters £10,000.) Yet whatever the qualifications, marriage to the viscount was an indication of Naunton's elevation on the social scale. After Sir Robert died, his daughter succeeded in rising even further on the scale, for after the death of her husband, she remarried the heir to the Pembroke earldom while one of her daughters by Bayning achieved the ultimate heights by marrying the last Vere Earl of Oxford. Her social *coups* probably had little to do with the Naunton family but rather were a function of Bayning money; the wardship of Viscountess Bayning's two daughters cost £10,000. Nonetheless, Sir Robert's tenure as a royal servant certainly paved the way for all the later social glory for his descendants.

To a certain extent his worth must be measured by how well he carried out his functions in this role. In one sense, he served his first royal master as much by what he represented as by what he did. For Sir Robert was part of a system that attempted to balance factions within the government. He was also part of a large, loosely structured group that opposed the Spanish and Roman Catholic interests, both at home and abroad. Through men such as Naunton, James sought to maintain the loyalty of the more extreme puritans, common lawyers and parliamentarians. The king hoped to show these men that some slight moderation of their opinions could lead to high office. He held up men such as Sir Robert as examples. He was at least willing to listen to people with a point of view similar to their own. James wanted them to believe that he objected much more to their style than their philosophy.

This broad-based system insured the king of more than just loyalty. It also gave him a wide choice of men who could perform the various tasks of both domestic and foreign business. Because of the wide spectrum of views represented, James could put the man most sympathetic to a policy in a position to carry it out. It is true that the king's choice of men was not invariably correct. The two best known favourites. Somerset and Buckingham, undoubtedly did the royal government more harm than good. The same could be said of Lake and Suffolk. Yet these errors were not the whole story. Men such as Bacon, Cranfield, Digby, Carleton, Calvert and Naunton were clearly successful as administrators and royal servants. The policy of an all-inclusive administration meant that during the period that Naunton was active as Secretary of State, the problem of friction between the executive and administrative branches of government was kept to a minimum. To the extent that James was able to instruct

132

his ministers to do what they wanted, he had been able to guarantee that his wishes were carried out.

Charles's accession to the throne spelled the end to broad-based government. The decline was not a sudden phenomenon, but a gradual withdrawal from several different areas. The first was definitely religion. The rapid rise of Laud, the support of the preacher, Montague, and the York House conference gave a sure indication that the Church of England and its leading personalities were going to take a rapid turn in a more conservative direction.

Naunton gave no indication of what he thought of the new king's ecclesiastical policy, though with his reputation among the puritan gentry of his county for being sympathetic to their point of view, his complete approval of the new policy is in doubt. Sir Robert had been educated at Cambridge under John Still, Master of Trinity College. Still opposed the puritanical Cartwright, but was more moderate in his views on this subject than his predecessor, Whitgift, had been. Though there is no proof that Sir Robert thought the same, it can be shown that as he grew older, he became progressively more anti-Romanist, and it would be surprising if he did knot interpret Laud and his ideas as leaning in the wrong direction.

Whatever his religious views at the outset of the new reign, the foreign policy must have pleased him. During the first three years there was an active war with both Spain and France, Naunton's two chief *bêtes noires* of the Christian world. Therefore, he must have been greatly surprised and eventually disillusioned to discover that the king and parliament were at odds over the best manner of handling the war. As one might expect from a man of Naunton's temperament, he sided with the king. Unfortunately for Sir Robert's relationship with the king, the chief advocate for an aggressive foreign policy was his patron, Buckingham. It was his influence on Charles that kept the wars going. The duke also shielded many of the aggresively anti-Spanish, puritanically inclined royal servants from their anti-war foes. Thus, when Buckingham was assassinated, not only the warlike foreign policy, but Naunton's last links with the king died with him.

There was now no major policy of government with which Sir Robert was in full agreement. He did not favour anyone who leaned towards Romanism as the Laudians seemed to do, and he did not want peace with Spain as most of the leading figures in the new government did. *Fragmenta Regalia* makes it clear that, though Naunton felt some parliamentarians had gone too far, he nonetheless thought the king should give them another chance and convene a new parliament. In this attitude, Sir Robert illustrates just how much he was outside the mainstream of the court's political life, and it is no wonder that Charles required his presence less and less at the Privy Council.

Under Charles the political centre of government had shifted in a more conservative direction than it had occupied under James. Men such as Wentworth now represented the effective outer limits of the government, whereas Windebank, Portland, and Cottington were very much in the centre. It is true that people such as Carleton managed to survive as influential ministers for several years after Buckingham's death, but their survival was at the price of changing their views, or at least remaining silent about any ideas that would annoy the king. There were, of course, those ministers who were unwilling to pay the price. The result was ostracism, the fate that overtook Archbishop Abbot. Such isolation could also be just the first step in forcing these men from office, as Sir Robert learned. The upshot of Charles's attitude was that he relied almost exclusively on men who accepted his point of view. Those in his government who did not, he tried to ignore. When it came time to replace these dissidents, it was not their political allies who were placed in their posts.

It would surely be an overstatement to call this conservative refocusing of royal administration the key event that caused the Civil Wars. Yet the fact remains that this action was a contributory factor. By removing men such as Naunton from his inner councils, the king forced these moderates into a neutral or antagonistic position. He also destroyed the bridge to the more extreme elements in the country, thus widening the gap between them. Whereas, in the beginning of the reign, they were willing to trust a man such as Naunton, and even elect him a county M.P., within a few years, most of Charles's principal ministers were viewed with grave suspicion and looked upon as threats to the security of the realm.

This situation was a decided change from James's reign. He had been successful in periodically attracting such men as Sir Edward Coke into his government (and there were few men who differed with James or who were more vocal about it than Sir Edward). Charles made only one effort in this direction, when Noy and Wentworth were brought into the government. In the long run, even this move made little difference because Charles seldom, if ever, entirely trusted any man who had opposed him. Even someone as able as Wentworth was excluded from the inner circle of royal advisors until 1640, when the final crisis of the reign had begun, and then it was too late.

As for Naunton, by 1635 he was undeniably an old, sick man, and thus there were other reasons besides political ones for dismissing him. Yet, despite Sir Robert's decline in his later years, he was a minister the crown found worth having. He was a hard worker who enjoyed the grind (even if he occasionally brought himself to the point where only a strong physic and an enforced holiday would restore his vigour). When dealing with foreign affairs, he showed a genuine and lively interest. Had he been able to devote his final years to this area, there is every reason to believe he would have performed well. Certainly *Fragmenta Regalia,* written in his last years, readily demonstrates that he retained his ability to think clearly, for it contains acute observations of men and events as well as a wry, if somewhat ponderous, humour.

Yet, whatever Naunton's assets, one cannot view his career as an example of a man who deserved to play a more major role than he did. His perspective was too narrow, his methods too slow, to permit him to become an able policymaker. Even a government devoted entirely to an anti-Spanish and anti-Romanist programme would have needed a quicker, more subtle mind than Naunton's to guide it.

In spite of this observation, given Naunton's clear capabilities in foreign affairs, one can only regret that he was not utilized more extensively in this field. In large measure, he was a victim of the governmental system and the social standards of his time. He was not well suited for the post of Master of the Wards, yet he was most anxious to obtain it because prestige, honour and money meant more to him than efficiency. Here he was merely reflecting the standards of the governing class of his day, and for him, those three matters were, by and large, the touchstones for this group. Sir Robert unquestionably would have made an excellent ambassador to any court hostile to the Habsburgs. Yet, since an ambassadorship was considered a lesser post than his former office of Secretary of State, he never made the slightest effort to obtain one. Naunton would rather have retired completely from politics than come back into government as less a man than he had been.

If the standards of the age are accepted as a fact of life, there were still other possibilities besides the Court of Wards. The ideal post would have been one similar to that which Carleton held in 1628. At this time Sir John Coke took care of the domestic affairs as one Secretary of State while Carleton (by then Viscount Dorchester) handled the foreign affairs as the other. The opportunity was certainly there in 1625 to do just that. War with Spain was virtually declared with Charles's accession that year, and there should have been no objections on either the king's or Buckingham's part to having two anti-Spaniards, Conway and Naunton, occupy the secretariat.

Despite the attractiveness of this idea from a practical point of view, it is highly unlikely that it was ever considered by any of the principals. For a start Naunton already had a post. Too many candidates were about and too few positions existed in the 1620s for any politician of the administrative rank to hold down more than one major office. Sir Robert could, of course, have turned down the position of Master of the Wards and waited for a more suitable post, but the dearth of offices made such an approach highly risky. Some kind of switch might have been worked out, but the mastership was a more lucrative and prestigious post than the secretaryship, and as stated before, Naunton was not going to take a step down. The result was that he remained in the Court of Wards, and the opportunities to utilize him efficiently slipped by.

In the final analysis of Naunton's worth as a royal servant, one can say that, under the right circumstances he performed as well as, if not better, than the other people then available. He was an able administrator with a particular talent for coordinating other people's activities and for acting as an intermediary. His talent showed itself best in the field of foreign affairs. Whenever Sir Robert was working in this area with other Englishmen, he performed the tasks required of him more than adequately. The real misfortune of his political career was that these circumstances did not prevail for very long. For eleven years as Master of the Court of Wards (in contrast to three active ones as Secretary of State), he occupied a post that could have been filled far more competently by others. It is true that thanks to the experience and skill of the other members of the Court of Wards, royal finances did not suffer unduly while Naunton was master, nor one suspects, did their own. Nonetheless, mediocrity was the best Naunton achieved at the Court of Wards. He had neither the inclination nor the ability for the work, and he often left it to others less scrupulous than himself.

Given the standards of the time, both Naunton and his royal master made the best of the existing situation. Yet it is regrettable that a talented man was utilized for eleven years in a way that took the least advantage of his talents. In all fairness it should be said that after Buckingham's death, given Charles's policy of conciliation with Spain, and no substantial aid to the Prince and Princess Palatine, even if Naunton had been foreign secretary, he still would have ended his days in isolation and bitterness. This observation does not mitigate the fact that Naunton clung too long to the mastership, and as a result he ended his life pitied and despised by many of his contemporaries. Surely that is too high a price to pay for survival alone.

APPENDIX A: FOREIGN CORRESPONDENCE

(All figures quoted are, by necessity, based on surviving documents. There is, of course, the possibility that there were other letters written.)

Empire correspondence:

Of the twelve letters sent by Carpenter, an English letter writer, one was definitely to Calvert and eleven were probably to him. None was definitely to Naunton. *Source:* SP/80.

Flanders:

Numerous letters are addressed to 'The Secretary of State' without any indication as to who read the letters, so no exact set of figures can be gathered. All that can be said with any certainty is that the first letter addressed to Naunton by name was dated 3 September 1618. Winwood, the previous secretary, had died on 27 October 1617, and Naunton was appointed to his place on 9 January 1618. Calvert was sworn secretary on 16 February 1619 and did not have a dispatch addressed specifically to him from Flanders until 15/25 November 1620. Judging by the handwriting on the backs of the dispatches, Naunton received the vast majority of the Flanders correspondence from around November 1618, even though dispatches were addressed to Lake until as late as 31 January 1619. *Source:* SP/77.

France:

From June 1618 to 21 October 1618 William Beecher, the English agent at Paris sent at least four letters specifically addressed to Lake and one to Naunton. Most are addressed to the Secretary of State, but the evidence of endorsements shows that nearly all of them went to Lake. There was then a break in the diplomatic relations between England and France after the Raleigh affair. When relations were renewed, Sir Edward Herbert was sent as the English ambassador. From 4 July 1619 to 19 January 1621 Herbert sent Naunton over seventy dispatches, while Naunton wrote over twenty to Herbert. In addition those three unaddressed dispatches probably went from Herbert to Naunton. Approximately ten letters in this period were addressed to Calvert; they were all of a complimentary nature. Herbert received a minimum of two letters from Calvert largely on matters of no political significance, i.e., seeing that James got his quota of French wine with no difficulty. *Sources:* SP/78; BL Add. 7082; PRO/30/53.

Germany:

Doncaster directed all his letters that went to a Secretary of State to Naunton. Bilderbeck, the agent who was apparently German and did what could best be called free-lance work, wrote to Lake until January 1619; from August 1619 until 1624, all his letters went to Naunton. There is evidence that letters were sent to Naunton before August 1619, but they have not survived. Nethersole wrote over twenty dispatches to Naunton and at least three to Calvert; two are uncertain. Naunton sent at least five to Nethersole. If Calvert wrote to Nethersole, none of his letters survived. Conway, Weston and Dickerson wrote about ten letters from Germany to Naunton, and Naunton wrote two to them. No letters exist at this time either to or from Calvert to these three ambassadors. *Sources:* BL Eg. 2592, 2593, 2394; SP/81.

Holland:

Naunton received his first dispatch from Holland on 4 February 1618. Between 24 February 1618 and 18 May 1618 Carleton and Lake exchanged a minimum of eight letters and Naunton and Carleton exchanged at least five. Carleton stopped writing to Lake in May 1618. From the date of Calvert's appointment until Naunton's suspension on 17 January 1621 Calvert and Carleton exchanged approximately twenty letters. Several of these were written after Calvert's accession to his office and were in effect letters of protest and rebuttal. During the same period, Naunton and Carleton exchanged an average of six letters a month. *Source:* SP/84.

Poland:

Two letters from Gordon, the English agent, went to Naunton; the rest went directly to James. *Source:* SP/88.

Savoy:

All letters went to Lake from Sir Isaac Wake until 6 August 1618. From then until Naunton's suspension approximately three letters go to either Lake or Calvert. Over forty dispatches were sent to Naunton during the same period. None of Naunton's dispatches to Wake has survived, but from remarks made in Wake's letters it seems he received approximately one letter back for every two or three he wrote to Naunton. *Sources:* BL Add. 18641, 18642; SP/92.

Spain:

From January 1618 to January 1619 twenty-one letters went from

Cottington to Digby or Lake and five went to Naunton. Aston wrote no letters to Naunton that survived and at least four that did to Calvert. The Public Record Office index for Spanish correspondence shows numerous letters from Cottington to Naunton, but an inspection of these letters has shown that they were addressed to 'The Secretary of State' and most probably endorsed by Calvert or his scribe. *Source:* SP/94.

Venice:

Wotton wrote only to Lake until July 1618. From 5 July 1618 until January 1619, Wotton wrote at least five letters to Lake and over twenty to Naunton. From 25 April 1619, the date of Wotton's first letter to Calvert, until 17 January 1621, no fewer than five dispatches went to Calvert (one went from Italy; four went from the Austrian provinces) and minimum of eleven dispatches went to Naunton (three from Italy, eight from the Austrian provinces). *Source:* Logan Pearsall Smith, *The Life and Letters of Sir Henry Wotton* (Oxford, 1907), vol. II.

APPENDIX B: PAYMENT OF AMBASSADORS AND AGENTS

The following chart shows salaries of English ambassadors and agents. It is divided into two periods: May 1611 to March 1614, and July 1617 to January 1621. The columns into which the chart is divided are self-explanatory, but special attention should be paid to the last column. It will be noted from the information found there that shortly after Salisbury's death, the orderly system of payment established by him rapidly deteriorated, and several payments were either grouped together or paid after the money was borrowed, or both. The improvement took place in Naunton's time and slightly before, though it never reached the efficiency of the Salisbury period. Nonetheless, the procedures noticeably improved. Carleton's and Herbert's salaries are eventually paid on time and Trumbull's and Wake's were nearly brought up to date.

Sir Robert Anstruther, Ambassador to Denmark

Pay Date & Reference	Sum & Details		Period Covered
21 Jan. 1612 E/403/1712, fo. 184	£ 160	— in part of £200	—
23 May 1612 E/403/1713	£ 40	— pension (£160)	¼ year
5 Dec. 1612 E/403/1714	£ 40	— pension (£160)	¼ year
23 Dec. 1612 Ibid.	£ 200	— embassy to Denmark	—
17 Apr. 1613 E/403/1715	£ 80	— pension (£160)	½ year

Sir Robert Anstruther, Ambassador to Denmark continued

Pay Date & Reference	Sum & Details		Period Covered
23 Apr. 1613 *Ibid.*	£ 40	— pension (£160)	¼ year
12 June 1613 *Ibid.*	£ 570	— final payment of £1070	—
11 Oct. 1613 E/403/1716	£ 40	— pension (£160)	¼ year
23 Apr. 1614 *Ibid.*	£ 80	— pension (£160)	½ year
10 Nov. 1617 E/403/1723	£ 100	— pension (£400)	¼ year
9 May 1618 E/403/1724	£ 100	— pension (£400)	¼ year
22 July 1618 E/403/1724	£ 200	— pension (£400)	½ year
14 Oct. 1619 E/403/1725	£ 100	— pension (£400)	¼ year
11 Jan. 1620 E/403/1725	£ 100	— pension (£400)	¼ year
13 March 1620 *Ibid.*	£ 500	— special services	—

Sir Robert Anstruther, Ambassador to Denmark continued

Pay Date & Reference	Sum & Details		Period Covered
25 Apr. 1620 E/403/1726	£ 100	— pension (£400)	¼ year
10 Nov. 1620 E/403/1727	£ 100	— pension (£400)	¼ year
6 Jan. 1621 Ibid.	£1000	— special services	—

Sir Isaac Wake, Agent to Savoy

Pay Date & Reference	Sum & Details		Period Covered
6 July 1618 E/403/1724	£ 92	— diet	June-Aug. 1617
	£ 91	— diet	Oct.-Nov. 1617
	£ 90	— diet	Dec.-Feb. 1617-18
	£ 200	— transportation	—
	£ 100	— secret service	Jan.-July 1617
	£ 150	— transportation	—
	£ 200	— secret service & transportation	July-Jan. 1617-18
6 July 1618 Ibid.	£ 92	— diet	Mar.-May 1618
10 Nov. 1619 E/403/1725	£ 150	— transportation & secret service (In part of £400)	Jan.-July 1619

142

Sir Isaac Wake, Agent to Savoy continued

Pay Date & Reference	Sum & Details		Period Covered
11 Jan. 1620 *Ibid.*	£ 250	— (final payment)	Jan.-July 1619
	£ 184	— diet	Mar.-May 1619
	£ 66	— diet (in part of £184)	June-Aug. 1619
13 May 1620 E/403/1726	£ 118	— as above	" " "
	£ 182	— diet	Sept.-Nov. 1619
	£ 100	— transportation (in part of £200)	" " "
9 Aug. 1620 E/403/1726	£ 182	— diet	Dec.-Feb. 1620
	£ 184	— diet	Mar.-May 1620

Sir Albertus Morton, Agent to the Princes of the Union

Pay Date & Reference	Sum & Details		Period Covered
19 Mar. 1618 E/403/1723	£ 125	— transportation	—
18 May 1620 E/403/1726	£ 400	— transportation (part of £500)	—

Sir Edward Herbert, Ambassador to France

Pay Date & Reference	Sum & Details		Period Covered
27 Nov. 1619 E/403/1725	£ 255-10/0	— transportation (in part of £397)	—
17 Dec. 1619 *Ibid.*	£ 142	— transportation (final payment)	—

Sir Edward Herbert, Ambassador to France continued

Pay Date & Reference	Sum & Details		Period Covered
	£ 486	— transportation	May-July 1619
	£ 57-6/8	— diet (final payment)	
13 May 1620 E/403/1726	£ 340	— secret service	May-Oct. 1619
	£ 200	— secret service	Nov.-Jan. 1619-20
15 Aug. 1620 E/403/1726	£ 368	— diet	Aug.-Oct. 1619
	£ 132	— transportation (in part of £400)	—

William Beecher, Agent to France

Pay Date & Reference	Sum & Details		Period Covered
1 Aug. 1618 E/403/1724	£ 180	— diet	Jan.-Mar. 1618
	£ 182	— diet	Apr.-June 1618
	£ 66-13/4	— secret service	Jan.-Mar. 1618
	£ 184	— diet	July-Sept. 1618
	£ 66-13/4	— secret service	Apr.-June 1618
13 Nov. 1619 E/403/1725	£ 90	— diet (final payment)	Oct.-Dec. 1618
	£ 62	— diet	Jan. 1619
	£ 17	— transportation (part payment)	
21 Jan. 1620 Ibid.	£ 103	— transportation (final payment)	—
	£ 66-13/4	— secret service	Oct.-Dec. 1618

144

William Beecher, Agent to France continued

Pay Date & Reference	Sum & Details		Period Covered
	£ 66-13/4 —	secret service	Jan.-Mar. 1619
	£ 33- 6/8 —	secret service	Apr.-May 1619
13 May 1620	£ 100 —	supplement	—
E/403/1726		(in part of £300)	

James, Viscount Doncaster, Ambassador to the Princes of the Empire

Pay Date & Reference	Sum & Details		Period Covered
28 Feb. 1620	£2500 —	embassy to Germany	30 Mar. 1619
E/403/1725		(in part of £12,412-6/0)	2 Jan. 1620
11 March 1620	£6912 —	as above (final payment)	,, ,, ,,

Sir Thomas Edmonds, Ambassador to France

Pay Date & Reference	Sum & Details		Period Covered
4 May 1611	£ 488 —	diet	Apr.-June 1611
E/403/1711	£ 180 —	secret service	Dec.-Mar. 1610-11
11 Nov. 1611	£ 100 —	secretary of French tongue	—
E/403/1712, fo. 51	£ 75 —	clerk of Privy Council	—
Ibid., fo. 53	£ 488 —	diet	Aug.-Oct. 1611
	£ 180 —	secret service	Apr.-July 1611
29 Feb. 1612	£ 488 —	diet	Dec.-Mar. 1611-12
Ibid., fo. 287	£ 180 —	secret service	Aug.-Nov. 1611

Sir Thomas Edmonds, Ambassador to France continued

Pay Date & Reference	Sum & Details		Period Covered
15 May 1612 E/403/1713	£ 488 —	diet	Apr.-June 1612
	£ 180 —	secret service	Jan.-Mar. 1612
22 Sept. 1612 *Ibid.*	£ 488 —	diet	Aug.-Nov. 1612
	£ 180 —	secret service	Apr.-June 1612
	£ 37-10/0 —	clerk of Council	—
30 Mar. 1613 E/403/1714	£ 600 —	extraordinary expenses	—
23 Oct. 1613 E/403/1716	£ 60 —	clerk of Council	—
	£ 66-13/4 —	secretary of French tongue	—
12 Jan. 1614 E/403/1716	£1212 —	diet	Feb.-Nov. 1613
	£ 540 —	secret service	Aug.-July 1612-13
5 Mar. 1614 *Ibid.*	£ 484 —	diet	Dec.-Mar. 1613-14
	£ 180 —	secret service	Aug.-Nov. 1613

Philip Burlamachi, merchant

Pay Date & Reference	Sum & Details		Period Covered
12 Jan. 1614 *Ibid.*	£ 66 —	interest on £1868 for Edmonds	20 Aug. 1613- 8 Jan. 1614
3 May 1617 E/403/1723	£ 484 —	diet	Dec.-Mar. 1616-17
	£ 180 —	secret service	Aug.-Nov. 1615

Sir Thomas Edmonds, Ambassador to France continued

Pay Date & Reference	Sum & Details		Period Covered
Ibid.	£ 52- 6/8 —	diet (final payment of £488)	Apr.-June 1616
Ibid.	£ 312-18/0 —	secret service	Dec.-Mar. 1615-16
Ibid.	£2400 —	expenses in Paris & Bordeaux (in part of £3000)	—
10 July 1617 Ibid.	£ 180 —	secret service	Aug.-Sept. 1615
31 Oct., 1617 Ibid.	£ 24 —	transportation (in part of £250)	
14 Apr. 1618 E/403/1724	£ 500 —	secret service	Apr.-July 1617
	£ 600 —	secret service and transportation	Aug-Nov. 1617
	£ 226 —	transportation (see 31 Oct.)	—
	£ 530 —	transportation	—

Sir Henry Wotton, Ambassador to Venice

Pay Date & Reference	Sum & Details		Period Covered
4 May, 1611 E/403/1711	£ 403-6/8 —	diet	Jan.-Mar. 1611
	£ 125 —	secret service	Dec.-Mar. 1610-11
	£ 640 —	transportation	
3 March, 1612 E/403/1712, fo. 292	£ 600 —	diet (Savoyard embassy) & other expenses	1 Dec., 1611- end
14 Mar., 1612 Ibid., fo. 304	£ 100 —	diet	Ibid.

Sir Henry Wotton, Ambassador to Venice continued

Pay Date Reference	Sum and Details		Period Covered
4 June, 1612 E/403/1713	£ 50	— pension (in part of £200)	—
31 July, 1612 Ibid.	£ 50	— pension (in part of £200)	—
28 Sept., 1612 E/403/1714	£ 250 £1079	— diet — transportation	Dec.-Aug. 1611-12 —
28 Sept, 1613 E/403/1715	£ 150	— pension (in part of £200)	—
11 Dec., 1613 E/403/1716	£ 50	— pension (in part of £200)	—
15 Jan., 1614 Ibid.	£ 50	— pension (in part of £200)	—
27 Sept., 1617 E/403/1723	£ 230	— diet (in part of £306)	Aug.-Oct. 1617
4 Mar., 1618 Ibid.	£ 125	— secret service	16 Jan.-17 Apr. 1617
19 Mar. 1618 Ibid.	£ 335	— part of £431 for diet & £125 for secret service	Nov.-Jan. 1617-18 July-Oct. 1617
4 May, 1618 E/403/1724	£ 86-13/4 £ 10	— diet (final payment) — secret service	Nov.-Jan. 1617-18 July-Oct. 1617

Sir Henry Wotton, Ambassador to Venice continued

Pay Date & Reference	Sum and Details		Period Covered
Ibid.	£ 125	secret service	Apr.-July 1617
Ibid.	£ 306-13/4	diet	Aug.-Oct. 1617
Ibid.	£ 275	post charges for secretary	—
Ibid.			
2 July, 1618	£ 296-13/4	diet	Feb.-Apr. 1618
Ibid.	£ 125	secret service	Oct.-Jan. 1618
	£ 306-13/4	diet	May-July 1618
	£ 125	secret service	Jan.-Apr. 1618
4 July, 1618	£ 250	pension	1¼ years
Ibid.			
14 Jan., 1620	£ 35	secret service (final payment)	Oct.-Jan. 1618-19
E/403/1725	£ 125	secret service	Jan.-Apr. 1619
	£ 186-13/4	secret service	Apr.-Aug. 1619
	£ 210	salary of embassy secretary	Jan.-Sept. 1618-19
	£ 7-10/0	secret service and posting	8-30 June 1619
	£ 166-6/8	transportation (in part of £800)	—
6 May, 1620	£ 100	pension (in part of £200)	½ year
E/403/1726			
9 June, 1620	£ 6-13/4	diet (final payment)	May-July 1619
Ibid.	£ 104-6/4	transportation (final payment)	Aug. 1619
	£ 683-13/4	transportation (final payment)	—
	£ 340	interest on loan	—
	£1000	interest on loan	—

Sir Henry Wotton, Ambassador to Venice continued

Pay Date & Reference	Sum and Details		Period Covered
27 June, 1620	£ 153-6/8	— extraordinary expenses	—
Ibid.	£ 100	— extraordinary expenses	—
	£ 150	— mourning (for Queen Anne)	—

Sir Dudley Carleton, Ambassador to Venice

Pay Date & Reference	Sum and Details		Period Covered
4 May, 1611 E/403/1711	£ 406-13/4 £ 250	— diet — secret service	Apr.-July 1611 Oct.-Apr. 1610-11
20 Dec., 1611 E/403/1712, fo. 155	£ 406-13/4 £ 250	— diet — secret service	Aug.-Nov. 1611 Apr.-Sept. 1611
28 Feb., 1612 *Ibid.*, fo. 282	£ 406-13/4 £ 125	— diet — secret service	Dec.-Mar. 1611-12 Oct.-Dec. 1611
E/403/1713	£ 406-13/4 £ 125	— diet — secret service	Apr.-July 1612 Jan.-Mar. 1612
16 Oct., 1612 E/403/1714	£ 406-13/4 £ 125	— diet — secret service	Sept.-Nov. 1612 Apr.-June 1612
23 Dec., 1612 *Ibid.*	£ 403-6/8 £ 125	— diet — secret service	Dec.-Mar. 1612-13 July-Sept. 1612
11 Jan., 1614 E/403/1716	£ 810 £ 375	— diet — secret service	Aug.-Mar. 1613-14 Jan.-Sept. 1613
Ibid. *Ibid.*	£ 250	— supplement	—

Sir Dudley Carleton, Ambassador to the Dutch Estates General

Pay Date & Reference	Sum & Details		Period Covered
5 July, 1617 E/403/1723	£ 306-13/4 —	diet	June-Aug. 1617
27 July, 1618 E/403/1724	£ 303-6/8 —	diet	Oct.-Nov. 1617
	£ 125 —	secret service	June-Aug. 1617
	£ 300 —	diet	Dec.-Feb. 1617-18
	£ 125 —	secret service	Sept.-Nov. 1617
	£ 125 —	secret service	Mar.-May 1617
30 July, 1618 Ibid.	£ 306-13/4 —	diet	Mar.-May 1618
	£ 125 —	secret service	Dec.-Feb. 1617-18
	£ 256 —	transportation & salary for secretary	May-July 1618
27 Nov. 1619 E/403/1725	£ 306-13/4 —	diet	June-Aug. 1618
	£ 37-6/8 —	transportation	—
	£ 125 —	secret service	
	£ 37-13/4 —	secret service	Dec.-Feb. 1618-19
	£ 300 —	diet	Jan.-Feb. 1619
17 Jan. 1620 Ibid.	£ 87- 6/8 —	secret service (final payment)	Dec.-Feb. 1618-19
	£ 306-13/4 —	diet	Mar.-May 1619
	£ 272 —	diet (in part of £306-13/4)	June-Aug. 1619
15 May 1620 E/403/1726	£ 33-13/4 —	diet (final payment)	June-Aug. 1619
	£ 306-13/4 —	diet	Sept.-Nov. 1619
	£ 21 —	messengers	
	£ 150 —	mourning (for Queen Anne)	—

Sir Dudley Carleton, Ambassador to the Dutch Estates General continued

Pay Date & Reference	Sum and Details		Period Covered
12 Aug. 1620 Ibid.	£ 500	— secret service	Mar.-Feb. 1619-20
9 Nov. 1620 E/403/1727	£ 303- 6/8	— diet	Dec.-Feb. 1619-20
	£ 306-13/4	— diet	Mar.-May 1620
	£ 306-13/4	— diet	June-Aug. 1620
	£ 125	— secret service	Mar.-May 1620
	£ 303- 6/8	— diet	Sept.-Nov. 1620
	£ 125	— secret service	June-Aug. 1620

Patrick Gordon, Agent to Poland

Pay Date & Reference	Sum & Details		Period Covered
4 May 1611 E/403/1711	£ 121-13/4	— diet	one year
14 May 1612 E/403/1713	£ 121-13/4	— diet	one year
18 May 1613 E/403/1715	£ 121-13/4	— diet	one year
6 July 1618 E/403/1724	£ 37-10/0	— pension (in part of £150)	—

Patrick Gordon continued

Pay Date & Reference	Sum and Details	Period Covered
27 Nov. 1618 E/403/1724	£ 187-10/0 — pension	—
6 May 1620 E/403/1726	£ 75 — pension (in part of £150)	½ year
23 June 1620 Ibid.	£ 300 — embassy to Poland	—

Sir Ralph Winwood, Ambassador to the Dutch Estates General

Pay Date & Reference	Sum and Details	Period Covered
3 May 1611 E/403/1711	£ 403-6/8 — diet £ 125 — secret service	Mar.-June 1611 Dec.-Mar. 1610-11
10 Aug. 1611 Ibid. (31 Aug. 1611)	£ 206-13/4 — diet	July-Sept., 1611
	£ 37-10/0 — supplement	¼ year
28 Feb. 1612 E/403/1712, fo. 283	£ 303- 6/8 — diet £ 140 — secret service	Jan.-Mar. 1612 Sept.-Dec. 1611
16 May 1612 E/403/1712	£ 303- 6/8 — diet £ 140 — secret service £ 100 — transportation	April-June 1612 Dec.-Mar. 1611-12 —

Sir Ralph Winwood continued

Pay Date & Reference	Sum and Details		Period Covered
16 July 1612	£ 306-13/4 —	diet	July-Sept. 1612
Ibid.	£ 140 —	secret service	Mar.-June 1612
3 Oct. 1612	£ 100 —	transportation	—
E/403/1714			
30 Nov. 1612	£ 306-13/4 —	diet	Oct.-Dec. 1612
Ibid.	£ 140 —	secret service	June-Sept. 1612
	£ 100 —	transportation	
7 May 1613	£ 300 —	diet	Jan.-Mar. 1613
E/403/1715	£ 140 —	secret service	Sept.-Dec. 1612
30 Oct. 1613	£ 112-10/0 —	supplement	—
E/403/1716			
8 Nov. 1613	£ 306-13/4 —	diet	July-Sept. 1613
Ibid.	£ 140 —	secret service	Mar.-June 1613
9 Nov. 1613	£ 306-13/4 —	diet	Oct.-Dec. 1613
Ibid.	£ 140 —	secret service	June-Sept. 1613
	£ 500 —	transportation	
11 Dec. 1613	£ 303- 6/8 —	diet	April-June 1613
Ibid.	£ 140 —	secret service	Dec.-Mar. 1612-13

Sir Walter Aston, Ambassador to Spain

Pay Date & Reference	Sum and Details	Period Covered
1 Jan. 1620 E/403/1725	£ 552 — diet	Nov.-Feb. 1619-20

William Trumbull, Agent to the Spanish Netherlands

Pay Date & Reference	Sum and Details	Period Covered
3 May 1611 E/403/1711	£ 91 — diet £ 18- 5/0 — postmaster	Apr.-June 1611 —
28 Feb. 1612 E/403/1712, fo. 283	£ 91 — diet £ 91 — diet	Oct.-Dec. 1611 Jan.-Mar. 1612
29 Feb. 1612 E/403/1712, fo. 284	£ 18- 5/0 — diet	—
16 May 1612 E/403/1713	£ 90 — diet	Apr.-June 1612
16 July 1612 Ibid.	£ 92 — diet	Aug.-Sept. 1612
30 Nov. 1612 E/403/1714	£ 92 — diet	Oct.-Dec. 1612
25 Mar. 1613 E/403/1714	£ 90 — diet	Jan.-Mar. 1613

William Turnbull continued

Pay Date & Reference	Sum and Details		Period Covered
30 Oct. 1613 E/403/1716	£ 63-17/6 —	diet	¼ year
8 Nov. 1613 E/403/1716	£ 255 —	diet	Apr.-Oct. 1613
4 Dec. 1613	£ 9- 2/6 —	postmaster	—
31 Oct. 1617 E/403/1723	£ 75 —	clerk of Privy Council	—
10 Nov. 1617 Ibid.	£ 53-15/0 —	postmaster	—
13 Apr. 1618 E/403/1724	£ 80 — £ 300 —	diet secret service	Apr.-June 1617 Jan.-Sept. 1617
8 May 1618 Ibid.	£ 26-10/0 —	postmaster	—
15 May 1618 E/403/1724	£ 50 —	clerk of Council	—
10 June 1618 E/403/1724	£ 92 — £ 90 —	diet diet	Oct.-Dec. 1617 Jan.-Mar. 1618
	£ 91 — £ 92 — £ 75 —	diet diet secret service	Apr.-June 1618 July-Sept. 1617 —

William Trumbull, Agent to the Spanish Netherlands

Pay Date & Reference	Sum and Details		Period Covered
20 Dec.1619 E/403/1725	£ 26- 5/0	— secret service (final payment)	Oct.-Dec. 1618
	£ 75	— secret service	Jan.-Mar. 1618
	£ 133-15/0	— secret service	Jan.-Mar. 1619
	£ 70	— secret service (in part of £133-15/0)	Apr.-June 1619
7 April 1620 *Ibid.*	£ 50	— clerk of Council	—
15 May 1620 E/403/1726	£ 28- 5/0	— postmaster	½ year
	£ 182	— diet (supplement)	July-Sept. 1619
	£ 63	— secret service (final payment)	Apr.-June 1619
	£ 133-15/0	— secret service	July-Sept. 1619
28 July 1620 *Ibid.*	£ 25	— clerk of Council	½ year
	£ 27- 7/6	— postmaster	¼ year
8 Aug. 1620 *Ibid.*	£ 184	— diet	Oct.-Dec. 1619
	£ 182	— diet	Jan.-Mar. 1620

Francis Cottington, Agent to Spain

Pay Date & Reference	Sum and Details		Period Covered
3 May 1611 E/403/1711	£ 91	— diet	Apr.-June 1611
17 Dec. 1611 E/403/1712, fo. 149	£ 150	— supplement	—

Francis Cottington continued

Pay Date & Reference	Sum and Details		Period Covered
1 Aug. 1617 E/403/1723	£ 120- 7/0	transportation	—
	£ 182	diet	Dec.-Feb. 1615-16
	£ 80	secret service	—
	£ 262	diet & secret service	Dec.-Feb. 1615-16
	£ 184	diet	Mar.-May 1617
	£ 184	diet	June-Aug. 1617
	£ 80	secret service	Feb.-May 1617
	£ 70	secret service	Feb.-May 1616
	£ 70	secret service	May-Aug. 1616
31 Oct. 1617 E/403/1723	£ 65	clerk of Privy Council	—

Francis Cottington, Agent to Spain

Pay Date & Reference	Sum and Details		Period Covered
10 Nov. 1617 Ibid.	£ 182	diet	Sept.-Nov. 1617
	£ 80	secret service	May-Aug. 1617
4 Dec. 1619 E/403/1725	£ 600	special services	—
19 Jan. 1620 Ibid.	£ 10	secret service (final payment)	Dec.-May 1617-19
	£ 352	diet	Sept.-Feb. 1618-19
	£ 20	diet (in part of £184)	Mar.-May 1619
7 April 1620 E/403/1725	£ 50	clerk of Council	—

Francis Cottington continued

Pay Date Reference	Sum and Details		Period Covered
15 May 1620	£ 150	— diet (final payment)	Apr.-June 1619
E/403/1726	£ 100	— secret service	May-Aug. 1618
	£ 150	— transportation	—
	£ 100	— Mourning (for Queen Anne)	—
6 July 1620 *Ibid.*	£ 12-10/0	— clerk of Council	¼ year
10 Aug. 1620 *Ibid.*	£ 184	— diet	June-Aug. 1619
	£ 182	— diet	Sept.-Nov. 1619

Sir Francis Nethersole, Ambassador to the Princes of the Union

Pay Date & Reference	Sum and Details		Period Covered
11 May 1620 E/403/1726	£ 100	— Pension (part of £200)	—
20 May 1620 *Ibid.*	£ 206- 5/0	— diet	Michaelmas 1619-Michaelmas 1620
	£ 100	— pension	—

Sir Edward Conway and Sir Richard Weston, Ambassadors to the German princes

Pay Date & Reference	Sum and Details		Period Covered
1 July 1620 E/403/1726	£ 800	— diet (£400 each)	From June 1620
9 Aug. 1620 *Ibid.*	£ 600	— Paid by Burlamachi for Conway, Weston and Wotton.	

Sir John Digby, Ambassador to Spain

Pay Date & Reference	Sum and Details		Period Covered
28 Mar. 1611 E/403/1711	£ 546	— diet	Apr.-June 1611
16 July 1611 *Ibid.*	£ 552 £ 125	— diet — secret service	July-Sept. 1611 Apr.-June 1611
31 Oct. 1611 E/403/1712, fo. 31	£ 552 £ 125 £ 200	— diet — secret service — Cottington	Oct.-Dec. 1611 July-Sept. 1611 —
17 Dec. 1611 *Ibid.*, fo. 49	£ 970	— transportation	—
29 Feb. 1612 *Ibid.*, fo. 288	£ 546 £ 125	— diet — secret service	Jan.-Mar. 1611-12 Oct.-Dec. 1611
16 May 1612 E/403/1713	£ 546 £ 125	— diet — secret service	Apr.-June 1612 Dec.-Mar. 1611-12

Sir John Digby continued

Pay Date Reference	Sum and Details		Period Covered
16 July 1612	£ 552	— diet	July-Sept. 1612
Ibid.	£ 125	— secret service	Apr.-June 1612
30 Nov. 1612	£ 552	— diet	Oct.-Dec. 1612
E/403/1714	£ 125	— secret service	July-Sept. 1612
7 May 1613	£ 500	— diet	Jan.-Mar. 1613
E/403/1715	£ 125	— secret service	Oct.-Dec. 1612
26 June 1613	£ 120	— secret service & extra-ordinary expenses (in part of £1203-17/0)	two years
24 July 1613	£ 546	— diet	Apr.-June 1613
Ibid.	£ 125	— secret service	Jan.-Mar. 1613
6 Aug. 1613	£ 552	— diet	July-Sept. 1613
Ibid.	£ 125	— secret service	Apr.-June 1613
7 Aug. 1613	£ 583	— final payment of 26-6-13	—
Ibid.			
18 Dec. 1613	£ 120	— diet (in part of £1092)	Oct.-Mar. 1613-14
E/403/1716		— secret service (in part of £490)	July-Dec. 1613
12 Feb. 1614	£ 200	— Ibid.	Ibid.
Ibid.			

161

Sir John Digby, Ambassador to Spain

Pay Date & Reference	Sum and Details		Period Covered
5 Mar. 1614 *Ibid.*	£1262	— *Ibid.*	*Ibid.*
12 Nov. 1619 E/403/1725	£4000	— special embassy (final payment of £7000)	—
20 June, 1620 E/403/1726	£2000	— transportation	—
8 Aug. 1620	£5000	— embassy to Spain (final payment of £7000)	—

John Dickerson, Agent to Juliers & Cleves

Pay Date & Reference	Sum and Details		Period Covered
3 May 1611 E/403/1711	£ 89	— diet	Feb.-Apr. 1611
10 Aug. 1611 *Ibid.*	£ 92	— diet	May-July 1611
28 Feb. 1612 E/403/1712, fo. 282	£ 92	— diet	Nov.-Jan. 1611-12
16 May 1612 E/403/1713	£ 90	— diet	Feb.-Apr. 1612
16 July 1612 *Ibid.*	£ 92	— diet	May-July 1612

John Dickerson continued

Pay Date Reference	Sum and Details	Period Covered
30 Nov. 1612 E/403/1714	£ 92 — diet	Aug.-Oct. 1612
16 Apr. 1613 E/403/1715	£ 92 — diet	Nov.-Jan. 1612-13
8 Nov. 1613 E/403/1716	£ 185 — diet	May-Oct. 1613
9 Nov. 1613 *Ibid.*	£ 89 — diet	Feb.-Apr. 1613
30 June 1620 E/403/1726	£ 200 — Secretary to Conway & Weston	—

APPENDIX C: PROFITS OF THE COURT OF WARDS, 1625-1634

The following chart shows the net profits (rounded to the nearest £5) of the Court of Wards for the ten fiscal years of Naunton's sole responsibility for them as master. The expenses deducted from the gross profits are those over which the Court of Wards had some control. Thus, money distributed by parliamentary authority, letters patent, or privy seals are excluded.

Naunton's role as master of the Court of Wards makes him generally responsible for its finances. Assigning him a specific part is a more difficult matter. In 1629, when the court's revenues declined to a marked degree, not only wardships (over which Sir Robert had direct influence) but payment of back debts and liveries all decreased. Bad harvests were a feature of these years, but their effect is difficult to evaluate. Nonetheless, when the good harvests returned in 1631, the profits began to climb significantly. It was once again not only wardships, but all the other money-making devices which yielded increased dividends. This uniform fluctuation could mean that some person, either inside or outside the court, was applying pressure or failing to apply pressure on the people responsible for collecting revenue. It should be pointed out that liveries and wardships, the two principal sources of income, were not dependent on one another in the same year. That is to say, liveries were sued either independently of any wardship or were sued when a ward or other heir reached full age. Thus, it is quite likely that some influence was brought to bear on the men who were responsible for both.

Though it is not beyond the realm of possibility that the other members of the Court of Wards took their lead from the master, it is nonetheless difficult to image Naunton taking the initiative without reference to his superiors. The lack of evidence, however, makes it impossible to determine his specific role in the overall financial management of the Court of Wards.

1625 [Wards 9/417]		1626 [Wards 9/417]	
Gross Profits	£44,540	Gross profits	£54,830
Fees, diet & allowances	990	Fees, diet & allowances	1,010
Exhibitions	2,050	Exhibitions	3,150
Money by decree	20	Money by decree	225
Running expenses	495	Running expenses	340
Total expenses	£3,555	Total expenses	£4,725
Net profits	£40,985	Net profits	£50,105

1627 [Wards 9/417]

Gross Profits	£57,150
Fees, diet & allowances	1,040
Exhibitions	3,105
Money by decree	790
Running expenses	415
Total expenses	£5,350
Net Profits	£51,800

1628 [Wards 9/417]

Gross Profits	£50,640
Fees, diet & allowances	1,020
Exhibitions	3,080
Money by decree	180
Running expenses	575
Total expenses	£4,855
Net profits	£45,785

1629 [Wards 9/417]

Gross profits	£42,895
Fees, diet & allowances	1,020
Exhibitions	3,100
Money by decree	120
Running expenses	480
Total Expenses	£4,720
Net profits	£38,175

1630 [Wards 9/422]

Gross profits	£45,185
Fees, diet & allowances	1,055
Exhibitions	2,765
Money by decree	75
Running expenses	435
Total expenses	£4,330
Net profits	£40,855

1631 [Wards 9/422]

Gross profits	£55,490
Fees, diet & allowances	1,060
Exhibitions	2,875
Money by decree	455
Running expenses	460
Total expenses	£4,850
Net profits	£50,640

1632 [Wards 9/422]

Gross profits	£56,885
Fees, diet & allowances	1,095
Exhibitions	2,810
Money by decree	1,555
Running expenses	505
Total expenses	£5,965
Net profits	£50,920

1633 [Wards 9/422]

Gross profits	£59,545
Fees, diet & allowances	1,080
Exhibitions	2,995
Money by decree	1,300
Running expenses	520
Total expenses	£5,895
Net profits	£53,650

1634 [Wards 9/426]

Gross profits	£52,370
Fees, diet & allowances	970
Exhibitions	3,225
Money by decree	795
Running expenses	515
Total expenses	£5,505
Net profits	£46,865

APPENDIX D: NAUNTON'S WILL

Introduction

There is nothing out of the ordinary about Sir Robert Naunton's will. Given his station in life, the amount of land and personal possessions involved is about what one would expect from a well-to-do member of the gentry. The only surprising element is that there was not more. Given what one finds in the will, it is easy to understand why Naunton was never offered a peerage. He simply did not have the necessary means to support such an honour.

Wills, however, are not easy documents to interpret. They may not contain all the property a man holds for fear of it ending up in the Court of Wards, along with his heir. On the other hand, there are those who leave very large bequests in order to appear as substantial men when, in fact, they do not have the means to fund all they have given away. It is difficult to tell where Naunton falls on this scale. It seems, however, from carefully reading the will and trying to interpret its tone, that it is more likely to lean toward the second category than the first. If this was indeed the case, then it is at least useful in giving one an outer limit; Naunton probably was not worth more than the will indicates.

Some funds he mentioned are undoubtedly genuine. One instance of this is money owed him by friends and relations. This totals just under £1000. Other categories are somewhat less certain. He grants his two nieces £500 per year after they are married, but does not say from where this money will come. All told, he bequeathed money and gifts totalling £2749. As for the pensions, their value is difficult to compute. Leaving aside a minister to supervise the poor, and counting only his wife and two nieces (who would receive £100 and £500 per year each respectively), if the former survived for twenty years and the latter for thirty, this would mean payments of £50,000. There is no way to know if the estate could stand that kind of expense, even if it were distributed over such a long period of time.

Perhaps the most interesting portion of the will deals with the attempt to set up a college at Cambridge in Naunton's name. In a sense, it is amazing that a man who had been around Stuart government for so long would be optimistic enough to believe that his heirs could really collect the £7,300 in back pensions owed him, especially to set up a college that would be organized by men who, at the minimum, had no great love for Charles's Arminians. What is even more unbelievable is that he let the pension remain uncollected specifically with this in mind, or at least so he claims in the will.

Perhaps Naunton had been careless about claiming his pension and thought that some pious cause, such as a college, might pry the money out of the government, whereas a plea from his heirs for themselves would not. Whatever his motives might have been, his project apparently never got off the ground. One can only presume that his guilt at not having a male heir outweighed all other considerations and caused him to try for the continuation of the Naunton name in a well-accepted manner.

[fo. 1] In the name of God Amen. I Robert Naunton knight being in good and perfect memory (thankes be to God [)] therefore doe make and declare this to be my last will, and testament, revoking hereby all former wills, and codicells whatsoever which heretofore I have made, and acknowledged, First I commend my soule with all humility and thankefulness to my most mercifull God, and Father, to my Deare Lord and Saviour and to the holy ghost my true comforter, and my Body to bee interred with my Tumestone in the Chauncell at Leatheringham in Suffolke, and that in such decent, and modest manner as shall seeme fitt to my executor in his discretion with the advice, and direccion of Sir Henry St. George, who is best acquainted with my pedegree, and what coates I do duely quarter, and for my wordly goods where with it hath pleased God to blesse mee it is my will, and [fo. 2] meaning that they shalbe disposed of as hereafter followeth. First I give unto my beloved wife Dame Penelope Naunton all her wearing Apparrell, her Chaine of gould, and Dyamonds which I bought for her, togeither with the rest of her Jewells, which I bestowed upon her to remayne in her Custody to use during her life, but after her decease I give the said Chaine and Jewells to my deare daughter the Lady Bayning, which herselfe formerly promised me to performe as of her selfe, though I had not soe hereby ordered it. Item I give unto her the use of all such plate as is used in my house, and as remaineth in her Custody during her life if shee shall so long keepe unmarried, and beare my name of Nanton, which after her decease or day of her marriage I bequeath to myne Executor with whome I have left an Inventary of the most part thereof signed with my hand. Item I doe give unto her likewise during her life all the rents issueing out of my Mannor of Twiford in the County of Lecester, and out of all my other Lands which I have within that County. Provided that shee, nor none other by her assignement shall committ anie manner of waste on the houses tymber or woods being or growinge thereupon, all which Tymber and wood I leave to bee disposed of by myne Executor. Item I bequeath unto her the use of my House at Pickadilla with the Barnes, stable and garden there during her life to be used by her, with my House at Charinge Crosse, which I have formerly assured to her with my Manor and Parke att Nelmes and other my Lands adioyning thereunto within the Parish of Hornchurch in the Countie of Essex in lieu of her dower. Provided that shee shall preserve the Game of Deare, and Conyes, and not fell, or cutt downe anie tymber or wood being or groweing within the Parke, nor plowe upp anie part thereof, nor fell or cutt Downe anie wood or tymber without the Parke, but only for her owne necessary Expenses within Nelmes Lodge. Item I doe further give unto her an anuitie of One Hundred Pounds per Annum, to be paid by Fifty Pounds every halfe yeare by my Brother William Naunton, Esq: his Executors or assignes who my will is shall give Bond for due payment thereof. Item my will is that my wife shall have the use of all my Housholdstuffe att Charing Crosse, after they shalbee inventoried, and [a] praised by direction of myne Executor during her life excepting all my Pictures, and Cabbenetts in my House, which I will shalbe removed by myne Executor to my house at Letheringham. Provided alwayes that my wife shall enioy noe part of anie thing in this my will devised to her unless shee shall quietly permitt myne Executor to take, and remoove all such goods out of both my Houses at Charing Crosse and Nelms to dispose thereof as in this my will hee is directed, and unlesse shee shall forbeare to make anie further clayme for dower by anie suite in Lawe to bee by her commenced for the same. Item my will is that my wife shall deliver all my Housholdstuffe at Nelms to myne Executor, with the rich furniture for a bedd, the Pillars the Double Vallances Tester, and Curtaines with the large Coverlett, and Counterpointe, all of Crimson branched velvett with gould Lace and fringe (which I caused to bee made at the Birth of my Daughter Bayning) all which I will shee shall deliver to my said Executor, upon Demand to be made by him or his assignes the which rich furniture I will shalbe remooved to Letheringham, and kept in myne house there as an Harloome, All which I committed to my wives Custody. Item my will is that myne Executor remooving Householdstuffe from Nelms to Leatheringham for furnishing of my House there. Item I doe give towards the maintenaince of seaven poore woemen that are to inhabite in myne Almeshouse built by mee at Leatheringham, to each of them one Load of wood, and foure markes in money yearely, the same to be taken, and raised out of my Lands, and tithes in Leatheringham, Hoo and Branston, whome I would have to gett the rest of their Living by their worke, and not to be maintained in idleness. Item I doe give, and bequeath to a preaching minister that shall discharge the Cure of Letheringham, and Hoo, a Lodging in the said Almeshouse, and fower nobles yearely for governing, and ordering the Poore therein, and his diett to be allowed him by them that shalbe [fo. 3] owners of my house at Leatheringham, and twenty Pounds more in money to bee yearely paid him by them for his maintenance, And I doe give Twenty Pounds more yearely to another preaching Minister that shall discharge the Cure at Chaffeild the said severall sommes of twenty Pounds and Twenty Pounds to be paid out of my Lands and Tithes of Leatheringham, Hoo, and Chaffeild. Item I give unto my daughter Bayning, and her heires, all my Estate in Cardiffe Forrest within the Countie of Carmarthen which I hould in fee farme from his Majesty and was sometymes the Land of Sir John Perret her Grandfather. Item I give to her my great guilt Cupp of the workmanshipp of Norrenberge which hath my Coate inameld, and her name ingreaven in it, which Cupp is in my studdy att Nelmes. Item I give unto her my two Cabbinetts and a silver Standish covered with a Case of Crimson velvett which all three does stand upon my two Tables in the Gallery at Nelms. Item I give unto her my Deske inlaid with Mother of Pearle, Covered with a Case of greene velvett which stands upon my Presse in my Gallery att my house by Charing Crosse. Item I give unto her a Cabennett consisting most part of Christall which is in my chamber att Leatheringham. Item I doe give unto my Lord Viscount Bayning her husband my best Cabinett of white Satten imbrothered, and my best Clocke once covered with crimson velvett, both which are in my Gallery at Charring Crosse. Item I does give unto my Brother William Naunton of Leatheringham Esq: my Mannor of Twyford in the Countie of Leicester, and all my other Lands which I have within that County, which Discended upon me from my deare mother and his, to have and to hold to him, and his heires males of his body lawfully begotten, and for want of such yssue, the remainder to be unto myne owne right heires, the rents onely of which Lands I have formerly given unto my wife During her life in Augmentation of Her Jointure, to be paid her yearely by my Brother. Item I doe give unto my fower nephewes his sonnes Robert, William, Henry & Thomas One Hundred Pounds a peece, to be paid unto them severallie att such tyme as their father shall find most fitt. Item I doe give unto my Neeces his daughters, Elizabeth, and Marie towards their advancement in marriage Five Hundred Pounds a peece, to be paid within one yeare after they shalbe married. Provided that it bee with the consent of their fathers, and of my noble freind Sir Thomas Glemham knight, or the Survivor of them if my said Neeces shall soe long lyve after their severall Marriages. Provided likewise that my Brother or his Executors, shall over and above this Legacy of myne paie, or cause to be paid to each of them Five Hundred Pounds more at the Daie of their Marriage, it being performed with his consent, or with Sir Thomas Glemham in case my Brother himselfe shall die before. Item whereas upon a late Accompt of my Cosen Robert Kempton Gent: taken by my brother there appeared to be due unto mee from my said Cosen Kempton the somme of one hundred pounds, and Seaventy Pounds or somewhat more, it is my will, and meaning that after defalcacion made for my daughters, and her Gentlewoemens board and for such other disbursements, as hee, or his wife have layd out for her use that the Surplussage shalbe freely remitted in respite of the great care, and faithfulness which they have showed the tyme of her abode with them. Item I Doe give unto my Coson Samuel Kempton their sonne all my right, and Interest which I have in that Lease of Barrington Hall Lands from Trinitie Colledge in Cambridge towards his better maintenance att the Temple. Item I doe give unto my Daughter the Lady Bayning, and to her heires my house at Charing crosse wherein shee was borne togeither with my Lease of my Houses barnes stables, and garden at Pickadilla, after my wives decease. Item I give unto my Cosen Winifred Gosnoeld widdow, the Forty Pounds which I lent her, And I doe give unto my Coson Mary Gosnoeld her Daughter One guilt Bowle with a Cover, of the value of Tenn Pounds. Item I doe give unto Mrs: Lucy Downing, a like guilte [fo. 4] bowle of the same valew. Item I doe give unto Mrs: Bracey for her paines shee hath taken with me Tenn Pounds. Item I doe give unto Thomas Lord, and George Verney my two Secretaries to each of them a guilte bowle with a Cover of Tenn Pounds valew. Item I doe give unto my sister Anne Jeffery widdow Fifty Pounds. Item I doe give unto John Sanderson Twenty Pounds, and to Robert Whitfield Tenn Pounds. To Martin Coleman, John Barradge, to Robert Manley, to George Coleston, to every of these Fyve Pounds, to William my keeper at Nelmes Fyve Pounds, To Toby my Gardiner, and Thomas Banbery each of them five Pounds, and to Susan my Brothers maid for her paines taken about mee in my sickness Five Pounds. Item I give to Thomas Ashbey Esq: That was my scholler in Trinity Hall forty Pounds, and to his Brother George Ashbey Esq: one guilt Cupp with a Cover of the value of Tenn Pounds, To Robert Bloyes my Godson, One Guilt Cupp of the value of Tenn Pounds. Item I doe give to Thomas Lower Esq: my wives sonne one Silver Tankard with his father['s] Armes engraven upon it, and one round Silver Bason with P.L. in the Bottome of it. Item I doe give unto the Poore of **Leatheringham, Hoo, and Chaffeild five Pounds a peece to each** Parrish, to be Distributed according [to] the discretion of myne Executor. Item I will that myne Executor doe give mourning blacks unto my Lord Bayning, and his Lady, and fower of their Servants, to himselfe, and all his Children, and two of his servants, To all myne owne servants, whom I have mencioned in this my will, and to Alice my maid at Charing Crosse, to whome I give likewise in money Five Marks, To Nurse Mills a mourning gowne, and Five Marks, To my wife, and to her

Chambermaid, each of them a black; To Mr: Thomas Lower, and Ciprian Southwicke; each of them a black to the preacher Mr: Dale whome I desire to preach att my funerall a blacke, and Five marks in money. Item my will is that the first fourteen hundred Pounds bequeathed to my brothers Children, shalbe paid by him or his Executors at such tymes as are formerly appointed in this my will, And the rest of my Legacies in money, to bee paid within three moneths after my decease, by him my said Executor. Item I will that my sayd Executor shall give Seaven blacks to my seaven Almes woemen such as he shall chuse and appoint, I founded them lesse to occasion my heires to encrease their allowances hereafter as their behaviour in their places shall Deserve: For my bookes, and Papers I referr the disposing of them to a Codicill, which I meane to annex hereafter to this my will. Item I doe nominate and appointe my brother Esq: to be my sole Executor of this my last will and Testament. And I doe earnestly intreate my approved worthie, and beloved freinds Henry Calthropp Esq: and Mr. Emanuell Downing to be the Supervisors thereof, and to assist him as Supervisors onely but not as Coexcutors, with their best helpe and Councell for the due execution thereof, to each of whome I bequeath for their faithfull Care, and assistance for the improving of that estate which I have hereby left unto him for his best profit, and advancement the Somme of Fiftie Pounds a Peece, and to each of them a blacke for themselves, and two blacks a piece for their servants. And for confirmacion of this my last will and Testament I have to every of the seaven Leaves thereof put my hand and Seale this Third Daie of March. In the yeare of our Lord God one thousand six hundred thirty-fower. Robert Naunton. Memorandum that this will consisting of Seaven sheets of paper was sealed every severall sheete a part with the signe mannual of the said Sir Robert Naunton with in named, & delivered as his last will and testament in the presence of us being witnesses thereunto. Thomas Lord, Lucye Downinge John Saunderson. George Verney.

A CODICILL to be annexed to my last will bearing date the Third Day of this Instant moneth of March. One Thousand Six Hundred Thirty Fower.

[fo. 5] WHEREAS I have heretofore by deed indented under my hand and seale made a Lease unto my Brother William Naunton Esq: of my two mannors of Hoo and Kettlebrough in the County of Suffolke togeither with the

Advowsons, and Patronage of the severall Churches of Hoo, and Kettleborough aforesaid with all the rights, members, and appurtenances to the said Mannor, and either of them belonging for the terme and tyme of fower score yeares as by the said deed bearing date the Eighteenth Day of August last past before the date hereof more at large doth, and may appeare; Whereas alsoe I have power reserved to mee in the deed of purchase of the said Mannors to lease the same for thirty yeares by my will, I doe therefore hereby will and bequeath unto my said Brother William Naunton Esq: the said Two Mannors of Hoo, and Kettleborough in the County of Suffolke, togeither with the Advowsons, and Patronages of the said severall Churches, and all the rights, members and appurtenances to the said Mannors of Hoo and Ketleborough, and either of them belonging, To have, and to hold both the said several Mannors, and advowsons, and all the premisses mencioned to be hereby demised withall, and singuler their and either of their appurtenances unto the said William Naunton his heires Executors and assignes for and during terme and tyme of thirtie yeares, to beginn ymediatly after the determinacion, and end of the foresaid Lease of Fower score yeares fully to be compleat and ended, yeilding, and paying therefore yearely One Pepper Corne att the Feast of St: Michaell the Archangell if the same be lawfully demanded. And whereas there is a debt of Seaven Hundred, and Fifty Pounds Due unto mee from Ann Twiford of Traventy in the Countie of Carmarthen widdowe, and payable at certaine dayes agreed upon betweene her and mee in wryting, for payment whereof shee hath made assurances of divers Lands which were her late fathers in the County of Salopp, I doe hereby give, and bequeath, my whole right, and Interest which I have to all, and every of the said Lands, if shee the said Ann shall not make due payment of the said debt at the tyme greed upon unto him my said brother William Naunton Esq: or his heires. I doe give unto my beloved Coson Sir Peter Hayman kt: one guilt bowle with a Cover of the valew of Tenn Pounds, which I would have my Coate of Armes and his to be ioyned in remembrance of our allyance. Item I doe give unto my worthie freind Edward Read Esq: One guilt Bowle with a cover, of the value of Tenn Pounds, wherein I would have my Coate of Armes engraven as in all other guilt bowles which I have bequeathed in my will to divers of my freinds. Item, I doe further give unto my Brother William Naunton Esq: my Tenement, and House at Snape, with the Smithes forge, and backside, with all and singuler the appurtenances thereunto belonging in the said County of Suffolke now or late in the possession of Robert Bowles. Robert Naunton. Memorandum that this Codicill, consisting of Two Sheetes of Paper was sealed and delivered, and annexed to the last will and Testament of Sir Robert Naunton upon the Fift Day of March one thousand six hundred Thirty fower. In the presence of us by him the said Sir Robert Naunton, Thomas Lord, Lucy Downing, John Saunderson.

ONE OTHER CODICILL to bee annexed to my last will bearing date the third of this instant March, One thousand six hundred Thirty Fower.

WHEREAS there is due unto me for the arrerage of my Pencion [fo. 6] granted mee by his late royall Majestie in reward of my faithfull, and Laborious services done him, thefull somme of Six Thousand Pounds as doth appeare by a Certificate under his hands of Sir Myles Fleetwood knight in his Majesty's Receivor generall of his Court of Wards, and Liveries, And whereas also there is likewise due unto mee by his said late Majesty's graunt one other Annuity of One hundred Pounds by yeare during my life, which I have forborne till it should growe to amore considerable somme, both which graunts are passed under the great Seale, and recorded in the Exchequer. The arreare of which annuitye comes to some Twelve, or Thirteene hundred Pounds as will best appeare by my last Acquittance given into the Exchequer for my last receite of my said Annuity, both which said debts I doe hereby give and bequeath unto my Brother William Naunton Esq: my sole Executor of my said last will and testament, to the Intent that hee my said Executor, shall imploy it faithfully and whollie to the founding, and erecting of a Colledge in the universitie of Cambridge where I had my first breeding, and where I lived with soe much happines and contentment, And I doe hereby humbly intreate the right honorable my Lord the Earle of Holland, and Sir John Cooke knight his Majesties principall Secretary that they wilbe pleased to further this my humble suite, and Desire with thier best indeavors unto his sacred Majesty as well for the speedy payment of both the said sommes (which I have soe long forborne) the rather out of my fixed intencion to consecrate these rewards of my Publique services to this publique, and pious use wholly when they should be raised to the greatest somme, as for his Majesty's gracious Leave, and Licence for the erecting of such a foundacion, which I doe the rather desire, that it may beare my name, because it hath not pleased God to graunt mee a male issue: Item my will is that when this Colledge shallbe built, and established that my Executor shall give in Plate befitting the use of the said Colledge to the full value of Two hundred Pounds. Item I doe give and bequeath further unto the said Colledge my whole Library of Bookes with my Two Globes, and all my Mapps which are at my Houses at Charing Crosse, and Nelmes Lodge: And for the scittnating pro- portioning, regulating, and ordering of the said Colledge with fitt Statutes for the Governing thereof I doe hereby commend the more perticuler care thereof unto the best direction of my welbeloved, and approved good freinds Mr: Dr. Collins Provoist of Kings Colledge, Mr: Dr: Ward, M[aste]r of Sidney Colledge; Henrie Calthropp Esq: and Emanuell Downing gent: with whome I have formerly advised touching the same, And if it shall please God that by the endeavour of my two honorable freinds the worke shall proceed, and take effect, I doe then hereby give unto his Lordshipp, and Mr: Secretary Cooke to each of them a Legacy of Fifty Pounds to be be bestowed in a Peece of Plate in remembrance of their pious assistance to this my poore designe, And I doe likewise give to my fower last named good freinds Twenty Pounds a Peece in remembrance of their like assistance. But if this whole worke shalbe opposed soe as it shall not take effect, then I doe hereby give, and bequeath both the whole debts before mencioned to my foresaid sole Executor: And I doe likewise hereby then give and bequeath my whole Library of Bookes, with my two Globes, and all my mapps, and all other my writings, Notes and Papers which are in my house by Charing Crosse unto the right honorable the Lord Viscount Bayning my beloved sonne in lawe. Robert Naunton.

Memorandum that this second Codicill consisting of three sheets of Paper was sealed delivered and annexed to the said Last will and Testament of Sir Robert Naunton upon the Sixt Day of March One Thousand six hundred thirtie Fower by him the said Sir Robert Naunton in the presence of us: Thomas Lord. George Verney. Lucy Downing. John Saunderson.

WORKS CITED

MANUSCRIPT SOURCES

Berkshire Record Office
Trumbull MS 33

Bodley Library
Fortescue MS Additional D 110
Tanner MSS 73, 74

Boughton House
Windwood's Original State Papers VIII

British Library
Additional MSS 7082; 17677 I, K; 18641; 36445; 38170; 38861;
    48091
Egerton MSS 1589, 2592, 2593, 2594
Harleian MSS 1580, 1581
Lansdowne MS 162
Stowe MS 176

Brussels, Archives Generales
PC 55, 56

Cambridge University Library
MS D.D. 12.20

Huntington Library
MS EL6055

Kent Record Office
Sackville MSS M 34, M 1007, M 7580

Lambeth Palace
Bacon Papers 654, 936

Münich; Geheime Staats Archiv
Kasten Blau 118/1, II

Paris; Bibliotheque Nationale
Fonds Francais 15988

Public Record Office
C 66: 2209,
E 403: 1711, 1712, 1713, 1714, 1715, 1716, 1723, 1724, 1725,
    1726, 1727, 1728
PRO 30:
24: 17
53: 1, 2, 3, 4

PRO 31:
3: 53, 54
12: 21, 24
Reg. 1: 28
SP13: 109
SP14: 99, 111, 118, 119, 139, 146, 158, 164, 168, 169, 171, 172,
    181
SP16: 104, 116, 121, 126, 192, 284
SP17: 90
SP38: 12
SP75: 5
SP77: 13, 14
SP78: 68, 69
SP81: 14, 15, 16, 19, 20
SP84; 73, 79, 82, 83, 84, 85, 86, 87, 88, 89, 91, 92, 93, 94, 95, 96,
    97, 98, 99, 106
SP92: 7
SP105: 95
Wards:
5: 40
9: 93, 95, 98, 99, 100, 162, 163, 207, 275, 417, 422, 426, 535, 543,
    544, 545, 546

PRINTED SOURCES AND SECONDARY WORKS

Acts of the Privy Council: 1615-16; 1618-19; 1619-21; 1621-23;
    1627-28; 1628-29; 1629-30
Aylmer, G.E., *The King's Servants* (New York, 1961)
Birch, T., *Memoirs of the Reign of Queen Elizabeth* (1756) I, II.
Cabala ... Mysteries of State (1691) 3rd edition.
Calendar of State Papers, Domestic: 1591-94; 1611-18; 1619-23;
    1623-25; 1626-49 Addendum; 1627-28; 1631-33
Calendar of State Papers, Irish: 1615-1625
Calendar of State Papers, Venetian: 1617-19; 1619-21; 1621-23;
    1623-25
Carter, C.H., 'Gondomar: Ambassador to James I', *Historical
    Journal* 7; *Secret Diplomacy of the Habsburgs, 1598-1625*
(London, 1964)
Clark, P., *English Provincial Society from the Reformation to the
    Revolution* (Hassocks, Sussex, 1977)
Coke, D., *The Last Elizabethan, Sir John Coke* (London, 1937)
Commons Journal I
Debates in the House of Commons in 1625, ed. S.R. Gardiner
    (Camden Society: Westminster, 1873)

Diary of Sir Henry Slingsby, ed. D. Parsons (London, 1836)

Dictionary of National Biography
Dietz, F.C., *English Public Finance 1558-1641* (New York, 1932)
Documentos Ineditos para la Historia de Espana (Madrid, 1936)
Edwards, E., *The Life of Sir Walter Raleigh* (London, 1868) I
Egerton Papers, ed. J.P. Collier (Camden Society: Westminster, 1840)
Eliot, Sir J., *Negotinum Posterum* (1881)
Evans, F.M.G., *The Principal Secretary of State from 1558-1680* (Manchester, 1923)
Fortescue Papers, ed. S.R. Gardiner (Camden Society: Westminster, 1871)
Fuller, T., *The History of the Worthies of England,* ed. A.P. Nuttall (London, 1662) III
Gardiner, S.R., *History of England* (London, 1901) III, V, VIII
Goodman, G., *The Court of King James the First,* ed. J. Brewer (London, 1839) II
Harlow, V.T., *Raleigh's Last Voyage* (London, 1932)
Hawkins, M.J., *Sales of Ward in Somerset 1603-1641* (London, 1965)
Haydn, *The Book of Dignities,* ed. H. Ockerby (London, 1894) 3rd edition
Hazlit, W.C., *The Coinage of the European Continent* (London, 1893)
Historical Manuscripts Commission Reports: *Buccleuch* I; *Cowper* I, II; *Downshire-Trumbull* IV; *Mar Supplement; Salisbury* VIII, XII; *4th Report; 12th Report*
Howell, J., *Epistolae Ho-elianae. The Familiar Letters* ed. J. Jacobs (London, 1890)
Hulme, H., *The Life of Sir John Eliot* (New York, 1957)
Hurstfield, J., *The Queen's Wards* (Cambridge, 1958)
Instructions to the Master and Counsaile of the Wards (London, 1610)
Larkin, J.F. & Hughes, P., *Stuart Proclamations* (Oxford, 1973)
Le Neve, J., *Fasti Ecclesiae Anglicaniae,* ed. T.D. Hardy (Oxford, 1854) I
Letters and Dispatches of the Earl of Strafford, ed. W. Knowler (London, 1739) I
Letters and Documents Illustrating Relations between England and Germany, ed. S.R. Gardiner (Camden Society: Westminster, 1865) I
The Letters of John Chamberlain, ed. N.E. McClure (Philadelphia, 1939), I, II

Lincoln's Inn Admissions Register, 1420-1779 (1896)

Mathew, D., *The Age of Charles I* (London, 1951)

Mattingly, G., *Renaissance Diplomacy* (London, 1955)

McGowan, A.P., 'The Royal Navy under the First Duke of Buckingham, Lord High Admiral 1618-1628', University of London, unpublished doctoral thesis, 1967

Moir, T., *The Addled Parliament of 1614* (Oxford, 1958)

Naunton, R., *Fragmenta Regalia* (Edinburgh, 1808)

Neale, J.E., *The Elizabethan House of Commons* (London, 1949)

Nicholas, D., *Mr. Secretary Nicholas (1593-1669): His Life and Letters* (London, 1955)

Nichols, J., *The Progresses, etc. of James the First* (London, 1828) III

Notestein, W., *Four Worthies* (London, 1956)

Notestein, W., *et. al., Commons Debates of 1621* (New Haven, 1935) IV

Official Lists of Sheriffs (London, 1898)

Official Return — Members of Parliament 1213-1702 (1878) I

Prestwich, M., *Cranfield, Politics and Profits under the Early Stuarts* (Oxford, 1966)

Oman, C., *Elizabeth of Bohemia* (London, 1938)

Rabb, T., *Enterprise and Empire* (Cambridge, Mass., 1967)

Rex, M., *University Representation in England 1604-1690* (London, 1954)

Russell, C., *Parliament and English Politics 1621-1629* (Oxford, 1979) 'The Warship of John Pym' *English Historical review* 84.

Smith, L.P., *The Life and Letters of Sir Henry Wotton* (Oxford, 1907)

Students Admitted to the Inner Temple 1547-1660 (1887)

Tawney, R.H., *Business and Politics under James I* (Cambridge, 1958)

Venn, J. and J.A. *Alumni Cantabrigiensis* (Cambridge, 1924) III

Wallace, W.E., *Sir Walter Raleigh* (Princeton, 1959)

The Way to be Rich According to the Practice of the Great Audley (London, 1662)

Wedgewood, C.V., *The Thirty Years War* (London, 1950) 5th edition; *Thomas Wentworth, First Earl of Strafford, 1593-1641: A Revaluation* (London, 1961)

Weiss, E., *Die Unterstutzung Friedrichs V. von der Pfalz durch Jacob I und Karl I von England in Dreissigjährigen Krieg* (Stuttgart, 1966)

Warren's Book, ed. A. Dale (Cambridge, 1911)

178

Whitelock, J., *Liber Famelicus,* ed. J. Bruce (Camden Society: Westminster, 1858)

Williams, F.B., *Index of Dedications and Commendatory Verses* (London, 1962)

Willson, D.H., *James VI and I* (London, 1956) *Privy Councillors in the House of Commons 1604-1629* (Minneapolis, 1940)

Winthrop Papers (Boston, 1929) I

Wotton, H., *Letters and Dispatches to James I and his Ministers,* ed. G. Tomline (London, 1850)

INDEX

Other volumes in this series

Copies obtainable on order from
Swift Printers (Sales) Ltd., 1-7 Albion Place, Britton Street, London EC1M 5RE